Diplomacy and its discontents

Diplomacy and its discontents JAMES EAYRS

UNIVERSITY OF TORONTO PRESS

© University of Toronto Press 1971
Toronto and Buffalo

Printed in Canada
ISBN 0-8020-1807-6 (cloth)
ISBN 0-8020-6121-4 (paper)
Microfiche ISBN 0-8020-0126-2
LC 73-163811

To Arthur Blanchette and Ed Ritchie

Preface

In 1965 I was invited to give the Alan B. Plaunt Memorial Lectures at Carleton University. 'As a subject,' its president proposed, 'I would suggest Canada's international relations or some fairly broad aspect of them. The audiences are usually of a kind not very appreciative of detailed scholarly exposition ... They usually include a large number of senior government people.'

It happened that the date set for the first of the two lectures coincided with that for a banquet commemorating the centennial anniversary of the Rideau Club; to that event, not mine, the 'large number of senior government people' for whom I'd gathered my thoughts ineluctably gravitated. But Ottawa is like a drum – albeit a kettle-drum – and word of what I'd said quickly passed around.

For foreign policy-makers especially that word was not to their liking. A former assistant under-secretary of state for external affairs felt obliged to publish a rebuttal: 'To the intellectual who refuses to serve the state because he fears he may be defiled by his service to the state, I say, "Go hang yourself, brave Crillon; we fought at Arques, and you were not there."' A former ambassador to the Soviet Union revealed that the lectures stirred in him 'a strong revulsion,' and advised the practitioner of foreign affairs on no account to read them: 'They will only raise his blood-pressure, without giving him the slightest help, either moral or practical, in the exercise of his exacting, often exasperating but essential and rewarding profession.' A former prime minister and secretary of state for external affairs took them to task for asserting that public service is uncongenial for the inquiring mind: 'One might as well say that the football squad is no place for the honour student in English because "the environment is alien."' (It was not for literature that Lester Pearson received his Nobel Prize – nor for logic either.)

These unflattering attentions from prominent persons helped to produce a modest but steady demand for my lectures after they were published in 1966 as *Right and Wrong in Foreign Policy.* Eventually they went out of print. Meanwhile I'd been developing, in essays, articles, and a series of radio talks published in 1967 as *Fate and Will in Foreign Policy,* a number of related issues to which my brief Plaunt Lectures had not paid full attention. The University of Toronto Press agreed to re-issue the lectures in the company of a selection of this other work. This book is the result.

For once it is unnecessary to offer the limp apologia that despite the grotesque disparity of the items making up one's collection they are brought together by a point of view or united by a common sensibility. For these discourses do hold to a single theme – the decay of diplomatic method, diplomacy and its discontents – with a tenacity that even their author has found disconcerting. Recalling Camus' definition of the intellectual as 'someone whose mind watches itself,' I have asked myself as well as I can whether what I have written is wholly in the spirit of free and disinterested inquiry. Am I, perhaps, in the grip of some ignoble obsession, my judgment – as one correspondent has alleged – warped by 'mixed private and public angers'?

Anyone free of public anger was either asleep throughout the sixties or responsible for what went on in them. But I nurse no personal animus that I know of. Long ago and far away I applied to the Department of External Affairs for employment, and was offered – too late for my acceptance – a job as a junior foreign service officer. So I have no grievance on that score – though there's another episode requiring explanation. The attentive reader of my strictures upon foreign offices for withholding diplomatic files may detect in them the tone of one who believes himself to have been badly treated by authority; and the attentive reader would be right.

It was not just a matter of being denied access to the files – though denials persisted for twenty years, and were on occasion ludicrous. (In 1958 the Department of External Affairs refused to allow me to read documents relating to its founding fifty years before; when my article appeared bereft of this important material, the official concerned offered his congratulations and assurance that none of the papers in his custody would 'significantly change the conclusions of your research.') There is more to it than that. As a condition of access to a collection in the Public Archives of Canada I was required to submit my notes to the Department of External Affairs to be 'vetted' for 'security.' The frail apparatus of its Historical Division collapsed beneath the weight of this responsibility: instead of censoring, it confiscated all my notes – of press clippings and other papers in the public domain as well as of those that were not – for sequestration in perpetuity. Months of work were wasted.

Hell hath no fury like a scholar scorned. But that too was long ago and far away. Policy has changed for the better since. The Department has made amends, showering upon me like manna its most precious memoranda. I bear it no grudge, harbour no ill-will. To its present director of Historical Division and its present under-secretary of state – the officials who have worked to achieve a new deal for students of Canadian foreign policy – I gratefully dedicate this book.

Those practitioners of diplomacy who think I exaggerate its discontents, or treat the craft of states too roughly, I do not chide for trying to extend the limits of the immunity to which they feel entitled. I only declare to them that elsewhere I have written of my own profession just as critically as of theirs.

The library of the Canadian Institute of International Affairs has provided me with courteous and efficient service, often beyond the call of duty; I am grateful for the help of its former librarian, Madelaine Grant, her successor, Jane Barrett, and Elizabeth Fox. My thanks to Heather Wright for secretarial assistance are long overdue but warmly conveyed.

To the University of Toronto Press I tender my appreciation of deft and expert assistance at every stage in the production of my book, with especial thanks to Rik Davidson for his interest and support, and to Jean Wilson for editing so rapidly and meticulously a rather unruly manuscript.

June 1971
Toronto   JE

Contents

Part I **THE DELIQUESCENCE OF DIPLOMACY**

1

The clearing of the chanceries

Readers of Lawrence Durrell's *Esprit de Corps,* written to while away the lon-
gueurs of a posting in some distant dreary capital, may recall his tale of the
evening when the entire diplomatic colony in Belgrade were invited by the
British ambassador to a party on a raft, specially constructed for the gala
event, which at the height of the ensuing revelry slipped its moorings and
edged from shore. 'The lighted raft hung like a fire-fly on the smooth surface
of the river and then slowly began to move downstream in the calm night air,
the candles fluttering softly, the band playing, and the corps dancing or smoking or gossiping, thoroughly at peace.' It was an enchanted moment, and the
ambassador was congratulating himself upon his social triumph when he remembered – the sweat starting out on him as he did so – that only a few miles
distant the river Sava met the swiftly flowing Danube forming by their conflu-
ence a whirlpool into the vortex of which the accredited representatives of
forty states, together with their ladies, were being inexorably drawn.

  That is one, possibly too drastic, way of reducing the diplomat surplus now
afflicting most of the countries of the world, including our own.

  There are other ways. One has just been put forward in Britain by the Review Committee on Overseas Representation.[1] This committee, composed of
a businessman (Sir Val Duncan, its chairman), a retired senior foreign office
official (Sir Frank Roberts), and an economist and *döppelganger* diplomat
(Andrew Shonfield), was invited by the foreign secretary 'to review urgently
the functions and scale of the British representational effort overseas ... in the
light of decisions on foreign and defence policy ... the balance of payments,

1   (Cmd. No. 4107, HMSO, London 1969)

and the changing international role which these imply for the United Kingdom.' It responded by producing a state paper as candid in its analysis and as radical in its recommendations as any since the Trevelyan-Northcote report on civil service reorganization more than a century ago.

The Duncan Report finds the British foreign service over-staffed and under-employed. One reason for the clutter is the indiscriminate opening of embassies in almost all of the fifty or sixty new states entering international society since 1945. Another reason is the assumption that while one mission may be smaller than another, all belong to the same species. This the Duncan Report rejects. Why, it asks, should the spectrum of diplomatic activity, and hence the scale of administrative complexity, be the same in the embassy at San José as it is in the embassy at Washington?

Accordingly it recommends dividing overseas missions into two different categories. The comprehensive mission may continue to run the gamut – handling inter-governmental relations, advising on foreign policy, helping one's nationals to clinch a deal or be released from jail, purveying intelligence, influencing foreign opinion. But the comprehensive mission should be confined to what is termed Britain's 'area of concentration' – western Europe and North America – where, it is forecast, most of the important diplomatic business of the seventies will be done; to the Soviet Union; and to China.

The selective mission is, with some exceptions, suited to the hundred or so other states relegated to the comparative obscurity of the 'outer area.' There British vital interests may be adequately looked after by small, highly specialized missions concentrating on a particular aspect of policy – trade, aid, defence, or whatever it may be.

There will be some countries, conceivably a fair number, where no mission at all is required. This is not because (as in the American diplomatic tradition) the local ideology is thought to emit an offensive smell, but rather because nothing goes on in 'Barataria' (the Duncan Report's fictive polity of marginal importance – a device not without hazard when new states keep coming on the scene with names like Zimbabwe, Namibia and, for all anyone can tell, Barataria) worth the trouble and expense of maintaining a mission there, even on a 'selective' scale.

But it is not just that there are too many missions. The chanceries are over-crowded. Too many people push too many pens across too many pieces of paper, filling them with worthless messages.

The Duncan committee would ruthlessly demobilize service attachés. They propose an immediate twenty-five per cent cutback in the British defence staff at Washington, they see little need for attachés in western European capitals which can be reached by air from Whitehall in an hour, they think they do more harm than good in those regions east of Suez from which military power has been withdrawn.

The committee also has it in for the embassy flack, known more decorously as the information officer. 'It will be desirable to curtail, quite severely, the attempt to project Britain's images and policies by the written word (handouts or press releases).'

These reforms the conventional foreign service officer can and will applaud. Ever since the British ambassador in Lisbon complained in 1840 that his attachés had nothing better to do than to read his despatches like newspapers, he has resented the intrusion of military officers, press officers, agricultural advisers, and so on down a lengthening list of specialist usurpers. It is when the conventional foreign service officer reaches chapter 4 of the Duncan Report ('political work'), with its annex J ('the evaluation and control of political reporting'), that his applause is stilled. For if the analysis is judged correct, if the recommendations are carried out, he may follow the military and press attaché into oblivion.

The Duncan Report calls into question his principal raison d'être: the necessity and worth of the despatches he sends back from abroad. These despatches, when they are not mere duplicates of what is contained in the great newspapers of record, fall into two kinds. There is the account of what the diplomat has been told, or asked, to convey to his government. Such a despatch is irreplaceable – a reporter or a businessman being an unreliable channel of communication – but not necessarily indispensable. Too often the network is clogged with gossip. 'It may not be without significance that when, during my fortnightly interview with the secretary of state in his office at noon today, I ventured to bring up the subject of the Chicago drainage canal, Mr Acheson betrayed even more asperity than is his wont ...'

The student of diplomatic history - the history, in A.J.P. Taylor's phrase, of what one file clerk said to another file clerk – will know how much of the archives is filled with twitter of this type; there is no reason to believe that this side of the thirty-year rule the proportion changes for the better. As with cybernetics, so with diplomacy: garbage in, garbage out.

Distinct from reporting what one foreign office wishes to tell another is the diplomat's appraisal of events. He tries to take the measure of a man, to discern the forces in a society. These he may wish to follow up by a magisterial 'Whither Barateria?' - if only to draw the fact of his existence to the attention of his superiors who might otherwise be oblivious to it. The fledgling foreign service officer writes his 'Whither Barateria?' for the same reason that the assistant professor writes his 'Political Culture in Central America' – except that with the FSO it is 'circulate or perish.'

Before me is a diplomatic calendar for June 1964. A typical week begins with Soviet aviation day on the 24th, moves on to proclamation of the independence of the Malagasay Republic on the 25th and is followed in quick succession by the Buddhist Festival of Pson on the 27th and Canadian Army Day on the 28th. Not all these events will feature entertainment as diverting as Polk-Mowbray's evening on the Sava, but even so they hardly provide a milieu suited to first-rate political analysis.

'The intensity and isolation of embassy life and entertainment,' writes one who knows them well, 'the formalities and protocol, all contribute to the diplomat's lassitude. Young British diplomats soon lose their curiosity, usually after their third posting, and achieve a lack lustre expression, an immunity to new experience and new people, and above all an absence of zeal.'[2]

It is upon such dispirited cohorts, at an annual cost of 105.8 million pounds sterling, that the British government relies for judgment as to what makes the world go round. But for not much longer – if Sir Val and his colleagues have their way.

'There are inherent difficulties in evaluating the political reporting work carried out by our diplomatic posts abroad. The nature of this work militates against any effective appraisal in absolute terms or any precise assessment of its cost effectiveness.' That much the authors of the Duncan Report are obliged to concede.

Common sense, as distinct from cost effectiveness, could have led them to conclude that diplomatic despatches are these days over-priced. The smallest possible 'selective' mission – two diplomatic officers to compose the cables, a clerk to encipher and decipher – runs $30,000 a year. That is a good deal more than annual subscriptions to those leading newspapers and journals of opinion from which any foreign office can glean what it needs to know about the background of world events. 'The truth is that one derives far more news from the press' – so wrote Lloyd George's private secretary in 1917 – 'than from every other source, and every day in the club one sees the long rows of high foreign officials going to the notice board to find out what is really happening.'[3] L.B. Pearson has testified that 'there are foreign correspondents of newspapers whose despatches can be as full, shrewd and useful as any diplomat's. Sometimes they are based on an even greater knowledge and broader experience of the country – and its people – about which they are both

2 Anthony Sampson, *Anatomy of Britain Today* (Hodder and Stoughton, London 1965), 318
3 Quoted in J.R.M. Butler, *Lord Lothian* (Macmillan, London 1960), 66

writing.'[4] It is said that during the New York newspaper strike the quality and quantity of diplomatic reporting around the world diminished perceptibly: without *The New York Times* to tell them what to say, the diplomats fell silent.[5]

The diplomat more than the journalist is inclined to be pro-junta. Everything conspires to make him so. He cannot, consistently with protocol, hobnob with the opposition, especially if it is under house arrest. He gets only one side of the story – often the losing side.

These impressions he faithfully conveys to headquarters. It is not that headquarters would be no worse off without them. It would be better off without them. Vietnam and Biafra are each in their way the products of the occupational hazards of diplomatic reporting from the scene. So much would common sense lead one to conclude. But Sir Val Duncan and his colleagues are not content with common sense. They have devised a scientific test, of sorts.

Taking advantage of a rupture of diplomatic relations with a number of other countries, resulting in the closing down of missions overseas, they have assessed what adverse effects, if any, have followed. They find it made no difference. The United Kingdom got along without the missions, as it had got along with them. The recipients of their advice were not paralyzed by being deprived of it. 'The user departments in the Foreign and Commonwealth Office made it plain that their main functions of action, decision, and policy-making had been little affected by the withdrawal of the posts in question.'

What lessons does the Duncan Report contain for the government of Canada? With sixty-seven missions in the field, from Moscow to Montevideo, plus nineteen consular establishments, Canada is wildly over-represented overseas in relation to her needs.

In earlier years those needs were constitutional rather than political. The Canadian diplomat was a pawn in the game of East Block versus Downing Street, each new embassy a milestone along the road from colony to nation. Our right of legation was first exercised in 1927 by exchanging ministers with the United States. But this was a step towards status, not substance.

'The qualifications for a successful diplomat in Washington,' wrote our first secretary soon after his arrival, 'are, in order of importance, (1) a good head for liquor and (2) a capacity for producing, orally and on paper, polite guff at a moment's notice. This,' he added, 'I found trying at first, but it is

4 *Diplomacy in the Nuclear Age* (S.J. Reginald Saunders, Toronto 1959), 16
5 'The bulk of political reporting is still spot reporting, also known as translating *Le Monde.*' *Diplomacy for the '70s: A Program of Management Reform for the Department of State* (GPO, Washington 1970), 468

becoming mechanical.'[6] It was much the same in London. 'No one here has any idea as to what the Canadian attitude is,' Pearson wrote after representing Canada for the first time, 'or even if there is a Canadian attitude. But I was reluctant to say that, so I chatted amiably for 15 minutes.'[7] There is a motto for a Canadian foreign office, but it would have to be disguised in Latin: *Horae quadrantum suaviter garriebam.*

Thereafter missions proliferated like toadstools in the dew. All parties agreed that more meant better. 'Is there any likelihood,' asked Mr Martin of Mr Green in 1960, 'of any mission being established in Baghdad?' Replied Mr Green to Mr Martin: 'This is a mission I would like very much to have established, and there are others too.'[8] But he did not explain how our vital interests are served by having our men in Baghdad, nor what role other than symbols of Canada's conspicuous consumption are played by a score of exotic missions in our numerous 'outer areas.'

Recent tribulations of the diplomatic profession – the fire-bombing of our embassy in Austria, the kidnapping of the US ambassador in Brazil – are useful reminders that missions these days are not so much mile-stones as mill-stones, hostages rather than status symbols.

A radical reorganization of the Department of External Affairs, undertaken in the spirit of the Duncan Report, could do much to improve the machinery of our diplomacy and the quality of our foreign policy. Most of its postings are expendable. Much of its work is redundant. Many of its officials are unnecessary. The name is 'External,' not 'Eternal.'

[September 1969]

6   Hume Wrong to Mrs G.M. Wrong, July 1927, Wrong Papers
7   Quoted in John R. Beal, *The Pearson Phenomenon* (Longmans, Toronto 1964), 55
8   Canada, *House of Commons Debates,* 15 July 1960, 6377-8

2

The ambassador as hostage

Into each life some rain must fall, but too much is falling into the diplomatic life. The modern ambassador is under severe occupational stress. Admittedly, most professions are tense these days, and academics are fond of singling out their own as one of special strain. But even the don, dissolving in self-pity as he faces the fusillade of chalk and insult by which his classroom's about to be 'liberated,' might concede that his predicament pales by comparison with the problems of the diplomat.

The don has tenure, the diplomat has immunity, both privileges are under attack. But while the traditional defences against violations of academic freedom – blacklisting the offending institution, solidarity among colleagues – are still secure against meddlesome governors (if not against mettlesome students), the traditional defences against violations of diplomatic immunity are in contrast crumbling. For they consist solely of whatever resources of restraint and courtesy a community may muster out of its sense of civic virtue and enlightened public policy. Of such resources the world today is running out – faster even than of gas, or of gazelles.

Last week's kidnapping of the West German ambassador to Brazil – unlike his colleague the ambassador to Guatemala, Mr Von Holleben at least emerged from his ordeal alive – reminds us once more of the truly savage levels to which we have allowed international comity to descend.

Peoples whom some anthropologists persist in calling primitive put us to shame in this respect, for among them the rules of diplomatic immunity are invariably observed. By one aboriginal culture after another – Arunta of Australia, Maoris of Oceana, Indians of North America – the person and mission of the tribal envoy are held sacred. Their ambassadors, writes an authority, 'were received with every mark of honor and respect, perfumed with incense, presented with flowers, and well lodged and entertained. Any insult or indignity offered them was a sufficient cause of war.'

There was a time when such hallmarks of civility were stamped as well on countries calling themselves civilized. But it was long ago and far away. In 1708, the Russian ambassador in London was arrested at the instigation of merchants to whom he owed money. He was quickly released, apologies were tendered, those harassing him were punished. But the ambassador, unmollified by these amends, had left in a huff, and nothing would do but that Lord Whitworth, British envoy at St Petersburg, be accredited for the special mission of conveying to Peter the Great in public audience the expression of the queen's regret and sorrow.

This episode was related in Satow's *Guide to Diplomatic Practice* in 1932 as if such punctillious apologies were still standard operating procedure among chancelleries, as if the molestation of an envoy was still an unheard of outrage. Neither were true. The image of the diplomat as effete pusher of cookies, dilettante of drawing-room and boudoir, obscured the extent to which his had already become a dangerous profession.

Four main hazards now haunt the diplomatic life. One is to be posted to a war zone and get caught in the cross fire, like the US vice-consul killed by a terrorist bomb in Cyprus in 1956, or the member of the US embassy in Saigon killed in a Viet Cong attack in 1965, or the US military attaché killed by sniper fire in Amman a few days ago.

Another is to be singled out by a crank or fanatic with some grievance, real or imagined, against the diplomat's government. A Soviet minister to Poland was gunned down in 1927 by a Russian monarchist; a Spanish diplomat was shot in the streets of Mexico City by a Cuban who had fought against Franco; the American ambassador to Japan was stabbed by a student in 1961; some aggrieved individual set fire to the Canadian mission in Vienna in 1969.

A third source of danger to the diplomat is where a foreign government fails, for one reason or another, to provide him with protection, to which he is entitled by the law of nations, and so becomes accomplice in, even instigator of, his harassment.

Communist governments, with their equivocal attitude to international law and secretive style of politics, are notorious offenders. In eastern Europe, the line between legitimate political reporting and espionage is drawn by the authorities erratically and without warning; the experience of a junior Canadian diplomat who, driving from Berlin to Warsaw in 1947, was imprisoned by the Russians for a fortnight, is unusual only for the duration of his detention.

Third world governments, with their revolutionary ideologies and anti-imperialist hang-ups, often turn a blind eye while mobs vent their frustration on representatives of white, neo-colonialist powers.

And the most persistent and systematic violations of diplomatic immunity take place in Washington, DC, New York City, and along Route 40 (the highway in between), where African and Asian envoys endure affronts, abuse, and muggings.

But it is the fourth, and latest, hazard which is most dangerous of all - the risk of being kidnapped by guerrillas, terrorists or other outlawed opposition groups. This tactic holds the gravest peril not just for the person of the ransomed diplomat but for the future of the diplomatic system.

The outbreak began in August 1969, with the abduction of the American ambassador to Brazil. That this case seems to be the first of its kind is not because of the sanctity of embassies, it is because of lack of organization and flair among those underground movements which stand to gain by trading captured diplomats for prisoners and pay.

Now they have been shown it can be done. Political kidnapping will become as common - and as successful - as political hijacking. And the usefulness of the diplomat as his government's public eye abroad will be at an end.

Already it is ending. To the blinkers which have always shielded the diplomat from reality - the cronyism of the diplomatic corps, the diplomat's desire to think well of the regime at whose pleasure he remains, the circumspection required by protocol - must now be added the screen of security.

In capital after capital, embassies are being hermetically sealed so as to protect their inmates. 'Ambassadors no longer wander around on their own,' a despatch from the field reports. 'Security men accompany them to social functions, shopping trips and diplomatic appointments. The daily itineraries of ambassadors are kept as secret as possible, and official limousines alternate their routes while taking ambassadors between their offices and homes.'

In US embassies, one official has revealed, regulations are so strict that 'we tell each other where we're going and what we're planning to do only on a "need to know" basis.'

Such working conditions breed paranoia - hardly an aid to dispassionate analysis. It is by no means confined to the missions of West Germany and the United States, the countries thus far singled out. 'Representatives of all Socialist countries are in danger anywhere in Latin America,' a Czechoslovak embassy official there has stated; while a Latin American diplomat, chattering with fright, told a reporter: 'The guerrillas are out to get us, host governments may refuse to help us, other embassies may be serving as lookouts for the guerrillas, and any one who looks at us sideways on the street may be planning to kill us. How do I know you aren't talking to me merely to lay a trap?'

If the diplomat must now be described as an honest man sent to cower abroad for his country, his usefulness is clearly at a close. He might just as well stay home. His government will learn more of the turbulent world by reading the daily papers. The foreign correspondent is today a more reliable purveyor of intelligence than the diplomat – not because he is braver, but because his employers, given the choice between their scoop and his safety, will choose the scoop every time.

Ottawa planners of Canadian representation abroad, please note well.

[June 1970]

'An honest man sent to die abroad for his country.' Sir Henry Wotton's definition of the diplomat had it 'lie,' not 'die.' But that was in the seventeenth century, when the person of the envoy was held in scrupulous regard not only in the law of nations but in their practice too. We practise differently today.

Not that the law allows us to. The prime duty of all governments to protect the diplomat and succour him in danger survives in international affairs not as some quaint relic of the past but in a recent affirmation. 'The receiving state shall treat him with due respect,' recites the Vienna Convention on Diplomatic Relations, 'and shall take all appropriate steps to prevent any attack upon his person, freedom or dignity.' Such was the pledge of forty-five governments – among them the government of Canada.

The government of Canada failed to prevent an attack upon the person and freedom of J.R. (Jasper) Cross, United Kingdom trade commissioner in Montreal. (The dignity of Jasper Cross, being an aspect of his character, lay beyond the reach of his abductors.) The government of Canada therefore had an especial obligation to put his safety before every other consideration.

It chose to put it somewhere else. 'Clearly these are unreasonable demands,' the secretary of state for external affairs declared of the kidnappers' terms for the release of their hostage. 'I need hardly say that this set of demands will not be met.'

Ransoms demanded by kidnappers always appear unreasonable to those who are asked to pay them. Kidnappers run grave risks, they must play for high stakes; their time runs out quickly, they must use their fleeting power while they can. So the kidnappers of Jasper Cross set a steep price for his release.

Steep; but in only one of their demands exorbitant. The government could not in good conscience tell the FLQ the name of its informer; that would have amounted to trading one life for another. (Trading one hostage for another would have been an ethical exchange; but Canadian ministers, less chivalrous than Latin, did not volunteer to put themselves in Mr Cross's place.)

None of the other demands lay beyond the pale of a reasonable propitiation where a man's life hangs in the balance. Hunted men at bay must bargain for abeyance of the hunt. Without safe passage to an asylum, the abductors could not deal; the logic of this demand the government recognized only after the family of Jasper Cross had endured five times the expiration of a deadline for his murder. Postal workers if re-hired for the occasion could have been fired when it passed. $500,000 in bullion is less than the $700,000 demanded by Guatemalan terrorists – who killed their hostage when they didn't get it.

What of the demand – copied from the Tupamaros of Uruguay – for publicity for FLQ ideas? At length the government gave in on this. The broadcast on Thursday night of an FLQ manifesto, and its reproduction in the press, has done more good than harm. Locating the lunatic fringe helps the vital centre find itself. Any society does well to know the minds of those who would subvert it.

The most vexing of the FLQ demands was that twenty-three convicted terrorists be sprung from Canadian prisons for sanctuary in Cuba or Algeria.

A bitter pill to swallow; yet other governments had swallowed it. Brazil released five prisoners to secure the freedom of the Japanese counsul Veneral in March 1969; fifteen prisoners to secure the freedom of the American ambassador in September 1969; forty prisoners to secure the freedom of the West German ambassador in June. Only last month the governments of Britain, West Germany, and Switzerland surrendered the hi-jackers in their custody to secure the freedom of passengers held hostage by Palestinian guerrillas.

Defying the kidnappers, by contrast, ended only in tragedy. Guatemala refused to release twenty-five prisoners to secure the freedom of the West German ambassador; Count von Spreti was murdered. Uruguay refused to release 150 prisoners to secure the freedom of an American technical assistance expert; Dan Mitrione was murdered.

All these precedents were at the disposal of that inner circle of federal cabinet ministers and senior civil servants upon whom, during their meetings throughout the week in the new east block operations room, the burden of decision had devolved. If Jasper Cross was not to be sacrificed at the altar of Canadian national pride, experience pointed to appeasement.

Expediency pointed the same way. One thing for a government with thousands of political prisoners – or political criminals – to balk at releasing a few; Canada's twenty-three would have just about cleaned out the cells. Once in Cuba or Algeria they would no longer be a drain on the taxpayer, a strain on their guards, an inducement to more abductions. The FLQ might have botched their getaway; there's many a slip between Dorval and Havana, Dorval and Algiers. Maybe Castro or Boumedienne could be induced to send them back.

Such arguments, if heard, made no headway at all. Neither Ottawa nor Quebec City were disposed towards an appeasement which might make it appear that the FLQ were right to depict its jailed murderers and robbers as no more guilty of a real crime than the victims of Soviet or Greek or Brazilian tyranny. They feared as well for the safety of the realm. To give in would give rise to an orgy of kidnapping and lawlessness. Diplomats would topple to terrorist attacks like falling dominoes. There must be no surrender to blackmail.

That is called paying the Dane-gold;
But we've proved it again and again,
That if once you have paid him the Dane-gold
You never get rid of the Dane.

Buoyed by such homely folk-wisdom, the government refused to give in. Its reward for such holy obstinacy was the kidnapping, minutes after the final deadline passed, of the Quebec minister of labour.

To place the welfare of society ahead of the welfare of Jasper Cross (and now the welfare of Pierre Laporte) is justified only if we could be as sure of the impact of the release of the FLQ political criminals upon the national interest as we are of the impact of bullets upon the brain. No such certainty exists. To combat evil the prime minister has embraced evil. A leader who, however somberly, sacrifices the life of an individual to any political abstraction is a leader who one day may sacrifice hetacombs of kulaks for the sake of some cherished principle. His followers will find themselves not in the happy valley of the just society, rather in the canyon of totalitarian rule.

If Jasper Cross is crucified, we cannot fairly charge the government of Canada with his killing; the FLQ's done that. But our government's decision may remind us of another centuries ago. 'I am innocent of this man's blood; see to it yourselves.' Pilate's ghost stalked its operations room last week.

[October 1970]

J.R. Cross, Esq.
c/o British Embassy
Bern, Switzerland

Dear Mr Cross,
    It would be entirely understandable if you are consigning all mail postmarked Canada this Christmas unread to your waste basket. Even so, I write (as many Canadians must be writing) to say how relieved and thankful we are

that you have emerged from your ordeal safely and fit and been reunited with your family. That is some light amid our encircling gloom.

Not long before your abduction I'd discussed in a column the collapse of the traditional defences against violations of diplomatic immunity – defences consisting 'solely of whatever resources of restraint and courtesy a community may muster out of its sense of civic virtue and enlightened public policy.' What I didn't understand was how short is the supply of civic virtue and enlightened public policy in Canada. I shared the prevailing parochialism and smugness which betrayed us into believing that it could not happen here.

It seemed strange that it was happening at 1297 Redpath Crescent. Your house in Montreal used to belong to my parents-in-law, so that the concern of my younger children, who often stayed there, was first aroused by their being able to imagine so vividly the route taken by your kidnappers – up the stone steps to the front door, past the tiled foyer, through the panelled hall, up the broadloomed staircase – the newel post carved in the shape of an owl's head – to the bedrooms beyond. Your abductors confess to having been unnerved by this unaccustomed opulence. Not sufficiently unnerved, alas, for them to have dropped their guns and run.

More striking for me at the time was the odd symbolism of your case. A Joyce or Nabakov could have a field day – the house high on Mount Royal under the cross, your name itself, your initials J.C., the threat of double-cross, indeed of crucifixion. 'I am innocent of this man's blood; see to it yourselves.' The words of Pontius Pilate seemed to reverberate down the ages. On hearing that our government had turned down the demands for your release I quoted them in an article arguing as forcefully as lay within my power the case for negotiating your freedom.

It appeared to me then, it appears to me now, that the case for negotiating your freedom was unassailable, expedientially and ethically. About the ethics of the case, you maintained at your press conference in London earlier this month a discreet restraint. About expediency, you seem to share the view of the government of Canada. 'If you let these chaps go to Cuba,' you argued, 'what guarantee is there that I would then be released?' The guarantee, surely, is the terrorists' vested interest in preserving kidnapping as an instrument of credible bargaining for the future. To welch on the deal is to degrade the technique. But the technique is highly prized. No terrorist group, accordingly, has broken its word about its hostages – not for reasons of honour, for reasons of power.

You then raised the issue of the role of the media. 'There's been a lot of talk about journalistic responsibility,' you said at your press conference. 'But people have a responsibility to the kidnapped, the chap in there ...' Amen to that.

During your harrowing sojourn in the Avenue des Récollets our press bore this responsibility badly. Its speculation about whether your messages had hidden meanings was either despicable or stupid. Believe, if you can, it was stupid only – the result of what a recent report on our mass media calls 'the archaic perceptions of cop-shop journalism.' (It's true that the London *Times* ran one of your notes over the caption 'Is Mr Cross indicating he is under duress?' but then Lanctot and Carbonneau weren't likely reading the *Times*.)

I feel obliged to declare and defend my own record in this regard, for I wrote and spoke about the crisis while you were still a prisoner. What I wrote was meant to help you; it didn't help, but couldn't harm you. On three occasions I was asked to talk on television. One was the day after your abduction; I refused, knowing that seventy per cent of kidnap murders are committed within forty hours of the kidnapping. Another was the day you were released; I refused again, knowing that until you were safe silence was golden.

The third occasion was the day following the murder of Pierre Laporte. This time I agreed. I planned to try to plead with the audience to bring pressure on the government to bargain for your release. These are some notes I made to keep me to this theme: 'Don't dissipate opportunity in academic or philosophical discussion. One life has been taken. Another remains in the balance. Appeal to the government, to the Prime Minister, to put aside false pride, all considerations of prestige and face. Not to become slave of policies well-intentioned, but poorly thought through. Results count.'

I spoke along these lines as best I could. My words were lost in the editing. I don't blame the producer for cutting them out, though I felt badly that they'd been cut out. Mercifully it turned out they weren't needed.

You may have heard of a move to admit you and your wife to the Companionship of the Order of Canada. All here seem enthusiastic, in the manner of hosts solacing themselves for having been so beastly to their guests. Personally I don't care for the spectacle of committees of senior public servants solemnly bestowing awards of state on one another. What we in this country owe you and yours is not decorations but damages.

As a taxpayer I'd gladly help foot the bill. It's obviously impossible to work out the amount of compensation owing to a person obliged for sixty days to 'live each day as if thy last' in the most starkly literal meaning of that line from the old hymn. But £1000 each day comes close to what the London literary agents are saying your story's worth to them and what the foreign office won't allow you to sell your story for. I'd make them 60,000 guineas, not pounds. Guineas have class. So have you.

Respectfully yours,
James Eayrs
[December 1970]

3

The correspondent and the diplomat

In the beginning, we find the correspondent and the diplomat at loggerheads. 'The beginning' is the nineteenth century, and the second half of it at that. It's only a hundred years, and then only in Britain and America, since the opinion of the public begins to matter very much to those who conduct foreign policy on its behalf. And only when public opinion matters to the policy-makers does the correspondent begin to matter to the diplomat. He matters because it is by what he writes that public opinion is informed and influenced, for better or for worse.

In the beginning, the diplomat thought it for the worse. And with good reason. Look at the role of the press in the two wars by which the long nineteenth-century peace was broken: Britain's war in the Crimea, America's war with Spain.

The official history of *The Times* of London exaggerates the paper's part when it claims that *The Times* 'made the war' in the Crimea.[1] But once the war got under way, *The Times* made its conduct very difficult for diplomats. It was the first war when correspondents took to the field to telegraph to their papers their first-hand accounts of the ebb and flow of battle, the conduct of campaigns, the incidence of casualties. Their despatches made lurid reading and boosted circulation. They dismayed the Foreign Office. 'If *we* could get such information,' a British diplomat lamented after reading an especially forthcoming account, 'it would be worth thousands to us.'[2] (Pounds or lives he didn't say.) The secretary of state for war warned all the London

---

1 *The History of The Times*, II, *The Tradition Established, 1841-84* (Printing House Square, London 1939), 190
2 Quoted in Olive Anderson, *A Liberal State at War* (Macmillan, London 1967), 72

editors of the danger of publishing military information in the despatches of
their correspondents. 'I have only to appeal to your patriotism,' he told them,
'to ensure a rigid supervision of all such [despatches].' If that was what he
really thought, he was sorely disappointed. *The Times* published its despatches.
The diplomats damned its correspondents. But no one put them in jail.

During America's war with Spain, the press was hardly diplomatic. That's
putting it mildly. It was the first war when the press drove its government into
a war it didn't want. The ace illustrator of the *New York Journal,* ordered to
draw war pictures from Cuba, complained to his proprietor that it was an impossible assignment, since there was no war in Cuba. William Randolph Hearst
thereupon cabled his celebrated reply: 'You furnish the pictures and I'll furnish the war.' And he did. When Admiral Dewey's battleships sailed into
Manilla Harbor and blew out of the water what one historian has called 'the
collection of marine antiquities that passed for the Spanish fleet,' Hearst ran
an exultant headline 'HOW DO YOU LIKE THE JOURNAL'S WAR?'[3] That was
an exaggeration only in the sense that it was as much Pulitzer's war as Hearst's.
When any of you next win a Pulitzer Prize for news reporting, awarded (according to the citation of its first recipient) for 'strict accuracy, terseness, the
accomplishment of some public good commanding public attention and respect,' you may find it useful to remember that your prize money derives
from an estate accumulated by one whose journalistic creed was 'Never be
content with merely giving the news.' If news didn't exist, it would be necessary to invent it. A reporter from Pulitzer's *New York World* accordingly in-
vented the news of Spanish atrocities in Cuba:

Blood on the roadside, blood in the fields, blood on the doorsteps, blood,
blood, blood! The old, the young, the weak, the crippled – all are butchered
without mercy ...[4]

There wasn't a shred of truth in any of this. But its purpose wasn't to purvey
the truth. Its purpose was to provide a pretext for intervention. At the end of
his list of fabricated atrocities, the man from *The World* asked a question of
his 800,000 readers: 'Is there no nation wise enough, brave enough, strong
enough to restore peace in this bloodsmitten land?' It was a rhetorical question, both he and they knowing the answer already. There was such a nation.
It was their nation. The United States of America soon invaded Cuba – not for
the last time.

3 Quoted in Thomas A. Bailey, *A Diplomatic History of the American People,* 3rd ed.
   (Appleton-Century-Crofts, New York & London 1946), 514
4 Quoted in ibid., 498

During this hey-day of yellow journalism the diplomat formed his image of
the correspondent. Naturally it was far from flattering. Journalism and jingo-
ism had become all but synonyms. The diplomat, accordingly, regarded the
correspondent not merely as a rival but as something of a saboteur.

He was in any case a rival. Tension between the two was built into their
respective professional objectives. The highest testimonial a foreign minister
could earn – so Bismarck observed as early as 1883 – was distress in the world
of journalism. 'Happy the people,' Walter Bagehot remarked, 'whose annals
are vacant, but woe to the wretched journalists that have to compose and
write articles therein.'

But there is more to it than that. It's not just that their jobs seemed more
competitive than complementary, the correspondent prospering at the diplomat's expense. It's that their professional styles differ so, their life styles differ so. In temperament, in attitude, in outlook, in ethos, the correspondent
and the diplomat are at opposite extremes, inhabit different worlds.

To the correspondent, publicity is always welcome. It is his life's work to
create it. Often as not he is its subject as well as its creator. A well known
Toronto evening newspaper – not the *Telegram* – is famous for what's called
'*Star*-man news': 'STAR MAN REACHES SOUTH POLE'; 'STAR MAN FINDS GERDA
MUNSINGER IN MUNICH.' To the diplomat, publicity is deadly, the air that kills.
It nips negotiations in the bud, it withers treaties on the vine. The diplomat
shuns the limelight: the very word (he recalls with a shudder) derives from
news photography during its formative phase.

Or take their attitude to time. (I mean the concept 'time,' not the weekly
newsmagazine.) The correspondent works to deadlines. He's accustomed to
immediate results: file today, in print tomorrow, feed-back the day after. The
diplomat also has his deadlines. But his product takes a lifetime to produce,
and even then he can't be sure. (Dean Acheson took to woodworking as a
hobby because, as he says, you know when you've made a table or a chair,
but how can you tell with a foreign policy?)

As with the professional style, so with the life style. The correspondent
lives flamboyantly, floridly, if not in fact, in fancy. He takes for his model his
master, who used to live like a monarch: Hearst, secluded in a castle midst his
magpie treasures; Pulitzer, shuttling the Atlantic in a yacht the size of a liner;
Northcliffe, killing salmon on three continents; Thomson, killing competitors
on four. The diplomat, in contrast, tolerates rather than relishes all this. Osten-
tation and display, like chandeliers and wine, are but the props of his professional stage, on which he appears only to sign state papers or to honour official
visitors. His real work is done elsewhere: a retreat in Whitehall, perhaps, where
the routine's austere enough – a procession of papers and callers, broken by a
quiet lunch at The Travellers' and a walk in St James's park.

Their demeanour of work and of life being so drastically different, the correspondent and the diplomat confront one another in a posture of mutual antipathy. The diplomat, George Kennan has written, sees his task as a menial task, 'tidying up the messes other people have made, moderating the passions of opinionated individuals.' Is it any wonder that this 'weary sceptic' (as Kennan well describes him) should so deplore the correspondent? Who makes more messes than the correspondent? Who is more opinionated? And so the diplomat takes of the correspondent a jaundiced view, seeing in him

the distillation of all that in human nature which is most extroverted, most thick-skinned, most pushing, most pre-occupied with the present, least given to a sense of historical proportion, least inclined to be animated by any deeper and more subtle philosophy of human affairs, and – by that same token – least inclined to look deeply into the realities of international life.[5]

From such a creature the diplomat did not feel he had much to learn. The Foreign Office official[6] who took on the job of bringing up to date Satow's classic *Guide to Diplomatic Practice* notes only with disapproval what he describes as 'a growing tendency ... to substitute for the discreet exchange of notes, tendentious press conferences and abuse over the air'; he resolutely refuses to sully the pages of the classic by offering to fledglings of the foreign service hints on how to exploit the new techniques of open diplomacy.

But this was to act like King Canute at low tide.[7] It was to act, moreover, contrary to the precept which diplomatists are taught at an early age – that which holds statecraft to consist in the constructive acceptance of the inevitable. For what could be more inevitable than the growing influence of the press upon the conduct of foreign policy? The correspondent might be an interloper in diplomacy, a meddler, a trifler, a trouble-maker. But there he was on the doorstep, indeed with his foot in the door. And behind him were a host of others – rude and cheeky chaps from Pathé and Movietone news, roistering photographers with flashguns, boisterous broadcasters with microphones. Whatever could you do with them? One's first impulse (if one was a diplomat) was to confiscate their horrid apparatus and throw them all in jail. But you couldn't do that, much as you might want to – not in Britain or America. So what *was* to be done?

Well, there was always friendly persuasion ...

5 'History and Diplomacy as Viewed by a Diplomatist,' in Stephen D. Kertesz and M.A. Fitzsimons, eds., *Diplomacy in a Changing World* (University of Notre Dame Press, Notre Dame 1959), 106
6 Sir Nevile Bland
7 Not really. Canute went through the motions of obduracy so as to impress upon his courtiers the futility of stubbornness.

A harsher name for that is the management of news. If you want the very model of a modern news manager, you will find him in the person of the foreign office press officer. Old-fashioned foreign offices didn't have press officers, for old-fashioned foreign offices didn't manage news. The Great War is the turning point. The first impulse of the Foreign Office in 1914 was to censor the news, not to manage it. That worked for a while, but not for very long. 'As the war went on,' the official Foreign Office historian tells us, 'grave objections were felt to the exercise of censorship by the Foreign Office ... and late in 1915 a radical change was made.' For the arbitrary hand of the censor there was substituted what the official historian calls 'gentle guidance.' This is how he says it worked:

The Press Bureau continued to send the Foreign Office copies of dangerous or doubtful despatches, and it was often possible ... to telephone to any given newspaper that they were about to receive a message on this or that subject, but that it would be better that they should not publish it, or a part of it, for the following reason, the true state of affairs being ...[8]

The diplomat found this device much too useful to allow it to lapse with the end of the war. The management of news was here to stay. Henceforth the diplomat would meet the correspondent on the correspondent's ground, using the tricks of the correspondent's trade, even hiring correspondents to do his own trade – on the theory that it takes one to know one. This practice has developed most fully in the United States where today the gentleman who meets the press on behalf of the White House or the State Department is, more often than not, himself a sometime gentleman of the press – a Jim Haggerty, or a Pierre Salinger, or a Douglass Cater. He is the voice of his master, to whom he has sold his pen, his brain, his soul.

Sometimes, though, the master himself may try to manage news on his own behalf. An obvious technique is to win the favour of the correspondent by flattery and patronage. Trying to make lapdogs out of watchdogs can be a risky business, because the watchdog's apt to bite the hand that feeds it. But when it works it works wonders, and some statesmen are prepared to run the risk.

It worked wonders, for example, for the prime minister of Canada when, in 1923, Mackenzie King decided to take with him to an Imperial Conference the respected editor of the *Winnipeg Free Press,* John W. Dafoe. Mackenzie King was elated when Dafoe accepted: 'I confess,' he wrote privately, 'that this has given me a feeling of security with respect to a fair and just represen-

8 Sir John Tilley, *The Foreign Office* (G.P. Putnam's Sons, London & New York 1933), 282

tation of Canada's position, which I have not thus far wholly enjoyed.'[9] Dafoe
was a bit uneasy, as well he might have been, about a possible conflict between
his role as correspondent and his new found role as an unofficial member of
the delegation. But this soon wore off. Mackenzie King had every reason to be
pleased with the experiment. Not only was his position at the conference sym-
pathetically reported in the *Free Press,* he acquired in Dafoe a degree of admiration few other newspapermen in Canada felt for him. 'My regard for
King,' Dafoe himself confessed years later, 'which is quite considerable, dates
largely from 1923.'[10]

Encouraged by this success, Mackenzie King sought to repeat it a few
years later by directly approaching the editor of the Toronto *Globe.* 'I should
be the last to wish *The Globe* or any newspaper to sacrifice the slightest degree
of independence' – so the Prime Minister of Canada commenced his attempted
seduction –

but I think I have seen enough of public affairs to know that a Government's
influence can be much greater in the causes it has at heart where it has a press
that is sympathetic and in whose co-operation in furthering its ends and policies it is possible to count. Similarly, I believe it to be true that a great public
journal can be vastly more influential in causing to prevail many of the views
and opinions of its editorial control where it has the confidence and co-operation of a Government in office ... After all, we have not only common ideals
to advance, but common enemies to fight. I believe,

Mackenzie King concluded, 'that an increase of confidence between us would
mean not only added personal joy, but added power to the cause each of us
has very much at heart.'[11] The *Globe*'s editor, W.G. Jaffray, did not respond
to this, perhaps because he derived little personal joy from Mackenzie King's
embraces, perhaps because the prime minister's offer consisted merely of a
trip to Ottawa to talk things over. He might have done better with an offer of
a royal commissionership. (The visitor to Canada cannot fail to be astonished
not only at the number of royal commissions created in this country, but also
at the number of journalists appointed as royal commissioners.)

Mackenzie King's assertion that 'a great public journal can be vastly more
influential ... where it has the confidence and co-operation of a Government
in office' is nowhere better demonstrated – or more disastrously – than in the
relationship between the British government and the London *Times* during

9 King to Sir Clifford Sifton, 30 Aug. 1923, King Papers
10 Quoted in Ramsay Cook, 'J.W. Dafoe at the Imperial Conference, 1923,' *Canadian
    Historical Review*, XLI, no 1, Mar. 1960, 21
11 King to W. G. Jaffray, 12 Aug. 1929, King Papers

the years before the Second World War. It's not just that *The Times* stood editorially for everything that may now be seen, with benefit of hindsight, as the wrong policies – for appeasing Hitler, for ostracizing Churchill, for firing Vansittart. We all make mistakes. No, *The Times'* offence is graver by far than that. It is so grave that its official history can only hint at the gravity:

The Editor and [his assistant] relied for their knowledge of the Continent less upon [their] Correspondents than upon certain personal sources, and thus the foreign policy pursued by *The Times* after the crucial year of 1936 became increasingly indebted ... [to] the Editor's ministerial friends, Baldwin, Chamberlain and Halifax ...[12]

There is one thing worse than an editor who prefers the views of ministers who happen to be his friends to the views of journalists who happen to be his correspondents. That is an editor who suppresses the despatches of his correspondent at the wishes of his ministerial friends. Thus far from his calling did Geoffrey Dawson fall. The official history of *The Times* passes over this sordid episode in silence, as an authorized biography of Judas Iscariot might skim lightly over the rather awkward bit about the thirty pieces of silver.

Harold Nicolson, who used to work for the Foreign Office, wrote at this time a widely read book on diplomacy, in the course of which he addressed himself to the problem of obtaining, as he put it, 'a satisfactory adjustment between the needs and rights of a popular Press and the requirements of discretion.' No trace of the travails of *The Times* darkens his sunny dispensation. 'The advantages of a free Press,' he wrote serenely in 1939, 'are so immeasurably greater than its disadvantages that this particular problem of democratic diplomacy need not cause anxiety. It is little more than a minor inconvenience.'[13]

Few people today – correspondents or diplomats – can think the matter should be left at that. Even those of us who would like to think it should be have to concede that it's a counsel of perfection – a distant star by which to plot our life's ideals, not a reading light by which to earn our daily bread. And there are many who don't like to think it can be left at that – who would resolve the tension between the correspondent and the diplomat by having the correspondent place himself at the disposal of the diplomat.

12 *The History of The Times, IV, The 150th Anniversary and Beyond, II, 1921-1948* (Printing House Square, London 1952), 905
13 *Diplomacy,* 3rd ed. (Oxford, London, New York, Toronto 1963), 99-100

Not all who are willing to compromise the freedom of the press are warriors in the Cold War. They include, for example, so sturdily independent a
spirit as Conor Cruise O'Brien who ranges himself squarely against the *ruat
caelum* position - 'let the sky fall,' the philosophical counterpart of 'publish
and be damned.'

If deceit is acceptable to win a war, why should it not be equally acceptable,
say, to preserve the peace? Or to ensure a greater measure of social justice or
social stability? How many lies [O'Brien asks rhetorically] might not justifi-
ably have been told to avert Hiroshima?[14]

Or, we may ask (improving on his rhetoric), to avert the death or mutilation
of one tiny child? And we answer, if there's any humanity left in us, as he
answers: whole systems of mendacity.

So the simple formula 'diplomats lie, correspondents catch them out' is
none too helpful here. Of course diplomats lie. We need no wise owls to tell
us that. Deceit is commonplace in foreign policy. And so what else is new?

Just this. Today, and never more so than today, honesty's the best policy.
The requirements of security, contrary to what diplomats tell us, do not conflict with the requirements of truth.

Diplomats tell us otherwise; some correspondents tell us otherwise. And I
cannot prove them wrong. The proposition that honesty's the best policy is
not to be established by some mathematical formula with the infallibility of
a computer. All I can do is to invoke some lessons of history - hypothetical
history at that. And appeal to your intuitions - which are known to be highly
developed.

Let's look closer at the O'Brien scenario. He asks us to lie to avert Hiroshima - short-hand for a hundred thousand dead, unspeakable suffering for as
many more again. And looking back in horror we are willing liars in that cause.
But what sort of falsehood might have spared those lives? None that I can
think of, and I've thought hard. What about the truth? On 16 July 1945, the
first explosion of an atomic bomb took place in the New Mexican desert. It
was witnessed by a correspondent, William Laurence of *The New York Times.*
But Laurence was no ordinary reporter, poised for the scoop of a lifetime. He
was under contract to the government, sworn to utmost secrecy, and included
among the witnesses only so as to record the event for posterity and to be better prepared to draft the press release once the bombs had fallen on Japan. And
so, the detonation over and the ghastly cloud subsided, he filed no story of this
news not fit to print. But what if he had? Suppose, instead of the delphic mes-

14 *Writers and Politics* (Pantheon Books, New York 1965), xvii

sages crackling across to Washington and Potsdam in code – 'The light in [Little Boy's] eyes discernible from here to High-hold and I could have heard his screams from here to my farm' – suppose there'd been banner headlines and detailed despatches. Might not the High Command in Tokyo, already divided on whether to fight on in a hopeless cause, have been swayed towards surrender? Might not Hiroshima have been averted? The questions can't be answered. But they can certainly be asked.

Thirteen years later another explosion shook the desert – this one a hundred times more destructive than the destroyer of Hiroshima. No correspondent witnessed the explosion – not because it was forbidden but because it was routine. Atomic testing had become a minor attraction for tourists, a minor inconvenience for the gamblers at Vegas. All the same there was a story here. The explosion was designed to ascertain how far from the scene the tremors of the blast might be detected. Much depends on the outcome. If not very far – a few hundred miles at most – the opponents of the proposed treaty to outlaw the testing of nuclear weapons could argue that the Soviet Union would violate the treaty by clandestine testing underground. But if the tremors could be detected at a safe distance – say a thousand miles or more – this argument was unconvincing and the chances for a treaty improved. The official report of the test, put out by the Atomic Energy Commission, stated that the explosion had not been detected more than 200 miles away. But at the time of the explosion, seismographical stations in Rome, in Tokyo and, as it happened, in Toronto, had registered its effects. A sharp-eyed correspondent in Washington, intrigued by the discrepancy, followed up the story and discovered not only that the blast had registered in these foreign cities, but that it had been picked up as well by no fewer than twenty US stations, one as far away as Fairbanks, Alaska – 2600 miles from the scene. But the evidence had been suppressed. The correspondent, I.F. Stone, publisher of the one-man independent *I.F. Stone's Weekly,* told the story in his newspaper. The Atomic Energy Commission said only that there had been an 'inadvertent' error. Which of them better served the national interest: the AEC by lying, I.F. Stone by publishing the truth? *That* question can be answered.

James Reston of *The New York Times* has confessed that he knew

for over a year that the United States was flying high altitude planes (the U-2) over the Soviet Union from a base in Pakistan to photograph military and particularly missile activities and bases, but the *New York Times* did not publish this fact until one of the planes was shot down in 1960. Was this a correct judgment? I think it was ...[15]

15 *The Artillery of the Press* (Harper & Row, New York 1967), 20

Bully for Reston and *The New York Times*. But consider. The news was suppressed until the first plane was shot down – until, that is to say, pilot Powers was in Soviet custody, until Khrushchev walked out of the summit conference in justifiable anger, until the infant *détente* lay strangled in its cradle. Might it not have been in the best interest of the United States, and the rest of us, had the facts been published when they first became known, so compelling the abandonment or at least the re-examination of so risky and provocative a policy?

My final example is very recent and close to home.

Last month a correspondent of the *Montreal Star*, Mr Gerald Clark, published a despatch which stated that

Canadian officers in the [International Control] Commission [in Vietnam] are betraying their trust by acting as informants for US intelligence agencies. They are passing on their first-hand experience of North Vietnam: on the effectiveness of US bombing attacks, and on other matters of military significance. A harsher way of putting it is that they are functioning as spies when they are supposed to be serving as international civil servants.[16]

It's hard to imagine a Canadian correspondent writing something more offensive to a Canadian diplomat than the words I've just quoted. Over the image of Canada – the image by which Canadian diplomats would like their country to be known to the world – they pour a bucket of tar; to which is added just for good measure a bale of feathers. For years, the Department of External Affairs at Ottawa has insisted that Canada's intimate alliance with the United States in no way impedes the performance of her international assignments, in no way impairs her reputation for impartiality, in no way erodes her effectiveness in mediation. The Clark despatch makes a mockery of this contention. So once again the diplomats are angry with the correspondent, who is charged with all the old familiar charges: indiscretion, irresponsibility, mischief-making. And worse: with lying. And even worse: with treason, or something close to treason.

Only the last is worth discussing. Certainly their anger isn't: foreign offices are quick to anger, especially at the expense of correspondents who do their job and do it well. As to lying, it is of course the diplomats who are lying, not the correspondent: notice, in this case, the government issues its denial first, mounts its investigation second. But as to treason? Here we are talking of the national interest, and it's still too soon to tell. In the short run, to be sure, the disclosures of correspondent Clark are damaging. But in the long run it may

16 'They are Functioning as Spies,' *Toronto Telegram,* 12 May 1967

prove otherwise. The momentary embarrassment of the Department of External Affairs may turn out to be very cheap tuition if it learns the proper lesson: that prolonged and intimate association of Canadian and American officials is not invariably beneficial for Canadian policy.

These examples prove nothing. But they raise doubts.

President Lyndon Johnson, frustrated in his efforts to win Walter Lippmann, the greatest of the correspondents, over to his side, once remarked with evident exasperation: 'Every time I pull my chair nearer that guy, he pulls his further away.' That this was the appropriate response the president did not, does not, will not understand. But not all presidents. President Johnson's predecessor understood it very well. Asked in the spring of 1962 what he thought of the correspondents of the Washington press corps, John Kennedy replied: 'Well I am reading them more and enjoying them less ... They are doing their task ... And I am attempting to do mine. And we are going to live together for a period, and then go our separate ways.'

[September 1967]

Among journalists, as among thieves, there is little scope for honour – though there is much honesty. The correspondent's occupation requires him to be an ingrate. Loyalty can never be his strong point. He bites the hand that feeds him. He will not take 'no' for an answer, still less will he take 'no comment.' He insists upon confirmation or denial. He insists upon opening up precisely those issues which those in charge fervently want closed. He is a trouble-maker for the policy-maker.

Such a paragon of a reporter has his beat in the Heavenly Kingdom; down below in history's cunning passages it is hard to keep this faith. Some earthly correspondents do not even try. There are even those who say they should not try. 'The responsible government official and the responsible reporter,' according to James Reston, 'when they do their best work are allies with one another.'[17]

So cosy a liaison is nearly always harmful to the press. 'Scotty ought to try harder,' a colleague writes of Reston's work, 'to share the news with the paying readers.' It may also harm the nation.

A loggerhead relationship between the correspondent and the bureaucrat is hardest to maintain in matters of national security, for the defence correspondent, more than other correspondents, feels obliged to feed his columns with morsels of information supplied by cronies within government. But cronyism brings its day of reckoning, if the correspondent is any good at all.

17 *The Artillery of the Press* (Harper & Row, New York 1967), 108

For one of the best a day of reckoning soon dawned. B.H. Liddell Hart, when military correspondent for the *Daily Telegraph* in Britain during the 1920s, enjoyed the run of the War Office. No visitor's pass for him, no need to clear interviews beforehand. Tea was proffered, sympathy expected. For a while, Liddell Hart accorded his hosts sympathetic treatment in his dispatches. Then a critical article appeared: the army had no armour, no armour was a scandal. The War Office retaliated by withdrawing his privileges; then, relenting, offered to restore them on certain conditions. 'I came to the conclusion,' Liddell Hart wrote in his memoirs, 'that these would be fettering. So from that time onward I never went to the War Office again ... I found that this abstention made little or no difference to me in the matter of keeping informed.'[18] Indeed it did not. Liddell Hart practised his profession of scrutinizing the profession of arms with mounting authority and influence; when he died in January 1970, statesmen on both sides of the hill paid homage to the man who, ten years before American pundits, had seen the need to limit war in the nuclear age. He had earned these tributes entirely on his own terms, being entirely his own man.

An instructive contrast is provided by one of his American colleagues. Phil G. Goulding covered military affairs in Washington for the *Cleveland Plain Dealer* from 1950 to 1965. Goulding patrolled his Pentagon beat on the buddy system, swapping discretion for secrets. A favourite buddy was Cyrus Vance, McNamara's right-hand man. Junkets as well as secrets were part of the pay-off: 'We renewed our 1957 acquaintanceship on a professional reporter-official basis, advanced it after he became secretary of the army, and eventually became friendly enough so that in the fall of 1963 he agreed to take me with him on a personal inspection trip of the army in Hawaii, Okinawa, Korea and Taiwan.' Goulding was already a veteran of this massage-parlour circuit, having navigated it two years earlier in the company of the chief of naval operations.

About the purpose of these junkets (though not about who paid for them) Goulding is frank enough: 'These private trips were quite worth while – not so much in the production of news stories en route as in gaining additional military background and developing friendships and professional associations for the future.' But there is no such thing as a free lunch, let alone a free round-the-world tour. 'On something like the Vance trip I behaved circumspectly, passing up hard spot "inside" stories which would cause trouble for our host ... Some information, received in confidence as a courtesy to Vance, or because we were with Vance, we kept in confidence indefinitely.' Thus

18   *Memoirs*, I (Cassell, London 1965), 120

Goulding practised what Reston preached. It helped create a military-media complex no less dangerous to democracy than that military-industrial complex which President Eisenhower warned about in his farewell address.

It is plain to see, and may have been plain for the *Plain Dealer* to see, that Phil Goulding was in the wrong profession. He did not stay in it. After a long party, he recalls, 'at perhaps 1 in the morning, I mentioned to Cyrus that it might be interesting to work in the Department of Defense.' Later that week the telephone rang. Later that month the defence correspondent became acting secretary of defense for public affairs.

To move from the visitor's side of a Pentagon desk to the chair of the man behind it is not like switching from the *Plain Dealer* to the *Post*; it is more like a priest changing places with his confessant, a surgeon with his patient etherized upon a table – a different world, not a different job. The reporter is expected to tell it like it is. The information officer is expected to tell it like his government wants it heard. How seldom these desiderata coincide, how often they diverge, are divulged in Goulding's recollections of four years as top flack in the Pentagon, US commissar of mendacity.[19]

The tyro PRO got off to a bad start. 'The plane did not enter the prohibited zone around Perrelatte': such was the text of his first press release. Not only had it entered, it had taken pictures of the French atomic energy plant. Hence his second press release: 'There was no intent to overfly any prohibited zone.' Maybe de Gaulle believed it; more likely not.

Then came the Palomares caper. A B-52 had crashed in Spain, one of its H-bombs was missing. For eighty days, while US troops and divers searched the area, the Pentagon kept saying 'No comment.' An information officer, asked why Geiger counters were being used, replied 'What are Geiger counters normally used for?' This gave away too much. 'We sent an immediate message to the air force commander,' Goulding recalls, 'to gag his gabby information officers.'

A year later another hydrogen bomber crashed, this time in northern Greenland. Our Department of Transport Air Traffic Control Centre in Moncton gave the show away. Goulding comments: 'Despite an agreement between two governments that nothing would be said yet, despite total silence in Denmark, at Thule, at Plattsburgh, throughout the State Department and throughout the Pentagon, the news of the crash popped out. It had not occurred to us to ask Moncton, New Brunswick, to keep still; indeed, we had been unaware that there was a Moncton, New Brunswick.'

19 *Confirm or Deny: Informing the People on National Security* (Harper & Row, New York, Evanston & London 1970)

The arrogance of ignorance.

Goulding's most saddening revelation is how he and his staff strove to discredit Harrison Salisbury's despatches from North Viet Nam exposing as a lie the US line that only military targets were being bombed. 'Each of the Salisbury pieces was duplicated and distributed within the government for line-by-line analysis ... Scores – possibly hundreds – of individuals in the Pentagon participated.' But they could not scupper the Salisbury statements, which simply told the truth.

Goulding describes this failure as 'a national disaster.' It was no national disaster, only a personal tragedy for those who like himself had strayed so far from the newsman's code as to try to betray a reporter in the field. 'It is incredible,' J.K. Galbraith remarks of them, 'that journalists, scholars, publicists, should join up with their natural enemies to espouse secrecy and reticence.' It is more than incredible, it is despicable. But the hacks and flacks of censorship are backing a losing cause. 'Those who are candid almost always survive. Those who seem for a time most successful in suppressing the truth eventually get buried by their efforts. We should be more grateful than we are,' Galbraith concludes, 'for whoever arranged things this way.'[20] Not even the military-media complex can manage all of the news all of the time.

[August 1970]

'It's all here: the story of our time – with the bark off.' So Lyndon Johnson boasted of the papers of his presidency embalmed in their buckram boxes at his Texas mausoleum. Yet to discover the extent of the rot beneath the bark – how President Johnson systematically and stealthily embroiled his country in a war he'd promised to avoid – an historian would have been obliged to wait for twenty years or more. Thanks to the US Defense Department for compiling the record, thanks to *The New York Times* for publishing its compilation, we can now read all about it.

A cliché to write of L.B.J. 'larger than life,' but so he is – even in his undoing. The Vietnam Archive exposes him as a titan of mendacity, bestriding the narrow world like a colossus of deceit. He and his courtiers emerge from the secret documents like characters in an amorality play, performers of *grand guignol* on a global stage.

Here is assistant secretary of defense John T. McNaughton outlining on 3 September 1964 how the United States could provoke North Vietnam into reprisals to which the Americans would then respond by bombing: 'The actions, in addition to US U-2 recce of DRV, US jet recce of Laos, T-28 activity in Laos would be by way of an orchestration ... to provide good grounds for us to escalate ...'

Here is assistant secretary of state William Bundy anticipating on 18 February 1965 how the administration's plot to provoke a wider war could possibly miscarry: 'We might well find the Soviets – or even the Canadians – sounding us out on whether we would stop our attacks in return for some moderation in VC activity. This is clearly unacceptable.'

Here is McNaughton again, defining on 24 March 1965 American goals in the war to come: '70 per cent – to avoid a humiliating US defeat (to our reputation as a guarantor). 20 per cent – to keep SVN (and the adjacent) territory from Chinese hands. 10 per cent – to permit the people of SVN to enjoy a better, freer way of life ... NOT – to "help a friend" ...' (So much for a deluded Prime Minister Pearson who ten days later was to assure his Philadelphia audience that the motives of their government 'were honorable, neither mean nor imperialistic,' that 'its sacrifices ... were not made to advance any selfish American interest'; so much for a deluding President Nixon who as recently as April of this year told his countrymen that 'never in history have men fought for less selfish motives – not for conquest, not for glory, but only for the right of people far away to choose the kind of government they want.')

And here is policy planning councillor W.W. Rostow blurring on 16 November 1964 the squalid nature of the enterprise by his flatulent philosophizing: 'I know well the anxieties and complications on our side of the line. But there may be a tendency to underestimate ... that limited but real margin of influence on the outcome which flows from the simple fact that at this state of history we are the greatest power in the world – if we behave like it.'

It was said of the servants of Weimar that by making peace they had stabbed Germany in the back. It may be said of these servants of Washington that by making war they had stabbed America in the stomach.

It is as if the basest of the Borgias, to whose misdeeds limits were set only by the inadequacy of the weapons at their disposal, had been able to trade their primitive poisons and daggers for the murderous equipment of the technetronic state. Not even the Borgias could have been more brutal. They certainly could not have been more blind.

In its attempt to prevent further publication of the documents, the Nixon administration says of *The New York Times* that it 'has prejudiced the defence interests of the United States.' In a sense that charge is true. Henceforth, as a direct result of *The Times'* disclosures, it will be harder for an American government to intervene by force in foreign countries, harder to go to war on a lie, harder to kill and maim on behalf of a fictive 'free world.' It will not be so easy for Washington to select options based upon deception, to manage violence with the old impunity. The disclosures do not guarantee – alas – that there will be no more Vietnams. But they make them less likely now. They have certainly frustrated one of the Johnson administration's war aims: 'To emerge from crisis without unacceptable taint from methods used.'

Was all this, then, news not fit to print? Did *The Times,* by publishing, debase the standard displayed daily on its masthead?

'All the News that's Fit to Print' implies there's news that's not. Such was its creed for many years. *The New York Times* is wiser now, it's learned its lesson well. All the news is fit to print, if it's news of government. Concealment as often as exposure proves harmful to the people. It is not the duty of the press to conceal, it is the duty of the press to reveal. Only those whose reputations suffer by its revelations now dare to disagree. 'Publish and be damned' has become 'publish and be praised.'

Damned or praised, the journalist has been taken off the horns of his dilemma. His course is clear. 'In what way can one's highest loyalty be given to one's country?' Alan Paton asks, and offers this reply: 'Surely in only one way, and that is when one wishes with all one's heart and tries with all one's power to make it a better country, to make it more just and more tolerant and more merciful, and if it is powerful, more wise in the use of its power.'

By seeing in the Pentagon Papers news that's fit to print, *The New York Times* has passed this test with flying colours – the colours not of a yellow journalism, but of the red badge of courage.

[June 1971]

4
'Rally round the file, boys!'

No one loves a commissar, or ought to. At his best he is a pitiable creature, robbing Peter to pay Paul - the quintessential bureaucratic act. At his worst, a hateful creature, beating Paul and Peter up. As with the collector of night-soil in a medieval town, such admiration as his activities arouse stems only from the feeling that someone has to do the dirty work.

Here is why commissars crave secrecy. Custodianship of society's secrets is their balm of Gilead, their source of psychic satisfaction. Armed with his security clearance, only the bureaucrat can look in the file, only the bureaucrat can read the magic messages. This exalts him over those who can't.

For those who can't wish they could. Secrets are fascinating. In times of turmoil their fascination becomes obsessive; but it flickers in tranquil times as well. It may be seen in the individual who will not believe what he reads in his newspaper, being addicted to inside dope. It may be seen in the diplomat who falls most eagerly upon data acquired by espionage, thinking black intelligence more beautiful.

Access means prestige, so the bureaucrat sets about augmenting it. First he adds to his store of secrets. For this purpose he wields a rubber stamp, or rather several rubber stamps. He narrows the arcane circle of those who need to know. Ideally, he alone would be cleared for top secret, but as a second best he admits a privileged few. There is no room in the circle for outsiders. An outsider, however loyal or reliable, might stumble on the topmost secret of them all - that the file is as bare of real secrets as was the emperor of real clothes, that the magic messages contain opinions no less commonplace than his own.

All bureaucracies are secretive, some more so than others. Canada's is more secretive than most. Totalitarian capitals apart, only official Canberra comes

close to matching that special air of furtive reticence which marks the Ottawa
mandarins off from other men. One wonders why this should be so. Perhaps
we have inherited the English vice; as Edward Shils observes, it is in Britain
more than in other democracies that 'the citizenry and all but the most aggres-
sively alienated of the elite do not regard it as within their prerogative to un-
mask the secrets of the government.'

Perhaps it is because of the trials of trying to eke out a civilized existence
in that 'sub-Arctic lumbering town transformed by a stroke of Victoria's pen
into a cockpit of malodorous politics' that the senior members of its bureaucracy huddle so exclusively together in their private retreats – the fishing camp
at Five Lakes, the card room at the Rideau Club – keeping their own company,
and secrets, more closely than is natural. Or perhaps it all goes back to that
grey morning of 6 October 1945, when the prime minister of Canada was told
by an agitated under secretary that 'a most terrible thing had happened.'

The Gouzenko affair cast a pall over Canada, out from under which we
have not come. The *Report of the Royal Commission on Security,*[1] so far
from helping to shake it off, pushes us back into the murk of administrative
secrecy of which other countries are working free. 'The administrative process
is surrounded by too much secrecy. The public interest would be better served
if there were a greater amount of openness.' 'Disclosure is a transcendent goal.'
These quotations are not from the Mackenzie Report. They are from the Report of the Fulton committee on the British civil service (June 1968) and the
US Freedom of Information Act (July 1968).

The authors of the Mackenzie Report (June 1969) are far from sharing
this philosophy. They have forgotten nothing since the Gouzenko affair. They
have learned nothing, either. International politics for them is still the politics
of cold war – 'détente,' they note in passing, 'has its dangers for security' –
still a zero-sum game in which secrets lost by one side are always a gain for
the other.

The notion that security can be subversive, that counter-espionage can be
counter-productive, is basic to deterrence; but their moss-back minds have yet
to grasp it. The notion that secret intelligence is likely to be bad intelligence
and hence harmful to the nation's interest – since, being classified, it is not
subject (as Richard Goodwin puts it) 'to the kind of debate and discussion
and contradiction and challenge which brings us closer to the truth' – has also
yet to cross those minds.

In its place we find the unsupported assertion – unsupported because in-
supportable – that 'classified information is of considerable importance to

1 Abridged (Queen's Printer, Ottawa 1969)

Canadian perception of the international scene.' Leaving aside how important is 'considerable importance,' that is just not true.

Far worse than the report's naïveté is its insensitivity to what is really precious. As between the secrets of the file and the secrets of the soul, the commissioners unhesitatingly rally round the file. Where there are grounds for doubt about an individual's loyalty and reliability, 'such doubts must be resolved in favor of the state.' Of the ethic expressed by Dean Acheson's 'I do not intend to turn my back on Alger Hiss,' the commissioners are heedless; of the view that these may be the noblest words ever uttered by a public servant they would be incredulous.

Instead, they enjoin teachers to rat on their students. The state, so far from staying out of the bedrooms of the nation, is to hide under its bedsprings. Telephones should be tapped, mail opened, eavesdropping is splendid if 'authorized personally and individually by the head of the security service.' The personal touch, the secret service with a heart. It is scant consolation to remember that people who listen at keyholes get only earache.

While the state should snoop on the public, the public can't watch the state. 'We would view suggestions for increased publicity with some alarm.' The Fulton commissioners, in contrast, reserve their alarm for the way bureaucrats may hide incompetence behind their veil of civil service anonymity. 'We think that administration suffers from the convention that only the minister should explain issues in public and what his department is or is not doing about them.' J.K. Galbraith, with experience in both camps, tells it like it really is: 'A man who will clam up because he is afraid that what he says will later be quoted is too craven to have anything worth saying. The public official who lowers his voice and pleads for strict confidence is invariably getting ready to say something repugnant to the public interest ...'[2]

The crowning irony is that a report written by commissars for commissars should turn out in the end to be a subversive document. Any university student who reads it, and is worthy of his subsidy, will be less eager than before to seek a career with the public service, let alone with the secret service. Of course there will always be recruits. But, as Rebecca West points out, 'the wrong people will get in. There are people whose special joy it is to be the wrong people, who get in.'[3] The quality of government will suffer. The publication of the Mackenzie Report, no less than its preparation, is a disservice to the 'security' of Canada – though not in the way its authors will imagine.

[July 1969]

2 *The Observer*, 28 Nov. 1965
3 'Unexplained Mysteries of the Vassall Affair,' *The Sunday Telegraph*, 28 Apr. 1963

Turn to the most recent volume of diplomatic documents published yearly by the US Department of State,[4] and you will find beginning on page 68 a top-secret 'Memorandum of Canadian-United States Defence Conversations held in Ottawa in Suite E, Chateau Laurier Hotel, December 16 and 17, 1946.'

Here is a state paper to make James Bond, had he come across it at the time, steady his hand with a double bourbon. An American delegation, gleaming with brass and expertise, is trying to persuade our civil servants to accept a US plan for northern defence against the Soviet Union – radar, bases, mapping, patrols, the lot.

The Canadians are clearly worried. They don't want to provoke the Russians. They don't want to snub the British. They don't want to alarm the public. Yet at George Kennan's masterly assessment of Soviet intentions, General Lincoln's high-pressure presentation of Soviet capabilities, L.B. Pearson, Arnold Heeney, and the rest can only murmur their misgivings.

Their main misgiving is how the proposed military measures may be concealed from public view. 'The cabinet,' Heeney tells the meeting, is 'anxious to have as much civilian "cover" for defence projects as possible.' Pearson points out that 'the entire problem was of far greater internal political importance in Canada than in the United States.' The Americans say that's our tough luck. In any case it would be impossible to 'civilianize' their top priority. 'Goose Bay,' declares US Colonel Van Devanter, is 'the only suitable base for very heavy bombardment groups and in fact could be said to be the most important all-round strategic air base in the Western hemisphere ... intended for offensive purposes.'

A Canadian historian, while duly thankful for this state department version, may suspect it does our statesmen less than justice. He will wish to check its record against our own. When he tries, he will soon be reflecting on Sir Walter Raleigh's dictum: 'Whosoever, in writing a modern history, shall follow truth too near the heels, it may haply strike out his teeth.'

The Department of External Affairs, like the US State Department, publishes a selection of its documents. Its program is moving with all deliberate speed – the speed of a heavily tranquilized snail.

The most recent item to be printed, while not lacking interest – it describes a meeting at which 'the Portuguese delegate made a most impassioned address, lasting for more than half an hour, during the greater portion of which he was shrieking at the top of his voice' – is dated 10 May 1919.

4   *Foreign Relations of the United States, 1946* (US Government Printing Office, Washington 1970)

What happens if the Canadian historian, finding nothing useful in External Affairs' books, asks to see the files? He gets what might be called 'the Nightingale treatment.'

In 1878 Florence Nightingale applied to the India Office to study its data on famine in Madras and Bombay. The applicant, already legendary as 'the lady with the lamp,' received the following reply: 'To open the records of a public office to the free inspection of a private individual, however distinguished for character and ability, would constitute a very inconvenient precedent.'[5]

Though not in any way a Nightingale, I've had the Nightingale treatment. 'Your desire,' wrote the under-secretary of state for external affairs to me in 1965, 'is to be given personal access to classified files – a privilege (not a right) – in contravention of established government policy and the regulations for the protection of such information. I would venture to suggest that scholars for centuries have written history with authority and truthfulness without having access to secret files.' Buzz off, buster.

But the times they are a-changin'. One by one, like washing flying from the line with a storm breaking, the arguments used by bureaucrats to keep their files inviolate are being blown away. Fifty-year, thirty-year, twenty-year rules, prescribing the period that must elapse between the writing of a document and its release, are more and more difficult to justify.

There's the argument that the files contain information of value to our rivals. That may still be true of personnel files cataloguing the quirks and foibles of public servants and useful to would-be blackmailers. It's not true of the rest. What with personal diplomacy and kitchen cabinets, foreign offices don't get the really important secrets. Governments read each other's mail, crack each other's code. If they don't – in an era of nuclear weapons and second strike strategies – they should.

There's the argument that to open the files will damage their quality. What diplomat would then express his mind in perfect candour? But that argument works both ways. When a diplomat knows he is to be read in a decade, it concentrates his mind wonderfully. 'The only people with serious grounds for objection,' writes J.K. Galbraith – a former diplomat himself, he knows whereof he writes – 'are those who, reflecting the oldest desires of public servants and especially of those concerned with foreign policy, would like to have a license for decorous inaction or error.'[6]

5 Quoted in Cecil Woodham-Smith, *Florence Nightingale* (Constable, London 1950), 544-5
6 *The Observer*, 28 Nov. 1965

And there's the argument that the recent past is too hot to handle. Wait, the historian is told – 'the impatient young historian' to a former Dominion archivist – until the dust settles. Otherwise his dentition will suffer, as Raleigh duly warned. Why study the Test Ban Treaty of 1963 when there's the Halibut Treaty of 1923?

Why? Because the times they *are* a-changin', their tempo's speeding up. To grub in the archives of fifty years ago, even of thirty years ago, has become an antiquarian activity – a papyrus approach in an electric age. 'No wonder,' writes the biographer of FDR, 'that in recent years doctoral candidates in history have tended more and more to choose dissertation topics dealing with the recent past.'

All this is gradually impressing itself upon a changing guard. The new under-secretary at External Affairs, the head of its historical division, are full of good will and good intentions. That is a revolution in itself.

But there has to be a catch. There is. Call it Catch 007.

If External seems willing now, Security is not. The events of October have led to stricter security checks all along the line. The scholar wanting to look in the files has to be fingerprinted, investigated, ideologically fumigated, cleared to top-secret by federal fuzz. Watching the muniments room of the nation is Constable Dudley Do-Right, RCMP.

Nor is he disposed to let the scholar in. 'We would view suggestions for increased publicity with some alarm,' states the report of the Royal Commission on Security. Yearly publication of documents 'should go far to meet the legitimate needs of researchers, and thus minimize requests for access to files.' The person who wrote that has never written history.

So where are we? Where we've always been. Helpful solutions to the access problem must be imposed from above, for no bureaucracy presides willingly at the declassification of its own secrets. The prime minister is fond of quoting Acton on power. He should try quoting Acton on access: 'To keep one's archives barred against the historians is tantamount to leaving one's history to one's enemies.' And to the US State Department.

[February 1971]

The state has no place in the bedrooms of the nation, but journalists have a place in the affairs of state – as peeping Toms at the window-blinds of government. Citizens should help, not hinder, such voyeurs – loan them ladders if need be – for on their gratification a just society depends.

Keepers of, and peepers at, official secrets had their ups and downs last week. Bad news for the secretive being good news for the rest of us, let's look at good news first – how a London judge and jury gave the back of their hands to the Official Secrets Act.

This cumbrous legislation is the secrecy fetishist's favourite reading, causing him to drool: 'Every person who obtains, collects, records or publishes, or communicates to any other person any secret official code word, or pass word, or any sketch, plan, model, article, or note, or other document or information that is calculated to be or might be or is intended to be directly or indirectly useful to a foreign power is guilty of an offence' – punishment for which may be up to fourteen years in jail.

Under this act (which dates from 1911 and has a diamond jubilee in August) a journalist was prosecuted last year. His alleged offence was obtaining and publishing in his newspaper a confidential document of the British military mission in Lagos on the progress of the Nigerian-Biafran war.

Counsel for the accused placed his defence upon the highest principle. 'Journalists and the press have an unfettered freedom to exercise their own judgment as to what they should publish however embarrassing it may be to civil servants and ministers of the crown. They are employees of the people, and it is not for them to turn round and say: "You will embarrass us, therefore you must not publish and if you do we will persecute you."'

The judge, moved by this appeal, reminded the jury in his summing up that freedom of the press takes precedence over the state's right to privacy. 'An opinion-forming medium like the press must not be muzzled. The warning bark is necessary to help in maintaining a free society. If the fangs of the watchdog are drawn, all that will ensue is a whimpering, possibly a whine, but no bite.'

The jury, deliberating briefly, brought in a verdict of 'not guilty.'

The Times, commenting on the case, remarked that the section of the act under which charges had been laid ought to be repealed, and reproached the prosecuting attorney-general for 'a serious error of judgment.'

All so very different from our own Dominion dear, where authority looks with favour upon more, not less, stringent safeguards for the secrets of the state. 'We have given some thought,' confess the royal commissioners on security in their 1969 report, 'to the ideal content of an Official Secrets Act.' Should an ideal act be drawn, as the London *Times* recommends, 'in the interests of more open and publicly accountable government?' Not at all. 'In our opinion, such an act should protect all classified information from any unauthorized dissemination, whether or not the purpose is prejudicial to the interests of the state.' Only a press of *Pravda*s could put up with that.

'Fifty-year, thirty-year, twenty-year rules, prescribing the period that must elapse between the writing of a document and its release, are more and more difficult to justify.' It may be so, but the British prime minister has imposed nothing short of a 100-year rule – on all cabinet papers relating to the abdication of Edward VIII. Historians must wait until 2036.

Why? In deference to the feelings of the duke and duchess? Not even the ageless Windsors can hope to last so long. Besides, in *A King's Story* ('the fault lay not in my stars but in my genes'), the duke has already told his side of it – if only to help finance his exile; it's fitting that the other side be told.

In deference, then, to the prince of Wales who, given today's divorce rate, could well face Edward's fate, could be the worse for full disclosure of the precedent? I think I hear Charles responding to that one: 'Come off it, chum – chuck that bosh!'

Nor is there any juicy gossip left. Details of the drama that swirled through Ciro's and the Kit-Kat Club, Belvedere and Balmoral, ultimately through Buckingham Palace and Downing Street, have long since come out in the wash of court tittle tattle.

In any case, historians aren't all that interested in court tittle tattle – former prime minister Baldwin telling Vincent Massey that 'he would like to have Mrs S. sent to the tower and beheaded,' or the impression the bachelor king made on bachelor King ('his hair quite thick and golden. He has lost the dissipated look ...').

Historians are more interested in how the crisis affected cabinet government, party politics, the British Commonwealth, church and state, Britain and Germany. These are important questions, historians have the need and right to know their answers.

Barring some geriatric miracle they won't know them in their lifetime. They must console themselves with a letter from Pliny the Younger which, being more than 2000 years old, lies beyond the Official Secrets Act of Rome: 'An author had begun a reading of a work of exceptional candor. Up came the friends of someone I won't name, begging and praying him not to read the remainder; such is the shame people feel at hearing about their conduct, though they felt none at the time of doing what they blush to hear. The author complied with their request. But the book, like their deeds, remains and will remain. It will always be read, and all the more for this delay, for information withheld only sharpens men's curiosity to have it.'

[February 1971]

5

'Live, and let Nelson Eddy live'

'Our information abroad has long been stumbling through a stunning sort of chaos.' This caustic comment and others critical of Canada's propaganda in foreign parts are recorded, with the air of a man who has made a discovery comparable to Dr Leakey's Zinjanthropus skull, in *To Know and Be Known,*[1] the report of the task force on government information. But this find is not at all remarkable. There is no reason to be surprised. There is not even reason, as will be shown, to be alarmed.

To convey to the outside world a coherent, credible, and flattering account of what government is doing lies beyond the power of any propagandist. Among ministeries of propaganda (commonly called ministries of information) are only varying degrees of ineptitude. It is an error to ascribe these to poor administration. Poor administration may make bad propaganda worse. But the best propaganda is no substitute for poor foreign policy. There are some things government can't do. One of them is to fool all of the people all of the time.

Totalitarian government thinks it can. Its propaganda ministry, straining every fibre of its monolithic being, rams its message down the throat of the foreigner, numbs his mind with some lurid image. But the effects of these wear off. The victim throws up, regains his senses of discrimination. The visage of Svengali fades, leaving behind it only a figure of fun, like Lord Haw-Haw, or a font of entertainment, like Tokyo Rose.

If the totalitarian propagandist tries to rape the masses, the liberal propagandist tries to seduce the masses. He does not hit people over the head with

1 (Queen's Printer, Ottawa 1969)

the blunt instrument of a big lie. He resorts instead to the techniques of friendly persuasion. As in courtship, so in propaganda: Candy is dandy, but liquor is quicker. The task force chides our Canadian liberal propagandist for his Whitman Sampler ways of wooing foreign friends: 'Print is still king ... It is as though television, film, and other audio-visual techniques and aspects of contemporary technology had simply never come into existence. It is enough to make one suspect that federal officials are still sending stuffed moose-heads to London.'

It is not quite so bad as that. What our federal officials are doing is sending stuffed trailer-trucks to Ouagadougou – a caravanserai of Canadiana designed to show francophone Africans that, contrary to what they are told, Quebec is not the Biafra of Canada. But that's beside the point. Suppose our propagandists perform as primitively as the task force says they do. Does this matter as much as the task force says it does?

Consider the United States Information Agency. Never has USIA been so fully packed, so free and easy on the draw. American propaganda has come a long way since the early fifties, when McCarthy's minions ransacked USIA libraries for subversive literature by Thoreau and Hemingway. It has come some way since the early sixties, when ambassador Galbraith complained to President Kennedy from New Delhi that its radio programming consisted 'of utterly irrelevant broadcasts about the progress of the grass silage industry, tedious and execrably written scripts on the American economy, or diatribes against communism. The latter,' Galbraith added, 'are perhaps the dreariest feature of all. I cannot hear them without pausing to consider whether the Communists have something, and Ed Murrow may well be turning me into a security risk.'[2]

No one today can reproach the members of the American propaganda community for indifference to the latest techniques of mass communication. The United States pavilion at Expo is one example of their handiwork. Another is 'The Silent Majority,' a fifteen-minute television film hastily distributed after the November moratorium to 104 countries in twenty-three languages in an attempt to persuade their people that Americans are still behind their president's policy for Vietnam. For sheer technical bravura and dexterity, American propaganda is the best in the world.

Yet for all the ceaseless flow of words and symbols, for all the mixed-media wizardry and McLuhanite gimmickry, the image of the United States, which it is the propagandist's duty to cherish and to burnish, has never been more besmirched. Just as there are stains no detergent can remove, so there

2 *Ambassador's Journal* (Houghton, Mifflin, Boston 1969), 109

are deeds no propaganda can efface. President Nixon did his best, timing the announcement of his decision to abstain from biological warfare to coincide with the revelations about the Song My massacres. But no counter-offensive is likely to obliterate, let alone diminish, the impact of the confession of Paul Meadlo, former private, US army: 'And we was going to put them in the hootch, and well, we put them in the hootch, and then we dropped a hand grenade down there with them. And somebody told us to bring them over to the ravine ... So we threw ours in with them ... And so we started pushing them off and we started shooting them.' A propaganda machine is not some kind of Laterna Magika through which Goya's 'Disasters of War' may be shown to the world as Tom and Jerry cartoons. The truth will out, and it has.

A great power drives its soldiers to butcher children; middle power butchery is confined to seal pups. We who live in a middle power may ruefully give thanks for this. Still, as the task force remarks, 'The campaign against seal hunting in the Gulf of St Lawrence has been one of the more persistent tarnishers of the Canadian image.'

Perhaps the new breed of public servant recommended by the task force – the career information service officer – will be able to offset the nasty things said about us last week by Miss Alice Herrington in a quarter-page advertisement in *The New York Times* attacking Canadians and their government for allowing the ice of the gulf to become each year 'a crimson patchwork, strewn with the skinless remains of what once were harmless, intelligent mammals that have died an agonizing, unbelievably cruel death.' More likely he will not. The cards are stacked against skilled apologists for butchery, whether of human beings or animals. The attitude of the attentive public, suspicious by now of super-publicists sent to lie abroad for their country, is no longer a willing suspension of disbelief.

Let us admit that the Canadian propagandist, whether ISO or FSO, has an easier time than his colleague in the USIA. He toils on behalf of a largely peaceable kingdom. Only exceptionally is he required to hide or justify crimes of state. His main job is to project a favourable image of our country so that we may get more than our fair share of skilled immigrants and wealthy tourists.

At this work the task force pronounces him no good. It reproaches the Canadian propagandist's persistent inability 'to correct a cliché image ... that is both irritating to Canadians and hardy as a weed. This is the Canada of Rose Marie and Maria Chapdelaine, land of ice, snow, Mounties, Eskimos, and not much else.' It looks to a new propaganda agency, which it wants to call Information Canada, to eradicate this unflattering image once and for all, substituting an image which does justice to second-century Canada and all the mod, hip, swinging, with-it, talented, creative people who live here.

The task force has a characteristically forthright word or two for those who think this game's not worth the candle. 'It may be argued, "So, okay, the government information services are a mess." So are a lot of things. Anyway, it's better to have a whole bunch of innocent bunglers in government information than one super-efficient propaganda machine.' Addressed to Canada's foreign propaganda, this argument is exactly right. Nor, in that context, does the task force offer any rebuttal. It fails to grasp to what extent a nation's image is shaped not by propaganda but serendipity, not by words but deeds.

So to the authors of *To Know and Be Known* I say: 'Live, and let Nelson Eddy live. And if the tourists turn up on Dominion Day with skis, just switch on the artificial snow machines.' And I commend to them a book which ought not to have escaped the task force bibliography – Daniel Boorstin's *The Image*.[3] Here, with one word changed, is its key passage: 'What ails us most is not what we have done with Canada, but what we have substituted for Canada. We suffer primarily not from our vices or our weaknesses, but from our illusions. We are haunted, not by reality, but by those images we have put in place of reality.' Or so it would be if the task force had its way.

[December 1969]

3 (Atheneum, New York 1962)

6

A foreign policy for beavers

Government White Papers – not to be confused with coloured books, so called for the covers (blue, green, orange, yellow) between which foreign ministries since the mid-seventeenth century have inserted tendentious selections of diplomatic documents, hoping to bathe their statecraft in the least unfavourable light – are rarely noted for precision of language and elegance of style. It would be surprising if they were. Posing as enunciators of policy, White Papers are really devices for concealment, and what they conceal is change.

'Pronouncements about fundamental policy changes are made to appear as vigorous endorsements of previous policies,' writes Anthony Sampson (the well-known anatomist of Britain) of how it's done at Whitehall, where white papering is a highly developed art form. 'Obscurity is encouraged to avoid offending previous ministers and officials.'[1] The process by which they are composed – more accurately, assembled – adds to their muzziness and murk. 'They are written from one department to another, full of mandarin language, and in the process of fooling the public, one suspects that civil servants begin to fool themselves.'

Given these characteristics of the genre, *Foreign Policy for Canadians*[2] – the government's statement of our new external policy, in the making since Prime Minister Trudeau took office – is by no means a discreditable document, especially if one makes the sort of allowance Dr Johnson did for the lady parson, judging not the tedium of her sermons but in admiring wonder that a being so handicapped could preach at all.

1 *Anatomy of Britain Today* (Hodder and Stoughton, London 1965), 299-300
2 (Queen's Printer, Ottawa 1970)

A conscientious effort has been made to communicate simply and directly, with a minimum of jargon and officialese. It is true that here and there the prose simply collapses under the weight of its argument, like a soufflé left too long in the oven. 'All this produces complex difficulties of targeting for any government wishing to set its objectives and assign priorities intended to deal with specific issues arising, preferably before they become critical' must mean 'It's harder than you think,' while 'The correct focus can only be achieved if all the elements of a particular policy question can be looked at in a conceptual framework which represents the main lines of national policy at home and abroad' translates as 'Don't forget anything important.' 'Implications' – a weasel-word much in demand by bureaucrats nervous in the vicinity of a conclusion – appears often in these pages. Wit, grace, passion, poetry, do not. 'Diligent but uninspired,' a pedagogue might comment, 'must do better next time. C plus.'

Higher marks go to the government for rounding boldly on the most cherished concepts of its predecessor – the more so because their staunchest defenders are members of the same party and even of the same cabinet. The chimera of 'influence' – for which Paul Martin paid so stiff a price by costly participation in European defence – is no longer to be pursued. Abandoned also is the search for a role. Gone, if not forgotten, is the Mackenzie King-Pearson obsession to be cast as 'helpful fixer' – variously known as golden hinge, linch-pin, bridge, or interpreter – when Great Powers start to quarrel. 'There is no natural, immutable or permanent role for Canada in today's world,' the White Paper asserts. 'Roles and influence may result from pursuing certain policy objectives – and these spin-offs can be of solid value to international relations – but they should not be made the aims of policy.' Here is more than the beginning of wisdom; it is a great leap forward.

In place of roles and influence we are to look in future to our vital national interests, more decorously described by the White Paper as major themes of policy. Six of these are then discerned and accorded the dignity of capital letters: Economic Growth, Social Justice, Quality of Life, Peace and Security, Sovereignty and Independence, Harmonious Natural Environment. (A minor flaw of this conceptual framework is treating Quality of Life and Harmonious Natural Environment as separate and equal: alone of the six categories they cannot possibly conflict.) The most significant decision conveyed by the White Paper is to rank them in that order of importance.

Priorities are crucial; abstract priorities, less so. Everything depends on how they are applied, on what may be deduced.

Ranking Social Justice ahead of Peace and Security naturally encourages the belief that we will be working from now on to expel the torturers of Greece from their membership in NATO. But Mr Sharp has already argued that Social Justice is better served by keeping them in NATO. Mr Sharp is entitled to that belief, as we are entitled to ours; but he must not be surprised when the overwhelming reaction to such perverse manipulation of the national priorities is cynicism and contempt.

At least one of the six stands so far as stated. Economic Growth comes first and foremost – not necessarily at the expense of Social Justice but at the expense of Social Justice if necessary.

The most urgent application is the policy for southern Africa. Here the Department of External Affairs displays all the delicacy of feeling it showed for a delegation of dons desiring economic sanctions imposed against South Africa by serving them Johannesburger Riesling at dinner. 'Total rejection of race discrimination and continuing trade with white regimes in southern Africa' is not for it an easy choice to be made in favour of the first, but rather a clash of 'competing national objectives, very closely balanced as to importance.' And it opts for trade.

Even as an abstract goal, the selection of Economic Growth as national policy objective Number One leaves much to be desired. Social philosophers on the leading edge of thought in every developed country are singing songs in praise of standing pat. Untrammelled dedication to enlarging gross national products and raising per capita income is under attack not on moral grounds alone but out of stark expediency. The young in age and young in heart are more and more repelled by the life-styles of materialism. For whom should our foreign policy for the seventies be fashioned if not for them? They will have to live with the results.

One returns again to the notion of style, for style is sometimes policy itself. The cover of the White Paper catches and holds its spirit perfectly. A glossy colour photograph of faces in a crowd – quite obviously, an Expo crowd: well-dressed, well-fed, well-mannered, attentive on-lookers at some outdoor entertainment.

And that is how the planners of our foreign policy see our place among the peoples – curious yet distant spectators at the pavillions of the nations, in the world, yet not quite of it, caring little about its suffering, sharing nothing of its squalor, a temperate zone of affluence amidst the wretched of the earth. What Auden wrote of other well-meaning and ineffectual folk applies to the White Paper makers' view of our life and time:

They attend all the lectures on post-war problems,
For they do mind, they honestly want to help; yet,
As they notice the earth in their morning papers,
What sense do they make of its folly and horror?[3]

[June 1970]

3   'A Healthy Spot,' in *Collected Shorter Poems, 1930-1944* (Faber and Faber, London 1950), 145

7

Principles for receivership

Arnold Heeney and Livingston Merchant, embarking upon their assignment
'of working out acceptable principles which would make it easier to avoid
divergences in economic and other policies of interest' to Canada and the
United States, were not dispassionate parties. They did not approach their
task as academics or commentators. They were neither supra-national nor
supernatural. They were flesh-and-blood representatives of their respective
governments.

Their work[1] is accordingly to be judged by different standards. There is
no such thing except in name as a Heeney-Merchant (or Merchant-Heeney)
Report. There is, rather, a Heeney product and a Merchant product. The
Heeney product is to be judged for its contribution to the promotion of
Canadian national interests. The Merchant product is likewise to be judged
for its contribution to the promotion of United States national interest.

In what follows – an assessment of the Heeney product – it is contended
that 'Principles for Partnership' (the title of the report which Arnold Heeney
signed for Canada) is not a contribution in the Canadian national interest. So
far from that, the principles which it enunciates are for us not principles for
partnership at all; they are rather principles for receivership, where what is
received is our sovereignty, where the United States government is the re-
ceiver-general.

Most of the critical commentary of the Heeney-Merchant Report has centred
on its paragraph 81 – indeed on one of two sentences in paragraph 81:

1 *Canada and the United States: Principles for Partnership* (Queen's Printer, Ottawa 1965)

It is in the abiding interest of both countries that, wherever possible, divergent views between the two governments be expressed and if possible resolved in private, through diplomatic channels.

Later on I shall have some critical things to say about this formulation. But first I want to comment on a lesser-known but to my mind no less important passage, in paragraphs 6 and 7. This is a statement of the frame of mind of the authors of the report, and supplies, I believe, the key to understanding the ideology of Heeney-Merchantism – why Arnold Heeney and Livingston Merchant came to hold certain truths self-evident:

6   ... Our method has been essentially that of a dialogue between two friends who have served together in both capitals and have had the good fortune to have represented their respective governments, each for two terms in the country of the other.

7   Our personal friendship, our association in the past in the joint affairs of Canada and the United States and our common concern for the maintenance and strengthening of the partnership between our two countries have greatly facilitated our present undertaking. They have also contributed to our work, and to this Report, an informal and personal quality which we believe is not inappropriate.

I believe it is highly inappropriate. The Heeney-Merchant exercise is not a form of brotherly love. The two ambassadors are not Kiwanians or Shriners engaged in confraternal celebration in Miami or Montreal. They are parties to a negotiation, of which the outcome is their extended communiqué.

Friendship may not be fatal to a negotiation, but it is rarely beneficial to it. Harold Nicolson's work on diplomatic method now seems to me much misguided,[2] but here he gets it right: 'Diplomacy, if it is ever to be effective, should be a disagreeable business ... It would be interesting to analyse how many false decisions, how many fatal misunderstandings, have arisen from such pleasant qualities as shyness, consideration, affability or ordinary good manners.'

Let us next look briefly at the two terms of Arnold Heeney's ambassiate in Washington. They yield clues to explain why he so uncritically endorsed the concept of Canadian 'partnership' with the United States.

The first term runs from 1953 to 1957 – the early Eisenhower years. Armistice in Korea had removed a major irritant from what Heeney and Merchant call 'the multilateral context.' Vietnam was but a name. Quemoy and

2   See below, 62ff

Matsu were dangerous enough, but Dulles could still josh about *his* off-shore island in eastern Lake Ontario, setting the Rideau Club to giggling. The long polar watch pumped cold cash into our economy. All things, if not bright and beautiful, were at least benign and bland.

Then came a second term – 1959 to 1962. Heeney now represented a different government, and spoke for a different mood. His mission as a middle power's middle man between John Diefenbaker and Howard Green, John Kennedy and Dean Rusk, while not perhaps mission impossible, was highly exacting. In the end it failed.

Reflecting on the failure of his mission, Heeney blamed anti-Americanism among his political masters. Anti-Americanism was for him an un-Canadian activity. He could not grasp that Diefenbaker had become prime minister precisely by playing upon a widespread popular concern that Liberals if re-elected would be insufficiently alert to what Dief in his campaign had called 'the depredations of Texas buccanneers.' The Texans who entertained the Heeneys in the gilded salons of Fort Worth seemed not at all like buccanneers, only like plutocratic Canadians. The countryside round Dallas recalled the southern Manitoba of Heeney's boyhood. How unnatural to be at odds with so like-minded a partner!

The metaphor of partnership is well suited to the era of the ascendancy of Texas in American national politics: 'partner,' or, rather, 'pardner' (as in 'howdy, pardner'), is a familiar greeting around ranch and corral.

The metaphor of partnership springs unopposed into the Heeney-Merchant Report. The metaphor not only figures in the title; it is used throughout the text, never with any justification or explanation. The authors assume that Canada and the United States are partners in some common enterprise, the terms of which are never disclosed, the nature of which is never discussed.

What is a partnership anyway? 'An association,' according to my dictionary, 'an association of two or more persons for the carrying on of a business, of which they share the expenses, profit and loss.' What, then, is the business of Canadian-American relations? What is this common enterprise in which we are engaged?

There are some of our mutual activities, I concede, for which the metaphor of partnership is not too misleading. Take continental defence, for example. The business in which we are jointly engaged is deterring Russians from nuclear attack. We share, very unequally, in the costs of this enterprise. We share, roughly fifty-fifty, in the profits – successful deterrence. It is an enterprise of unlimited liability, for if it fails we both stand to lose not just our shirts but our homelands.

The metaphor of partnership works well enough in describing our joint efforts to prevent a Soviet bomber attack on North America. Notice that it does not work so well in describing our joint efforts to prevent a Soviet missile attack. And that it doesn't work at all in relation to the threat of Chinese aggression.

If we are not yet partners in defence of North America against China, we are certainly not partners in the business of selling wheat to China. Nor may our respective concerns with Cuba be meaningfully described in terms of partnership. Nor yet our respective concerns with Vietnam. In fact, so small a fraction of our affairs with other countries fits the metaphor of partnership that its retention in public discussion of the Canadian-American relationship is a disservice to understanding.

How is it possible that the distinguished company of North American statesmen who, following the Heeney-Merchant lead, persist in discussing the affairs of Canada and the United States in terms of neighbourhood and partnership could get their terms so wrong?

It's not because they're ill-informed. They're often very well-informed. It's not because they're ill-intentioned. They have the best intentions in the world.

It is that they view the subject from the vantage point of who they are and what they do. They are politicians and statesmen, not political scientists and historians. Their job is different. Their perspective is different. Their assumptions are different. Their questions are different. It's not surprising that they come up with different answers. The job of politicians and statesmen is to keep communities together as going concerns. This job involves them in what may be called, politely, socially necessary deceptions. That is, they tell lies. No more often than they have to, perhaps, but as often as they have to. Civilization being what Keynes once said it is – 'a thin and precarious crust erected by the personality and will of a very few and only maintained by rules and conventions skillfully put together and guilefully preserved' – the keepers of civility resort to the perpetuation of myth and the fabrication of fable. They cannot allow themselves the luxury of pursuing truth at whatever cost. The cost – not to themselves but to the society in their charge – may be too great. Their task is not to expose reality to view. Often it is to hide it from sight.

The job of the political analyst is, or ought to be, very different. It is not his job to keep communities from falling apart or from falling out. It is to understand what holds them together. If he does his job well he is bound to be an unpopular figure. Always he is prying open old wounds. Always he is re-opening precisely those issues which his society would prefer to remain closed. To the policy-maker he must seem to be a trouble-maker. He is an ingrate. He bites the hand that feeds him.

Is there any wonder that there should subsist a certain tension between the policy-maker and the intellectual? It is no wonder at all. They are working at cross purposes. Often they get in one another's way. Sometimes they accomplish each other's ruin.

In police states the policy-maker has it all his own way. The intellectual becomes a lapdog, or else he goes to jail. In our own societies their confrontation is less crudely resolved. But, to the extent that each is faithful to his calling, it remains a confrontation.

And this is why documents such as the Merchant-Heeney Report, or the report of the committee of congressmen produced under Representative Tupper's leadership, can be, at one and the same time, so satisfying and so disappointing. They have as their purpose the promotion of good relations. To the extent that this objective is realized, the policy-makers of each country have reason to be satisfied. But the promotion of good relations is not the same thing as the promotion of scholarly inquiry. It may be an article of faith of the liberal creed that there is no necessary conflict between the two. So much the worse for the liberal creed.

In a frame of mind that is fairly described as mutually admiring, the friendly diplomats sat down to distil from their experience some rules for running the North American partnership during years to come.

Only a mandarin like Heeney, raised to the highest power, could presume to reduce to numbered paragraphs a relationship so convoluted and so volatile. But then such a mandarin in the presence of the Trinity would not hesitate to work out respective spheres of jurisdiction for Father, Son, and Holy Ghost. Heeney did not hesitate before attempting his only slightly less presumptuous task.

One of his numbered paragraphs – number 81 – got him into trouble. Look at it again:

It is in the abiding interest of both countries that, wherever possible, divergent views between the two governments should be expressed and if possible resolved in private, through diplomatic channels.

By 'diplomatic channels' it is fair to assume that the authors of this passage – one a former ambassador to the United States, the other a former ambassador to Canada – mean ambassadorial channels – embassy to embassy, rather than the personal diplomacy of visiting ministers. Here occupational bias gets the better of analysis.

Sometimes a diplomatic channel aids the flow of negotiation. Sometimes it does not. Consider the testimony of Richard Neustadt on the point. He is writing, from his perspective as former special assistant to President Kennedy,

of the breakdown of Anglo-American communication at the time of the Sky-
bolt missile crisis of 1962:

The British embassy in Washington and ours in London teem with ministers,
counselors, and secretaries of assorted rank, to say nothing of special-purpose
aides from a variety of government departments. These spew vast quantities
of information back and forth across the ocean. But rarely is it information
of the sort to shed much light on ministerial motives. Most members of those
massive staffs deal with official counterparts who often cannot comprehend
what moves their Minister, still less his colleagues. Even the minority of staf-
fers actually engaged in what our State Department terms "political" affairs –
that is, diplomacy – are mostly Foreign Service Officers themselves and deal
for the most part with Foreign Offices. But games of governance in Whitehall
and in Washington are played routinely, day by day, outside of and around
those Offices, through budgetary channels, legislative channels, and promotion channels in a party context. From these the Foreign Service types are
relatively shielded. Accordingly, they often are insensitive – nobody's fault –
to the very stakes most likely to move Ministers from day to day.[3]

What is true of the British embassy at one end of Massachusetts Avenue is just
as true of the Canadian embassy at the other. The business of Canada is too
important to pass invariably, even 'where possible,' through diplomatic channels. Budgetary channels, legislative channels, even 'promotion channels in a
party context' may move matters more quickly to our advantage.

So much for the Heeney hypothesis on venue. What of the hypothesis on
privacy?

'It is in the abiding interest of both countries that, wherever possible, divergent views between the two governments should be expressed and if possible
resolved in private ...' Compressed in this short statement are three distinct
propositions: 1 a proposition about propaganda; 2 a proposition about negotiating technique; 3 a proposition about diplomatic style.

1 No justification is attempted in the Heeney-Merchant Report for the
proposition that it is in our 'abiding interest' to refrain from appealing to US
public opinion when the views of the two governments diverge. But it is easy
to understand why the two ambassadors advance it as an axiom. Career diplomats instinctively shy away from propaganda. 'Regular diplomatic officials,'
George Kennan has explained, 'tend everywhere to view propaganda with dis-

---

3 Richard E. Neustadt, *Alliance Politics* (Columbia University Press, New York &
London 1970), 132-3

taste and scepticism. The profession of diplomacy induces a weary detachment, foreign to all political enthusiasm and *ex parte* pleas. Propaganda smacked of overt interference in the domestic affairs of other countries – something that went strongly against the grain of diplomatic tradition.'[4]

It is not surprising, then, that L.B. Pearson, reared in that tradition for a quarter of a century before entering politics, endorses the Heeney-Merchant injunction to eschew appeals to public opinion on the part of governments. As early as 1954, Pearson spoke disparagingly of 'international public relations.' Diplomacy is

more than monologues at international gatherings, or public press conferences, or calculated leaks to frighten potential adversaries or "put the heat on" reluctant friends, or even political quiz programmes before the microphone or camera. There should be more room for and greater reliance on quiet and confidential negotiation ... If Moscow, by the crudity of communist diplomatic methods, and by its incessant and direct appeal to peoples over the heads of governments, makes this procedure difficult or even impossible, we should keep on trying to restore it. In any event, we need not follow these communist tactics of propaganda diplomacy in conferences and negotiations between friends.[5]

Pearson reiterated this view as prime minister in an open letter to some 400 members of the faculty of the University of Toronto who had urged upon him a more forceful disaffiliation of Canada from US military operations in Vietnam than his government had so far seen fit to espouse. 'Confidential and quiet arguments by a responsible government are usually more effective than public ones ... Too many public declarations and disclosures run the risk of complicating matters for those concerned.' And again in the House of Commons on 10 May 1967:

I do not think that as a responsible government it would be wise or desirable or necessary for us to publicly condemn or publicly proclaim ... There is imposed on us the obligation not to unless it is inescapable; otherwise I believe we would not be able to act in a way in which our suggestions would be listened to by the United States government when we put them forward through the channels of diplomacy.

---

4   *Soviet-American Relations, 1917-1920*, II, *The Decision to Intervene* (Princeton University Press, Princeton, NJ 1958), 191
5   Lester B. Pearson, *Words and Occasions* (University of Toronto Press, Toronto & Cambridge, Mass. 1970), 124-5

Not to publicly condemn or publicly proclaim may be good manners. But is it necessarily the best policy? It runs counter to all the folk wisdom about squeaky wheels getting grease, about nice guys finishing last. This is not only true about international society, it is especially true about international society.

The great beast of state has too thick a hide, too many other preoccupations, to prick up its ear attentively whenever a Canadian minister sidles into one of the antechambers of power and there, quietly courteously, diffidently, decorously, recites from his confidential brief his confidential case. It may have been like that in the good old days – the days when the State Department, as Kennan recalls with great nostalgia, 'was a quaint old place, with its law-office atmosphere, its cool dark corridors, its swinging doors, its brass cuspidors, its black leather rocking chairs, and the grandfather clock in the Secretary of State's office' – and, he might have added, recalling the incumbent of that time, the grandfather figure in the secretary of state's office. But it's not like that any more. The atmosphere is less that of a law-office than of bomber-command; the corridors are neither dark nor cool; cuspidors are out and computers are in. And in place of Charles Evans Hughes we have Dean Rusk, of whom it is written: 'When Assistant Secretaries brought him problems, he listened courteously, thanked them, and let them go; they would often depart little wiser than when they came.' Where senior American diplomats fail to make an impression on so experienced a stone-waller, who are Canadian diplomats to succeed? You have to go higher than that, speak louder than that.

Higher than that means the president. Sometimes he is sympathetic, sometimes he is not. It is reported that President Johnson once responded to the representative of some less-developed land: 'What's the idea of someone like you asking the leader of the Free World a chicken-shittin' question like that?' The power of the presidency, joined to the personality of its incumbent, make for an atmosphere in which the conversation is frank and friendly only so long as the chief executive permits it to be so.

The Heeney-Merchant Report often mentions partnership; not once does it mention pollution. That is a glaring oversight. Purifying the North American environment is an enterprise for partnership if there ever was one. Canadians and Americans must work together at it if the work is to be done.

But that is not all. The appeal of government to people – government on both sides of the border to people on both sides of the border – is a potent weapon in the war against waste and smog and spill. To keep it hanging on the wall is to lose the war by default. Quiet diplomacy has no place in an ecological crusade.

So some ministers are starting to realize. In November 1970 the minister of energy, mines and resources addressed himself to the problem of controlling trans-national pollution. 'It is to be hoped,' J.J. Greene declared, 'that the great and powerful nation which can afford to travel to the moon and at the same time spend $50 billions a year and more for war will soon be able to afford to clean up its stinking, fouling tons of waste before dumping it into its friendly neighbour's back-yard.' Words like these in a public speech were not, he knew, what the Heeney-Merchant Report prescribed. But he'd given its principles for partnership a try, and he felt that they had let us down. He had been, he said, 'restrained, private, responsible and diplomatic. But the response to my quiet diplomacy has been rhetoric rather than result.'

2 Distinct from the Heeney-Merchant admonition to refrain from propaganda is its admonition to negotiate in secret.

This admonition merely betrays naiveté about the negotiating process. Bargaining knows no hard and fast correlation between secrecy and success. Sometimes it is good tactics to keep the terms of trade to the negotiating parties. Sometimes it is good tactics to let them out.

Fred C. Iklé's *How Nations Negotiate* had been published for a year when the Heeney-Merchant Report was published. Doubtless such experienced negotiators felt they had nothing to learn from an academic treatise on their life's work. More's the pity. They could have learned from Iklé what they ought to have learned from experience – that 'no matter what preferences one might have regarding secret versus open diplomacy, one must realize that each party will try to move toward or press for that form of negotiation from which it expects the best results.'[6]

3 The Heeney-Merchant Report embodies an approach to foreign policy, a diplomatic style. Foreign policy is for professionals. Amateurs are to keep off the grass. The report is hostile to participatory diplomacy. The public is to be seen and not heard. The report is partial to protocol. In the era of the sit-in, it still turns to Satow – that courtly guide to diplomatic practice for former generations.

The report thus points towards the past; and while not without its charm, the past is not the direction that our foreign policy ought to point. Some words of wisdom from the US State Department are a useful antidote to Heeney-Merchant antiquarianism:

6 (Harper & Row, New York, Evanston & London 1964), 135

The communications gap between foreign policy operators and the public, especially citizens in the more remote areas, intellectuals and youth, is still widening. Negative and often conflicting public attitudes are sometimes treated as immutable instead of capable of change through programs to develop understanding and support. Public mistrust on the one hand and elitist tendencies on the other can in combination promote and prolong continued division.

Internal insularity strongly affects the climate in which interaction between the Department and the general public takes place ... It causes the Department of State and its Foreign Service Officers to view the outside world from a detached perspective tinged with suspicion, defensiveness and even alienation ...[7]

'Detached,' 'tinged with suspicion, defensiveness and even alienation' - that is a fair description of the perspective from which the authors of the Heeney-Merchant Report look out upon the world. It is a perspective of which the Canadian foreign policy-making community ought to purge itself as quickly and as thoroughly as may be decently thought possible.

[March 1971]

---

7 *Diplomacy for the '70s: A Program of Management Reform for the Department of State* (US Government Printing Office, Washington 1970), 386

8
Trade, not braid

Now the day is over,
Night is drawing nigh,
Shadows of the evening
Steal across the sky.

The strains of Baring-Gould's fine old hymn, floating from the Peace Tower carillon into the offices of the East Block next door, provide a plaintive summer evensong for any foreign service officer still toiling at his desk. Here is a man who, like Hemingway before him, has survived to read his own obituary. It may be found in *Foreign Policy for Canadians*[1] - the government's White Paper released on 25 June - under the heading 'Organizing for the Seventies.'

Aesopian language and lurching syntax are clues to how grave is the conclusion struggling to emerge. At length, through the murk of the official prose - 'The pace of change renders more complex and urgent the problems of planning and implementing a coherent policy aligned with national aims'; 'An integrated management system cannot be established immediately or easily'; 'The new system must be developed harmoniously and above all keep its capacity for adapting to an evolving international situation' - may be read the writing on the wall: 'The government has decided that there should be maximum integration in its foreign operations.'

So the Department of External Affairs is to go the way of the army, navy and air force - not into oblivion but into homogeneity. It has travelled far and high since its humble beginnings sixty years ago, when a deputy minister, two clerks and a secretary shared an annual budget of $14,950 and an office above

1 (Queen's Printer, Ottawa 1970)

a barber shop on Bank Street. Forty years on, with Lester Pearson as its minister, its placement at the federal table put it closest to the salt. To its ranks candidates for public service most eagerly sought admission: from them came the most powerful civil servants in the land.

Nothing speaks more eloquently of power than feeling free to help a rival. Towards the end of the war, top people at 'External' began to worry about the Department of Trade and Commerce – not because it seemed too strong but because it seemed too feeble. 'Weakness in the senior personnel of Trade and Commerce,' the Under Secretary of State for External Affairs noted, 'is a matter of some concern to other departments who have to concert policy with them. It has also the unhappy result of producing a rather defensive state of mind and something approaching an inferiority complex within the department.'[2]

Their cure for this disease was to recommend the appointment of a forceful personality as its deputy minister. In the event, the services of their nominee were required elsewhere, and Trade and Commerce continued to flounder until rescued in 1948 by C.D. Howe.

Since then its star has shone ever more brightly, while that of External has gone into a decline. The reversal in their respective fortunes didn't happen all at once. In 1952, the question was put to its under secretary whether he thought 'the time has arrived when External Affairs should take over the trade commissioners.' Arnold Heeney responded archly: 'I am afraid that to answer the question would require a degree of diplomatic skill of which I am not capable.'[3] Today the question might best be put the other way around: Has the time arrived when the trade commissioners should take over External Affairs? A.E. Ritchie must truthfully answer: It has, and they are.[4]

It is not just the new mercantilism of the White Paper, with its philosophy of 'trade, not braid,' that's put External in the shade. It is as well the distress now being visited upon the entire diplomatic profession. One after another, the traditional missions of diplomacy are becoming redundant, or else next to impossible to perform.

Negotiating is more and more the mission of officials of the department or agency directly concerned with the subject at hand – labour, immigration, wheat, atomic energy. They fly out from their capital in large, four-engine aircraft; or bombard His Ex. by telex from home base.

2 Norman A. Robertson to W.L. Mackenzie King, 23 Dec. 1943, King Papers
3 Canada, House of Commons Standing Committee on External Affairs, *Minutes of Proceedings and Evidence,* no 2, 8 Apr. 1952, 34
4 It is only fair to cite Mr Ritchie's rejoinder: 'You got me wrong. My truthful answer is: "It hasn't and they aren't."' However, the deputy minister of Trade and Commerce has since been made high commissioner in London.

Propaganda seems pointless in a world already deafened by too much din. Reporting is hard when blinkered, which the diplomat is so heavily that he can barely make it from bar to buffet without colliding with his kind.

Perhaps he has borne these afflictions no worse than any professionals faced without early warning by the prospect of obsolescence. But his chief difficulty is of his own making. This is his failure to adjust to a dramatically changed international environment. A truly modern diplomacy, an authority observes, 'must protect and advance the national interest not primarily by the usual processes of negotiation and communication with stabilized states, but rather through developing contact with and exerting influence upon powerful but still largely inchoate political forces. This definition of the diplomatic task puts notions of sovereignty, protocol, non-intervention, and many other familiar considerations in a radically different framework.'[5]

How far from making that adjustment are most members of the profession may be judged from an aide-mémoire filched from last month's diplomatic pouch out of a beleaguered nation. 'The ambassador of Liberia, dean of the diplomatic corps, presents his compliments to their excellencies, the ladies and gentlemen, heads of diplomatic missions, and has the honor to inform them that the ambassador of Sweden, his excellency Bo L. Siegbahn, has expressed the desire that his tray should be engraved on its back instead of on the front, as is usually done. Therefore, the ambassador of Liberia, dean of the diplomatic corps, hereby submits this matter to their excellencies, the ladies and gentlemen, heads of diplomatic missions, for their reaction, at their earliest possible convenience.'

Meanwhile, as the traditional diplomats go through the motions of their potty protocol, like a ballet company finishing Swan Lake in an earthquake, the commercials are taking over. Foreign operations will centre more on manifests than manifestoes, on bills of lading, than on bills of rights, on 'cheap tin trays' carried in the holds of freighters than on sterling silver trays (whichever side engraved) presented to departing ambassadors. Being 'in trade,' no longer a badge of bureaucratic inferiority, is where the action is.

Presiding cheerfully over the dissolution of his own empire is the secretary of state for External Affairs. But then Mitchell Sharp was always a Trade and Commerce man at heart. 'On revient toujours à ses premiers amours.' That is why the minister can publish so that his department may perish. It is a pleasant enough division of labour – for him.

[July 1970]

5 Waldemar A. Nielsen, *African Battleline: American Policy Choices in Southern Africa* (Harper & Row, New York, Evanston, & London 1965), 138-9

9

The selling of the think-tank

Of all the gimmicks for governing the country sold to a too credulous press and public by Prime Minister Trudeau and his snake-oil merchants in the Privy Council office, none is more spurious than the design for an institute for re-search on public policy laid out by Ronald S. Ritchie.[1] Would you buy a second-hand think-tank from this man? The government of Canada has just bought it for you, at a cost of up to $10 millions.

For a politician tagged as trendy, Mr Trudeau is badly out of touch with the *haute couture* of intellect. Think-tanks and futurology, so far from being fash-ionable, have become as *démodé* as knee-length skirts, as out-of-date as spats.

Not just dated but discredited as well. Futurology has been exposed as fraud, think-tanks as a frill. 'The whole system of contracting out has become an empty ritual,' an American critic wrote as long ago as 1968, 'the magic of chateau-cloistered expertise is on the wane.'[2]

One reason for their falling out of favour is that their work is often shoddy. Many public policy research institutes lack any form of quality control for an output largely classified. Meant for a client's eye alone, it escapes detached evaluation.

In 1968 the US General Accounting Office looked in on the Hudson Insti-tute (along with RAND the most prestigious think-tank of them all, the one in which the prime minister's aides are required to immerse themselves from time to time) to find a major client profoundly disenchanted. 'The author did not have sufficient knowledge of the subject area,' 'many of the report's assump-

1 *An Institute for Research on Public Policy: A Study Prepared for the Government of Canada* (Queen's Printer, Ottawa 1971)
2 H.L. Nieburg, 'The Profit and Loss of Herman Kahn,' *The Nation,* 13 May 1968

tions were obvious or unproved,' 'superficial and not of much value,' 'unsupported guesses that serve only to distract' – such were the disparaging remarks of the Office of Civil Defense about the research it had paid Hudson to conduct on its behalf.[3]

Another sample of think-tank thought to come to light in which it would not ordinarily have been exposed is revealed in the Pentagon Papers. The Institute for Defense Analysis (cited in the Ritchie Report as 'able to attract competent staff by the challenge of the work') prepared for the Pentagon, its principal patron, a study of why a year and a half of bombing by the US Air Force hadn't brought Hanoi to its knees. 'North Vietnam has basically a subsistence agricultural economy,' IDA concluded after vast investigation, 'that presents a difficult and unrewarding target system for air attack.' Rather than bomb, IDA recommended, the United States should build, and what it should build is an 'anti-troop infiltration system' featuring 'a constantly renewed mine field' seeded with '20 million Gravel mines per month, possibly 25 million button bomblets per month,' the up-keep of which is put at $800 millions a year.[4]

The Vietnam War is the first to be waged by think-tanks; one hopes to God it will be the last. But even without that blotch upon their copy-books they would have been discredited.

Think-tank findings tend to bias. When the Hudson Institute prepares a report for the Grumman Aerospace Corporation on the future for manned carrier aircraft in the 1980s, does it tell its client that manned carrier aircraft may have no future in the 1980s? Does it so much as allude to the possibility? It does not. Instead, with the characteristic Hudson blend of ingenuity and ingenuousness, it devises a series of scenarios in which manned carrier aircraft more than ever go off into the wide blue yonder of the 1980s – if need be from floating platforms anchored to reefs or shoals (a feat made feasible by 'our tremendous engineering capability and offshore construction experience, combined with our fantastic sea logistic capability').[5]

Think-tank research cannot be disinterested. The institute comes first, the client a close second, the truth a poor third. We should accept their findings, Kenneth Boulding rightly warns, 'with the same kind of reserve that, shall we say, we might greet a study of the Reformation by Jesuits based on unpublished and secret documents in the Vatican; there is the same combination of honesty in the value system and bias in the commitment.'[6]

3   Ibid.
4   Quoted in *The Pentagon Papers* (Bantam Books, New York 1971), 508
5   Frank E. Armbruster, *A Study of the Probable Environment of Manned Carrier Aircraft in the 1980s: Interim Report* (Hudson Institute, Croton-on-Hudson 1970), appendix 1, p 4
6   *Conflict and Defense* (Harper & Row, New York 1962), 332

If think-tank impartiality is suspect, so is think-tank methodology. When since the mystic cults of Pythagoreans have mathematics been so abused on behalf of public policy?

Think-tank research runs to quantifying the unquantifiable. 'Herman Kahn once said to me: "You're 98 percent right",' a critic of his Hudson Institute recalls: 'I wonder how he arrived at that percentage.'[7] One might wonder as much about the percentages peppering the Pentagon Papers: 'US aims: 70% – to avoid a humiliating US defeat ... 20% – To keep SVN (and the adjacent) territory from Chinese hands. 10% – To permit the people of SVN to enjoy a better, freer way of life.' How much 'better,' how much 'freer'?

Think-tank research runs to extrapolating trends. But extrapolation is not prediction; futurology's persistent confusion of the two reminds Robert A. Nisbet of a mad scientist 'predicting giants at age twenty on the basis of growth rates at age ten.'[8]

Such a confusion may account for Herman Kahn's forecast of an economic growth rate of 10.8 per cent a year for Japan during 1981-5 – a figure tossed off with the assurance of one who has lived through the future he predicts, but Kahn has been nowhere near it. 'The unscholarly elements in [his] work,' writes the Australian strategist Hedley Bull of it, 'the tipsterism, the appeals to non-evidence and hints of vast studies under way at the Hudson Institute that would support his conclusions, are not extrinsic ... but are an essential part of his equipment as ... "a professional futurologist".'[9]

The professional futurologist lacks the power to predict but possesses the power to persuade. Professor Howard Perlmutter, made famous by forecasting that some 300 super-corporations will dominate the global market of the 1980s while medium-size corporations go under, says managers of medium-size corporations can hardly wait for his briefings to end so that they can get busy on their mergers. 'It doesn't matter what will happen,' futurologist Perlmutter declares. 'What does matter is what people think will happen. In that way they will make it happen.'[10]

Exactly. That is why Herman Kahn ought not to make oracular pronouncements that Japan will become a nuclear weapon power. That is why the Canadian government ought not to have allowed eighty of its senior servants at a seminar of the Institute for the Future at Middletown, Connecticut, to toy with – let alone to arrive at – the conclusion that Quebec will leave Confederation. They will only help to make it happen.

7 Quoted in Michael Davie, 'Shadow of a New Big Brother,' *The Observer,* 10 Jan. 1971
8 'The Year 2000 and All That,' *Commentary*, vol. 45, no 6, June 1968, 63
9 *Survival,* July 1971, 249
10 Quoted in Richard Spiegelberg, '1985 – the day of the super-giants,' *The Times,* 29 Mar. 1971

Biased in approach, flawed in methodology, think-tanks have suffered the final ignominy of redundance. After a first flurry of infatuation, governments have turned cool. Out-house research – who needs it?

Effective public policy research must be in-house public policy research. You have to do your own. 'Planning is a waste of time,' Henry Kissinger has testified, 'unless it is done by the people who have got to execute it. Unless you can get the attention of the top policy-makers, you are just writing theoretical exercises.'[11]

There's enough research in the system already. That 'urgent need to seek out more data,' of which the Ritchie Report has managed to convince the government of Canada, simply doesn't exist.

Data is coming out Ottawa's ears, it is up to its chin in the stuff. More is too much. 'Utilizing outside experts and research institutes' – Kissinger's testimony again – 'adds another burden to already overworked officials. It tends to divert attention from the act of judgment on which policy ultimately depends to the assembly of facts which is relatively the easiest step in policy formation. Few if any of the recent crises ... have been caused by the unavailability of data. Our policy-makers do not lack advice; they are in many respects overwhelmed by it.'[12] Ours are too.

Producing new ideas – the think-tank's raison d'être – is grossly over-valued. Policy-makers do not need new ideas. 'The ideas necessary for good government,' Hans Morgenthau points out, 'are part of the public record.' The basic Canadian problems – what to do about the French fact, American domination, pollution, unemployment – will not be solved by new ideas. The quest for political novelty, the pursuit of administrative innovation, are part of the disguise by which an irresolute leader seeks to conceal from his people the extent of his irresolution. What policy-makers do need is the courage of their convictions, and the right convictions. No institute of public policy research – however lavishly funded, staffed, and housed – is going to help them there.

Among the useful roles which the United States performs for Canada is that of social laboratory where inventions, as useful here as there, are tested and proven at no expense to us. We ride free on their research and development. We can take advantage of their successes, avoid their failures.

One of their failures is futurology. Years of experiment with long-range planning, large-scale research, institute brainstorming, think-tank 'schlock science,' have caused them to start calling it off.

11 Press briefing, 16 Sept. 1970
12 *The Necessity for Choice* (Harper & Brothers, New York 1960), 351

'The future-predicters, the change-analysts and trend-tenders,' writes Robert A. Nisbet, 'say that with the aid of institute resources, computers, linear programming, etc., they will deal with the kinds of change that are *not* the consequence of the Random Event, the Genius, the Maniac and the Prophet,' adding: 'There really aren't any; not any worth looking into.'[13]

'National planning does not work,' asserts a contributor to the current issue of *The Public Interest* (once almost a house organ for futurology), 'because no large and complex society can figure out what simple and unambiguous things it wants to do, or in what clear order of priority or how to get them done,' and goes on to quote Nabakov approvingly: 'What we do at best (at worst we perform trivial tricks) when postulating the future, is to expand enormously the specious present.'[14] And another contributor to the same issue calls for an attitude of 'utter agnosticism' towards the claims of long-range planners and the boosters of bigness and growth, conceding that 'since such a way of thinking about the future runs counter to that which the West has wholeheartedly espoused since the 18th century ... it will be something of a miracle if this new agnosticism comes to prevail.'[15]

The intellectuals' disillusionment with the claims of futurology is taking a toll of future-oriented institutions in the United States. In 1969, the US State Department disbanded its Policy Planning Council.[16] Twenty years of long-range foreign policy prediction by planners freed from day-to-day operational responsibility had shown it to be a waste of time and money. Contracts for out-house research are drying up as clients realize that think-tanks (in the words of an American critic) are no more than 'a means for spending money while rationalizing useless, unread and often uncirculated results,' 'a collaboration subsidized by the tax-payer' in which it is hard to tell whether the think-tank is working for the government or the government is working for the think-tank.[17]

Canadian policy-makers, far from being warned off by this experience, are coming on strong – infatuated with futurology despite its exposure as a racket.

Prime Minister Trudeau's keynote speech at the Liberal 'thinkers conference' in November 1969 was a paean to technocratic futurism, with its allusions to 'the refinements of our techniques for forecasting and planning,' to the need for planning to 'operate in a scale of time which is sufficient to permit it to alter the future,' to a political system in which methodology rather

13 'The Year 2000 and All That,' 66
14 Aaron Wildavsky, 'Does Planning Work?', *The Public Interest,* summer 1971, 104
15 E.J. Mishan, 'Making the Future Safe for Mankind,' ibid., 60-1
16 See below, 128-30
17 Nieburg, 'The Profit and Loss of Herman Kahn'

than principle is what divides the voters: 'A party which shows that it is capable of coming to grips with long range questions about the future of our society will have a new claim to the respect and the support of the people of Canada.'[18]

The prime minister's bemusement by the claims of futurology is leading to the creation of future-oriented institutions in Canada. In 1969, the Department of External Affairs created its Policy Analysis Group in response to what it calls 'an expression of concern by the present government that the elements of Canadian foreign policy should be settled with an orderly coherence in a rational form, be sensitive to changing conditions and priorities, and in tune with the future.' That same year, the prime minister received a report on the feasibility of setting up an institute 'where long-range research and thinking can be carried into governmental matters of all kinds.' The Ritchie Report concluded: 'With the experience of institutes and governments in the United States and Western Europe as a guide, there is every reason to believe that the time is now ripe for creation in Canada of a public policy research institute.' In 1971, the prime minister accepted this conclusion.

Minerva's owl, Hegel wrote despairingly, takes her flight only in the gathering dusk, but in Canada she can't so much as leave the ground. Why is our government placing so much faith and funds in the sort of institution that elsewhere has been discredited?

Partly because we have yet to shake off the remaining vestiges of a colonial mentality which, distrusting our own judgment, looks to the metropole for models. There it is traduced by the meretricious, like a half-wit playing Crown and Anchor at a fair.

Partly because of our prime minister's cast of mind which, moulded in the *cours classique* four decades ago, bearing still its ultra-rationalist imprint, was only in the dangerous years of later middle age exposed to the send-ups of American social scientism, to be by these bewitched.

Mainly because of a conflict of interest. The government sought counsel from those – to judge from the Ritchie Report's list of counsellors, only from those – who had a vested interest in endorsing the project. What would happen, the economist E.J. Mishan asks ironically, if futurology were phased out? 'We should have to give up our toys! A hundred thousand academics would have to abandon their hopes of status and recognition.'[19]

18 'Technology, the Individual and the Party,' in Allen M. Linden, ed., *Living in the Seventies* (Peter Martin Associates Ltd, Toronto 1970), 6-7
19 'Futurism: And the Worse That Is Yet to come,' *Encounter,* Mar. 1971, 9

But not in this Canada of ours. 'The major component of the institute's staff,' the Ritchie Report promises,

is likely to be social scientists – economists, political scientists, historians, sociologists, psychologists ... The professional staff would have to be backed up, of course, by secretarial, stenographic, clerical, accounting and other support personnel. They would need access to library and computer facilities. They would have to travel ... The institute would have to seek out and pay for research work done by outside scholars ... These too would have to travel ... The institute should surely be, within a reasonable time ... [staffed by] 80 to 100 professional personnel [with] an annual budget of the order of $5 million.[20]

What a cornucopia of goodies to gorge on for the so-called 'action intellectuals' in whom contracts for research arouse the avarice of a magpie and the morals of an alley-cat. To such a breed the public policy research institute would be in any case attractive, but the kind of action offered by the campus these days will make it irresistible. An almost audible relief is theirs at moving from the turmoil of the academy into their 'suitable headquarters building' with its 'own distinctive working quarters':

Hide me, O my saviour hide,
Till the storm of life is past.
Safe into the haven guide,
O receive my soul at last.

What of the universities they will leave behind? The Ritchie Report hopes to enlist only the best talent among 'highly regarded scholars.' Pull 80 to 100 highly regarded scholars out of Canada's social science faculties, and there would be nothing worthwhile left. Our universities would no longer be able to perform one of their vital functions – principled and radical criticism of society.

Could the Liberal party, with its successful record down the years of co-opting critics in the bud, have planned it all that way?

[August 1971]

20   *An Institute for Research on Public Policy,* 46-7

10

The deliquescence of diplomacy

A fundamental change is taking place within world politics. It may be described as the decline of diplomacy. Or, better, as the deliquescence of diplomacy – deliquescence in its dictionary meaning of melting away into nothingness, fading away into limbo.

I construe this prediction as the third instalment in a three-fold attack upon the diplomatic profession. Elsewhere I have charged it with moral turpitude,[1] and again with inefficiency.[2] In what follows I bring against it the charge of irrelevance.

This is perhaps the gravest charge that may be laid. Tell a man he's immoral, and he may feel a glow of satisfaction at being thought a rogue. Tell him he's inefficient, and he may console himself by reflecting that the inefficient, along with the meek, will inherit the earth. But tell him he's irrelevant – obsolete, redundant, no longer needed, in a word deliquesced – and there is no glow, no consolation, to be had. Deliquescence is a down trip.

The deliquescence of diplomacy has its causes in the changing *style* of negotiation, in the changing *technique* of negotiation, and in the changing *milieu* of negotiation.

To the question 'How should nations negotiate?' there are two general sorts of answers. The first answer derives from the tradition of classical diplomacy, and is best stated, perhaps, in that chapter of Harold Nicolson's well known little book, *Diplomacy*,[3] in which he describes, as so many have before

---

1 In *Right and Wrong in Foreign Policy;* see below, 165-91
2 In *Fate and Will in Foreign Policy;* see below, 81-162
3 (3rd ed., Oxford University Press, London, New York, & Toronto 1963)

him, the qualities of the ideal diplomat. This is what he says these are: 'The basis of good negotiation is moral influence and that influence is founded on seven specific diplomatic virtues, namely: - 1 Truthfulness - 2 Precision - 3 Calm - 4 Good Temper - 5 Patience - 6 Modesty - 7 Loyalty.'

When Nicolson praises these qualities, as he does in lapidary language, it is not as ends in themselves, not for virtue being its own reward. It is rather because he expects they will secure the best results, produce the greatest payoff. His book is really a set of variations on the theme that 'honesty is the best policy,' and that 'nice guys finish first.'

The second answer to the question 'How should nations negotiate?' is very different from Nicolson's answer. It is given most baldly, most boldly, in T.C. Schelling's *The Strategy of Conflict*. Schelling does not go so far as to contend that lying, imprecision, excitability, bad temper, impatience, immodesty, fickleness - the mirror-image opposites of Nicolson's seven cardinal negotiating virtues - are the keys to a successful diplomacy. He only contends that on occasion they can be. He observes that sometimes honesty is the best policy and sometimes it is not. He points out that there are times when nice guys finish first, and times when they finish last. He does, however, give the strong impression that the world is becoming more and more a place in which nice guys, if they do not finish last, finish well on down the line. And so he advises nice guys - the statesmen of the western world - that if they wish to survive the sordid stratagems of their opponents, they would do well not to appear so nice. They should not, he says, be above soliciting 'advice from the underworld, or from ancient despotisms, on how to make agreements work when trust and good faith are lacking and there is no legal recourse for breach of contract.'[4]

If the diplomatist of the old school reads his Schelling as perceptively as once he read his Nicolson, his Mona Lisa smile will be frozen on his face. This is no mere case of newcomers crowding his environment, making the working conditions less pleasant. He's put up with that before, he can put up with it again. It's a case of a new environment crowding out the old, making it impossible to do his job under any conditions, for the job no longer exists to be done.

For what's now required of him is to be adept at techniques altogether offensive to his taste. He is required to lie, to cheat, to dissemble and, the better to employ such measures, 'to solicit advice from the underworld, or from ancient despotisms.' But these are not the oracles the smooth diplomatist can easily or profitably consult. He did not enter the foreign service to live a life like Tamburlane's, or a life like Genghis Khan's. He can't model himself on a Dillinger, or even on Bonnie and Clyde. To the extent that he's conscious of his

4 (Harvard University Press, Cambridge, Mass. 1960), 20

predicament, and of its causes, a sense of his irrelevance hangs about him like a shroud. The modern diplomatist is thus a man under stress.

Typically he develops one or other of three defence mechanisms. Perhaps he'll pretend to himself, and try to get others to believe, that nothing really has changed. 'What are the essential qualities,' asks Escott Reid, a former Canadian foreign service officer, 'which a diplomat must possess?' And he answers as Nicolson answered: 'The first quality is honesty.'[5] That remark is beyond comment, as it is beyond belief.

Or he will seek consolation in the camaraderie of his profession. This is the reaction of Lord Strang, the former head of the Foreign Office, who writes in his memoirs as follows:

The thirst for world domination, the belief that it can be attained and the abandonment of all moral restraint in the attempt to achieve it [are] part of the environment in which the Foreign Service officer lives and works, and it is small wonder if he has sometimes been distressed and revolted by it ... To work in such an environment would hardly have been tolerable had it not been ... for the comradeship, in times good and bad, which colleagues in the Foreign Service afford to each other ...[6]

This is a true confession, for which the student of the subject is duly grateful. Diplomacy, he learns, is a dirty business, but fortunately for those engaged in it they are such a happy band of brothers that it hardly seems to matter, as they hardly seem to notice.

A third mechanism of defence against the stress which assails the modern diplomatist, caught as he is in the crossfire between the ideals and the practice of his profession, is to turn against its ideals and revel in its practice. For this a certain hardness of heart, and of nose, is required, and not all diplomatists possess them. One who does is Dean Acheson. The North Vietnamese, Mr Acheson remarked not long ago, 'don't want to negotiate. I say that's fine. I hope they stay that way.'[7] This is as if a surgeon, having successfully implanted the heart of patient X into the body of patient Y, were to utter a prayer for it to stop beating.

The stress of the modern diplomatist, however he may defend himself against it, is made no easier to bear by the reflection that if he won't learn from the underworld there are plenty of others who will. Not just the specialists in violence and the agents of deceit – those who staff the Pentagon, the

5 'The Conscience of the Diplomat: A Personal Testament,' *Queen's Quarterly,* winter 1967, LXXIV, no 4, 580-1
6 *Home and Abroad* (André Deutsch, London 1956), 305
7 'Acheson on Negotiation,' *The Reporter,* 28 Dec. 1967, 28

CIA and MI 5 - but within the precincts of his own profession he will find those fledgling Achesons - eager and ambitious public servants - who are not only willing to learn from the underworld, but can teach it a trick or two.

My first reason for predicting the deliquescence of diplomacy is this change in the *style* of negotiation. My second reason has to do with a change in the *technique* of negotiation.

The Johnson administration was often charged with failing to pursue, as seriously as it might, negotiation with Hanoi. This charge is wide of the mark. The Johnson administration has been negotiating with Hanoi. But the kind of negotiation engaged in is not the kind we used to know.

It doesn't take place around green baize tables. No carafe of Vichy water, no demi-tasse of coffee, aid and comfort the discussions. For the discussants are ten thousand miles apart. They communicate by sending and receiving signals. The signals are gradations of violence. Selection of targets, scale of attack, tell the recipient what the sender wants to say. Smooth diplomacy delivered despatches to a chancery. Rough diplomacy delivers bombs to a refinery - the very rough, to a hospital.

Such unholy communion is called tacit negotiation. Tacit negotiation is negotiation without negotiators, foreign policy without foreign offices, diplomacy without diplomatists. In tacit negotiation you let your weapons do your talking. The Marines are your ambassadors. Their mortars are your message. Asked what he would do in Vietnam, Dean Acheson replied: 'I would use this question of bombing as a military and other tool ... And as you do weaken them, and as they do want to stop, this particular weapon will be used less or not used at all. You don't have to talk to them about it, you just have to do it ...'[8]

Tacit negotiation's nothing new. Nelson called a man-o'-war 'the best negotiator in Europe.' There's always been interaction between arms and influence, ever since men began taking up arms to acquire influence. What's new is not the method but the popularity of the method, the pervasiveness of the method. And its popularity and pervasiveness derive from recent refinements of the method.

One is a refinement in doctrine. Even as recently as the Second World War, people thought there were only two postures - so to speak - in which to have international intercourse. One was a posture of peace. The other a posture of war - in Hobbes' phrase, 'the posture of gladiators.'

8 Ibid., 28-9

So restricted a repertoire offered little scope to tacit negotiators. All they could do was to transmit variations on the theme of 'If you don't quit now, we'll blow the hell out of you.' The Second World War was accordingly a war of saturation bombing, of final solutions, of unconditional surrenders. 'When men become locked in battle' – so said one of its most famous generals – 'there should be no artifice under the name of politics which should handicap your own men.'[9]

The author of this dictum was General MacArthur. For attempting to apply it to his conduct of the war in Korea he was stripped of his command. For the Korean War was a different sort of war than the military had got used to. It was a limited war, a war of status quo and stalemate, a war of sanctuary and redoubt, a war of weapons that were not fired and of generals who were fired.

The Korean War was limited war; the Vietnam War is escalated war. If Napoleon's soldiers carried in their knapsacks a field-marshal's baton, Johnson's chiefs of staff carry in their briefcases a collapsible version of Herman Kahn's escalation ladder. *On Escalation: Metaphors and Scenarios*[10] is a handbook for tacit negotiators, showing how they may proceed, step by step, rung by rung, from the innocuous posturing required by 'Solemn and Formal Declarations' (Rung 3), through the more provocative 'Super-Ready Status' and 'Large Compound Escalation' (Rungs 11 to 13), and so onwards and upwards, if no one backs down, into the wide blue yonder of nuclear conflict culminating, at Rung 44, in 'Spasm or Insensate War' – a strategist's nightmare, or a strategist's Nirvana. One is never quite sure which.

Kahn provides the cryptography for escalated war. The equipment – for sending and receiving the signals – comes out of the arsenals of North American democracy. These bulge with the merchandise of death, and of incapacitation. In escalated war, it is as important to be able to disable and disfigure, to defoliate and incapacitate, as to be able to destroy and exterminate. Even more important. For in escalated war, violence is inflicted not insensately, indiscriminately, as on Dresden or Hiroshima, but precisely, minutely, as degrees of temperature are calibrated on a sensitive thermometer. Like certain forms of high temperature therapy, the patient will be cured when his body-heat's up to 106°. Cured – or killed.

Escalated war requires a code, it requires the means of transmission. It requires as well command and control, so that the master signaller in the Kremlin

---

9 Quoted in Robert Endicott Osgood, *Limited War: The Challenge to American Strategy* (University of Chicago Press, Chicago 1957), 177
10 (Frederick A. Praeger, New York 1965)

or the White House may transmit with a minimum of garble or of noise the message of the moment to his adversary. This is not a job for soldiers, nor is it a job for diplomats. It is a job for political leaders. During the Cuban missile crisis, President Kennedy was in radio-telephone contact with the bridge of the USS *John R. Pierce.* (It may turn out that President Johnson was in radio-telephone contact with the bridge of the USS *Maddox*; and he must bitterly regret not having been in radio-telephone contact with the bridge of the USS *Pueblo.*) Only other demands upon his time prevented President Johnson from personally directing the mission of each aircraft attacking North Vietnam, from take-off through bomb-run to touch-down; but these did not prevent his selecting the targets for each night.

So the foreign office is displaced by the operations room. One should not blame President Johnson for the faltering morale of his State Department. Morale was as low under Kennedy, who did what he could be revive it. But the more he tried to breath life into it, the more rigor mortis set in. Kennedy seems never to have understood that his State Department was beyond resuscitation. President Johnson, however, understood only too clearly. Rusk was the perfect man for the job. It consisted not in presiding over the nation's foreign policy: rather, it consisted in presiding, like the last of the viceroys, over an empty palace from which vitality and power had long since departed.

The deliquescence of diplomacy is being brought about most drastically not so much by changes in the style or the technique of negotiation as by changes in the milieu of negotiation – changes in the nature of the states system itself.

People have been predicting the demise of the states system for so long – and have been confounded in their predictions so often – that it will seem foolhardy to offer the prediction once again. I know very well how daunting and how contradictory to my argument the evidence at first sight may appear. The states system has more than doubled its membership within the last few years. It doesn't seem at all to matter how tiny the territory, how meagre the resources, how few the people of these newcomers: sand-spit or atoll, rock-pile or slag-heap, they take their place of equal status with the proud and the powerful. The United Nations, intended by its charter to be the plaything of the great powers, has become instead the plaything of the flower-powers, manipulated by mini-states and micro-states which cannot even pay the rent.

All this being so, it would appear that, as time goes by, the world is going to need more and more of what it is that diplomats do, and larger numbers of diplomats to do it. But this appearance is misleading, for three reasons.

The first is that the very proliferation of micro-states and mini-states now adorning the modern international system will cause the older and more powerful of that system to turn away in disgust and disenchantment. They will renounce the procedures, the protocol, and the institutions by which the upstarts have been able to stake out and make good their preposterous claims upon the rest. Here is a perfect example of the dialectical process of social change: the profession of diplomacy is destroyed by the overproduction of unmarketable foreign policies, much as Marx believed that the profession of capitalism would be destroyed by the over-production of unmarketable commodities.

A second change in the environment of foreign policy, in the milieu of negotiation, making for the demise of diplomacy, is the shift – already visible – from the nation-state to the urban centre as the significant focus of political activity.

By the year 2000 – some soothsayers have said – the United States will be so transformed that its life will be dominated by, and centre upon, three massive regional enclaves. One is bounded by San Diego and San Francisco on the west coast; a second central enclave by Chicago and Pittsburgh; a third on the east coast, by Boston and Washington. (Some wag has called them San-san, Chipitts, and Bowash, for short.) These giant conurbations each contain upwards of twenty or thirty million people. In many respects their concerns will transcend in importance those of the national state entity out of which they arise. Already they exist in embryo. Already they have begun to conduct what may be called functional foreign policy – both with each other and with comparable regions in other parts of the world. On their agenda will be inscribed those problems of direct and pressing interest to their populations. These will have little to do with the classical concerns of traditional diplomacy, maintaining or manipulating the balance of power behind the façade of the moment – the United Nations, or NATO, or whatever it may be. They will have to do with problems of the pollution of the atmosphere, problems of race relations, problems of traffic control and of drug control, problems of civilian defence, even problems of foreign aid – the whole absorbing paramount task of assuring the millions of lives under their respective jurisdictions the means not just to life, but to the good life – as Aristotle said a city-state should. For what I am predicting – and it is no very startling prediction, for it is already taking place – is the rediscovery and rehabilitation of the city-state, the replacement of the nation-state by the city-state, the supplanting of *patria* by *polis*, or rather by *megapolis,* as the significant actor on the world stage.

In this shape of things to come, the fate of the classical foreign office is preordained. Its future is limited, its days are numbered. Only the grace with which it leaves the scene is yet in doubt. It may fold its tent, and silently steal away; or else, and more likely – since no bureaucracy gives up without a fight –

it will unwillingly be reduced to an anachronism, whose sole surviving functions are ceremonial, having as little to do with the content of policy as the Bureau of Indian Affairs or the Warden of the Cinque Ports. By the year 2000 it is possible that the principal duty of the State Department may be custodianship of the Great Seal of the United States, which is no longer affixed to documents of national importance for the excellent reason that there will no longer be documents of national importance. The important documents will be signed, as the important things will be done, down at Megapolitan Hall, by the city governors and the urban managers who are the real men of power. The Sam Yortys and the John Lindsays of the twenty-first century will not hanker for the presidency; for their prerogatives as mayors of megapolis will transcend the powers of the presidency, if any presidency is left.

A third change in the milieu of negotiation which will render tranditional diplomatic activity all but obsolete, if not entirely obsolete, is the emergence of the individual to a significant role in world politics.

The individual – and I think of him primarily as the ordinary guy, not as pope or potentate or prime minister – has fared wretchedly in the practice of international politics; and until recently he has not fared very well in theory either.

The dominant theory treats the individual as a creature of the state to which he belongs. The international system is a state-system, in which the individual, wrenched from the context of the state which gives him status, is as out of place and as dangerously exposed as a pedestrian on a highway on a rainy night. The individual cannot sue a foreign government for damages. If, while travelling abroad, he is unjustly arrested or imprisoned, his country, not his family or his person, is assumed to be the injured party. In affairs of state he has no business to meddle. Foreign policy is made on his behalf. If he doesn't like it he has to lump it.

In the United States the role of the individual in the domain of diplomacy is circumscribed by law. The Logan Act, passed more than a century ago by Congress, makes it an offence to try to negotiate with a foreign government. In Canada we have no such law. But convention no less effectively than legislation puts the individual in his place. On the entrance to the East Block in Ottawa is prominently, if figuratively, displayed a large sign. It says: 'No trespassing.' One should not be misled by protestations to the contrary. About a year ago – last 4 December – the then Secretary of State for External Affairs outlined what he conceived to be an appropriate part for the individual in world affairs. He may travel abroad, as a tourist. He may trade abroad, as a merchant. And he may comment on what the Department of External Affairs does on his behalf, as a journalist, or a professor, or a writer of letters to newspapers. That is as far as it goes. And it does not go far enough.

For there is another tradition besides the states-centric tradition – one more hospitable to individual initiative, one more responsive to individual need. This tradition sees the individual not as an atomic particle within the impermeable matter of the territorial state, nor as an object over which governments haggle only for their own advantage, nor yet as an auxiliary to officialdom. It sees the individual as the sovereign member of the community of man. It is the tradition invoked by Edmund Burke when he observed that 'in the intercourse between nations we are apt to rely too much on the instrumental part ... Men are not tied together by paper and seals.'[11] It is the tradition invoked by those who, from their sanctuaries of concern, speak out against the juggernauts of state power on behalf of their innocent victims. It is the tradition of humanism, set against, and defying, the tradition of statism. It is flower power vs nation power.

This humanistic tradition – despite many appearances to the contrary – is gradually gaining ground, at the expense of its rival. Its progress may be detected in the promotion to the role of actors on the international scene of otherwise unexceptional people. Here I am thinking not so much of those who make a career of it – those professional peace-marchers and border-watchers who move in a frenzy of well-publicized para-diplomatic activity around the airports of the states system, pausing only long enough to autograph their books. I am thinking rather of the ordinary citizen, distinguished from his fellow-citizens by the intensity of his concern for peace and by his realization that, for the first time in history, it lies within his power to affect the prospects for peace.

This is not at all because modern international society has become any more moral, any more humane, any more sweetly reasonable, than what it is displacing. On the contrary, there is much evidence that, every day in every way, governments behave worse and worse. They lie, they cheat, they dissemble, they maim, they kill for what they conceive, often quite mistakenly, to be the national interest.

No, it has nothing to do with a higher morality. It has everything to do with an improved technology. Technology, in an inspired paradox, acts as an after-burner for the humanist tradition, a booster-rocket for the individual whom it springs free of the coils of the states system in which he has for so long been held prisoner. Technology enables the individual to make his mark

11 'Letter on a Regicide Peace,' quoted in Martin Wight, 'Western Values in International Relations,' in Herbert Butterfield and Martin Wight, eds., *Diplomatic Investigations* (George Allen & Unwin, London 1966), 97

upon events by placing at his disposal resources previously monopolized by foreign offices.

The requirements for setting up your own department of external affairs in your basement are remarkably modest. You need only be reasonably literate, fairly persistent, moderately affluent.

If literate, the individual will find in the public library more data about the states system than was possessed, barely a generation ago, by all the intelligence sections of all the foreign offices in the world. If persistent, he may state his case, via television, to an audience more vast than any foreign office flack could ever hope to reach. If affluent, he may conduct foreign policy on his own. A few dollars sends a cable to a foreign capital. A few more can summon the mighty to the telephone. A few hundred will stake any one to a peace mission. A few thousand will mount a mercy mission. The very rich, like Cyrus Eaton, may convene their own disarmament conferences, even their own peace conferences. The day may not be too far distant before the individual may set himself up in the sticky business of tacit negotiation. H. Rap Brown, arraigned in the United States for taking a revolver across a state line, is reported to have said: 'Just wait till I get me an atom bomb.' We will not have to wait long before the individual, if he does not go nuclear on his own, is able to transmit by more conventional means the violent signals of his protest.

Such changes, without question, are on their way. But they may not be changes for the better. The global village, should it come to that, may only offer greater scope to global village idiots. I would rather hope for global village Hampdens. But that is the expression of a faith, not of social science.

[December 1968]

Part II **FATE AND WILL IN FOREIGN POLICY**

1

Left and right

Fate and Will are dealt with by Karl Marx in a famous aphorism: 'Men make their own history; but they do not make it just as they please.' I have found it useful to reformulate the aphorism as follows: Foreign ministers make their own foreign policy; but they do not make it just as they please. By 'foreign ministers' I mean not only the political heads of foreign offices – secretaries of state, or secretaries of state for external affairs. I mean all those personages – prime ministers and presidents, under secretaries and foreign secretaries – who are the custodians and executants of their countries' foreign policies.

When foreign ministers (thus understood) pick up their portfolios for the first time, we find them full of gusto for the tasks that lie ahead. They breathe confidence and optimism. They talk grandly of new brooms and new ideas, of fresh starts and fresh approaches. By the reverses of the past they are undeterred; by the failure of their predecessors they are undismayed. Uplifted and exuberant, they plunge into the fray.

It doesn't take long for this mood to disappear. A year later, two at most, and our hero is a changed man. His gusto has gone, his exuberance has faded, his optimism vanished. In their place we find guardedness, caution, reserve. Where the fledgling foreign minister talked excitedly of possibilities and opportunities, of initiatives to be seized and battles to be won, the veteran dwells gloomily upon drawbacks and difficulties. If he is still at all disposed to confide in anyone outside the charmed circle of his profession, it is only to say how hard it is to be a foreign minister, how narrow is his room to manoeuvre, how few his options are, how manifold the constraints, and oh! how heavy. He no longer depicts himself bestriding the narrow world; he depicts himself cabin'd, cribb'd, confin'd, bound in. Never mind that the modern foreign minister travels in a week as far as Franklin or Palmerston travelled in a lifetime. We see him at the airport, we see him on the jet. Literally he is on the move: figuratively he is in a rut. And he is the first to tell us so. 'No, gentlemen,' he dictates to the cluster of reporters who greet him on arrival, 'I am not a magician, I am only a foreign minister. I have no panacea, I have no magic formula.' Indeed he does not. Another conference over, he pauses at the ramp. 'We had a good conference,' he says to unseen millions, 'a very good conference, in my opinion. I was glad of this opportunity to exchange views with the Premier, whom I had not seen for too long. Our discussions were very cordial, very frank. Of course, I am not in a position to disclose more at this time.' And with that he is up the ramp and into the plane. And this is called progress.

Modesty may be a virtue. False modesty is not. The experienced man of foreign affairs assuredly is modest when reciting what he can do for us. But is he being falsely modest, unduly diffident? It could be much worse than that. Is he deliberately downgrading our expectations of his performance so that, should our hopes be dashed, we will not take it out on him? Does he debauch the currency of diplomacy so that we, the customers, will not expect it to buy too much? Is his self-depreciation a self-inflicted wound – a scar to stir compassion and allay anticipation? Is his modest role – the role in which foreign ministers cast themselves – really the product of necessity, imposed by objective limitations upon his country's power and his own talent? Or does he set his sights too low?

Foreign policy is the art of the possible. How much is possible? What have we a right to expect of foreign policy and of foreign ministers? What part of statecraft belongs properly to Fate, and what is left for Will?

Machiavelli, in a famous passage, puts the proportion at roughly fifty-fifty. 'It is not unknown to me,' he writes, 'how many have been and are of opinion that worldly events are so governed by Fate and by God that men cannot by their prudence change them.' He confesses that at times he has felt that way himself. 'Nevertheless,' he adds, 'that our freewill may not be altogether extinguished, I think it may be true that fortune is the ruler of half our actions, but that she allows the other half or thereabouts to be governed by us.' That was in the sixteenth century. In our own century, statesmen would have us believe that the scope for Will in foreign policy has steadily diminished; while the scope for Fate, they say, has correspondingly increased. Instead of 50:50, they tell us it is 40:60; in their more pessimistic moods, even 20:80.

I have no mathematically exact, even culinarily exact, recipe for combining the ingredients of Fate and Will in foreign policy. But it is my purpose in these talks to argue that the statesmen of the sixties possess more freedom than they are ready to admit; and that, by the same token, the constraints upon their freedom are not so onerous as they would have us believe.

Communist foreign ministers – they are more motley than monolithic these days, and getting motlier by the moment – communist foreign ministers receive from their doctrinal legacy ambiguous advice upon this matter.

In classic Marxism – the Marxism of Marx himself, and of Engels – freewill and determinism, freedom and necessity, Will and Fate, are delicately balanced in a precarious equilibrium. Men make their own history: they do not make it just as they please. The formula is oracular. It permits as much as it restricts. Perhaps it was meant to. In any event, a communist could manipulate it much as he wanted, depending on his purpose and on his temperament. If these were such as to dispose him to the quiet life, he could throw his weight upon the scale of determinism. He could stress the power and the inexorability with which the juggernaut of history moved up on its predetermined track. He could stress the sternness and the ruthlessness with which the dialectic treats those who do not treat it with respect. If, on the other hand, he yearned for action, he could throw his weight upon the scale of freewill. The dialectic assures the communist ultimate victory: it does not excuse him from the obligation to fight to attain it. And, if he puts his mind and heart into the fight, he can do much to attain it.

Marx himself wavered uncertainly between these polarities. Lenin, once he found himself, never wavered. He threw his weight upon the scale of freewill. He threw it there so hard and so recklessly as to tilt the Marxist balance between Fate and Will into a grotesque asymmetry. Men make their own history. Men make their own history just as they please.

Lenin's motive in stressing so radically the voluntaristic aspect of Marxist doctrine is plain enough. He was blessed (or cursed) with a revolutionary temperament. He was not the sort of man to accept with the necessary fatalism the Marxist prescription for Russian revolutionaries. He had no intention of lying content in the lap of the dialectic, of floating like flotsam on the tide of history until such time as it beached him (more likely, his descendants) upon the shores of the promised communist society. He had either to abandon Marxism, or to change it. Being a Marxist, he did not abandon it. He did change it.

If historical materialism means anything at all, it means that the world is moved not by the deeds and misdeeds of individual men and women, not by heroes or by villains, but by impersonal forces and structural changes working themselves out within society in a manner largely beyond influence and wholly beyond recall. Historical materialism lays down its iron laws, chief among which is that the forces of production inherent in a given society must reach full development before the next stage of social change takes place. Revolution in Russia required the industrialization of Russia. Russia had to become capitalist before she could become communist. That was too long for Lenin. He

looked to Will to redeem Russia's Fate. In place of impersonal forces and
structural changes, great men and inspired leadership. To Marx, leadership
was important; to Lenin, leadership was all-important. The right leader can
work miracles. He can make a socialist revolution in a feudal society. He can
foment a proletarian revolution without a proletariat.

It wasn't just theory. Smuggled into Russia as human contraband, Lenin
attained power within a year. No wonder Trotsky, the Soviet Union's first
Commissar for Foreign Affairs, his leader's example before him, confidently
expected the communist revolution to sweep far beyond Russia alone, into
eastern Europe and thence western Europe, and into the Americas soon
enough. No wonder he replied, when asked in 1919 what his foreign ministry
would do, 'We will issue a few revolutionary proclamations and shut the shop
for ever.' Who needs foreign ministries, who needs foreign policies, with capitalist societies falling like washing from a clothes-line with a storm breaking?

The storm broke; but the line with its washing held. Capitalism and the
old order remained intact. And the Bolsheviks, unprepared by their doctrine
for its persistence, didn't know what to do next. To their rescue came not the
old oracles but a new leader. The theory and practice of 'socialism in one
country,' Stalin's contribution to the communist canon, reasserted the pri-
macy of Will over Fate, of mind over matter, of leadership over circumstance.
It was an innovation no less daring than Lenin's, and scarcely less dramatic in
its result. For the next ten years, between the mid-1920s and the mid-1930s,
Stalin's dictatorship drove and cajoled the Soviet people – those who survived –
into prodigious feats of productivity. By a perverse and wholly un-Marxian in-
version of historical materialism, human effort was deployed to create, out of
poverty and chaos, that economic base needed to sustain a socialist super-
structure.

But the overfulfilling of norms, the overcoming of obstacles, the overturn-
ing of barriers, proceeded only on the home front. Abroad it was different.
The seeming intractacability of events beyond the frontiers of the Soviet
homeland had caused Stalin to urge the comrades to concentrate their effort
within those frontiers. In the cause of domestic policy, Will came into its own.
In the cause of foreign policy, Fate was given charge. The early fervour faded.
The initial manifestations of enthusiasm – the Bolshevik delegation, en route
for Brest-Litovsk, stopping their car by the first peasant they saw so that he
might join them, with full plenipotentiary authority, as a bona fide representative of the toiling masses; the designation of the first Soviet diplomatists as
polpreds, in preference to merely bourgeois 'ambassadors'; Trotsky's exuberant promise to close the foreign office altogether – these were soon displaced
by more conventional characteristics. 'With the waning of the first fine careless

rapture,' Harold Nicolson has mocked, 'the style, the behaviour, the external appearance and the urbanity of the representatives of Soviet Russia approximated ever closer and closer to that of pre-war Balkan diplomatists.'

As with form, so with content. It is not hard to find fault with Soviet foreign policy over the years. But it is hard to fault it for recklessness and irresponsibility. Amoral, yes: witness the Nazi-Soviet Pact of August 1939. Ruthless, certainly: witness the crushing of the Hungarian uprising in November 1956. Truculent, always: witness the shower of notes that fell upon the capitals of NATO throughout the 1950s, threatening their destruction. But, by and large, rarely if ever, adventuristic. The great exception was Khrushchev's decision, in 1962, to place offensive missiles in Cuba. The alarm and consternation produced in Washington by this foolhardy act was replicated in Moscow. Khrushchev was made to pay for his folly with his job.

For the foreign minister as hero-figure, the Soviet stage offers little scope. But the role is not unknown elsewhere in the communist theatre.

Few political acts require greater confidence in Will's capacity to conquer Fate than the declaration of independence. For declaring, then securing, the independence of his tiny country, Joseph Broz Tito has assured himself a niche in whatever Hall of Fame may commemorate heroism in foreign policy. Nor is he eastern Europe's only candidate. Rumania's Ceausescu is another. Poland's Gomulka, still another – though the voluntaristic quality of Polish foreign policy may be more open to question.

There is no questioning, however, the voluntaristic quality of the foreign policy of the People's Republic of China. What was it, in the words of the communiqué of 27 October 1966, which caused 'the guided missile to fly normally and the nuclear warhead accurately to hit the target at the appointed distance, effecting a nuclear explosion?' Not the privations and suffering of 700,000,000 Chinese, not the exertions of scientists and technicians, certainly not the technical assistance of Americans and Russians, but 'the brilliant illumination of the thought of Mao Tse-tung.' Mao's thought, credited likewise with every achievement of modern China since the liberation, is China's antimissile missile system, enabling her to survive even the horrors of thermonuclear war. 'On the ruins of destroyed imperialism,' her leaders have stated, 'the victorious peoples will create with tremendous speed a civilization a thousand times higher than under the capitalistic system.' Not even Nikita Khrushchev, for all his daring and panache, was willing to concede as much. There operated within the modern states system constraints so powerful that the mightiest of its member-governments did well to yield. 'If you have not lost your self-control, and sensibly conceive what this might lead to,' the Soviet chairman cabled to John Kennedy on 26 October 1962, then, Mr President, we and you ought not now to pull on the ends of the rope in which you have tied the knot of war, because the more we pull, the tighter the knot will be tied. And a moment may come when the knot will be tied so tight that even he who tied it will not have the strength to untie it, and then it will be necessary to cut that knot; and what that would mean is not for me to explain to you, because you yourself understand perfectly of what terrible forces our countries dispose.[1]

Can one imagine Chairman Mao, or Chairman Lin Piao, writing like this to President Johnson? One cannot imagine it; and therein lie the perils posed for man's Fate by China's Will.

To cross the spectrum, moving from the far left to the extreme right, is, it seems, to enter upon a realm where the dichotomy of Fate and Will in foreign policy, indeed in any policy, has lost all relevance. A foreign minister who boasts, as Hitler boasted, that he goes his way with the assurance of a sleep-walker does not know, does not even care, whether he is the master or the servant of destiny. A foreign minister who boasts, as Mussolini boasted, that 'we fascists have had the courage to discard all traditional political theories, and we are aristocrats and democrats, revolutionaries and reactionaries, pro-letarians and anti-proletarians, pacifists and anti-pacifists,' might just as well have added to his litany of paradoxes 'determinists and anti-determinists.' Fate and Will were but words to weave into the rhetoric of the moment, images by which to mesmerize the masses – or the Reichstag. 'Fate, for reasons which we cannot fathom,' Hitler declaimed there on 13 July 1934, 'condemned our peo-ple to serve as the field on which these politicians could make their experiments – as the rabbit in the hands of the vivisector ... In what land were the scales of Providence more often brought into use, and where more frequently was the verdict passed that the object weighed had fallen short of the due weight?'[2] National Socialists, however, refused to be weighed – not because they might be found wanting but because Fate, however fickle to their predecessors, could not be other than a friend to them. 'We are the fortunate ones: we have been chosen by Fate.' 'Fate in its grace gave to us men selected and chosen.' 'Fate has granted me great successes.' Yet, just as often, it was to Will, not Fate, that Hitler ascribed the victories of the past and appealed for victories in the future. He developed this theme, in the sober fashion best calculated to im-press his audience of British and American journalists, on 4 December 1931:

1 Quoted in Elie Abel, *The Missile Crisis* (Bantam Books, Philadelphia & Toronto 1966), 152
2 Quoted in Norman H. Baynes, ed., *The Speeches of Adolf Hitler,* I (Oxford Univer-sity Press, London & New York 1942), 292

One must not say ... that a people's fate is solely determined by foreign Powers ... Weak and bad Governments have at all times made play with this argument in order thus to excuse and explain their own failure ... Their plea has always been,"Anyone else in our position could not have done otherwise": For what could he begin to do with his people in the face of conditions which are fixed once for all and have their roots in the world beyond Germany's frontiers ...

But the foreign minister worthy of his trust could do, said Hitler, a great deal:

The essential thing is the formation of the political will of the nation as a whole: that is the starting-point for political action. If this formation of will is guaranteed in the sense of a readiness to devote all a people's energies to the attainment of any national end, then a Government, supported by this common will, can choose the ways which lead to success ... It matters not which problem of our life as a people we wish to attempt to solve ...

Thirteen years later, when (as Hitler might have said) Fate had turned against him, his belief in the power of Will to overcome impossible odds assumed the proportions of a mania, in the clinical sense of the term. He summoned fresh divisions to do battle with the enemy at the gate. But the fresh divisions were only phantoms of a demented mind. Here is the occupational hazard of the extreme voluntarist in foreign policy.

To speak of the illustrious de Gaulle on the heels of so odious a company is to seem insulting; but that is far from my intent. We move at once from the gutter to the pedestal, from the sewer to the fountain, from the scum to the sublime. Yet, all the same, there are some faint affinities.

We find in the early de Gaulle a deference for destiny, a respect for reality, more characteristic of determinists than of voluntarists. Here is the young officer writing in obvious admiration of the foreign policy of Louis XIV. It was a policy

of circumstances; it avoided abstractions, but liked realities; it preferred what was useful to what was sublime, what was opportune to what was resounding; for each particular problem it sought a solution which was by no means ideal but practical; it had few scruples regarding choice of means, but its greatness consisted in keeping an exact balance between the desired objective and the power of the State.

The creed of a pragmatist. Thirty years on, when de Gaulle has become France, and France de Gaulle, the pragmatic streak is not entirely extinguished. Here is the general addressing his people on 20 December 1960: 'France must espouse her times and adapt herself to the circumstances, full of hope, but brutal, that are reshaping the universe.'

But the pragmatic streak in Gaullism doesn't run alone. Accompanying it, mixing with it, often overwhelming it, is the creed of a voluntarist. It emerges as dominant whenever the general recalls his experience during the Second World War: 'Limited and alone though I was, and precisely because I was so, I had to climb to the heights, and never then to come down.'[3] For de Gaulle, as for few others, grandeur is not a delusion but a fact.

Nevertheless, when Will is elevated to such a height, there is also the danger of vertigo, of losing one's balance and one's footing, of relinquishing one's grip upon reality. 'Perhaps my mission consists in being the last flight towards the summits in our history. Perhaps I shall have written the last pages in the book of our greatness.' Perhaps.

The voluntarist strain in Gaullism makes a strong appeal to the leaders of newly independent states in Asia and in Africa; and it is easy to see why. 'Between the two colossi who confront each other with all the might of their frightening power,' Morocco's ambassador to Paris declaimed a few years ago, 'has emerged a man who understands freedom, the self-determination of peoples, their right to live and survive in respect for their own genius. This catalyst of the world, which should be called Third, is General de Gaulle.'[4]

Afro-Asian Gaullism – Third World voluntarism – is not so monolithic as all that. Consider three notable practitioners: Nehru, Nkrumah, Nasser.

Of the three, Nehru is infinitely the most complex. One might expect the heir to the mantle of the Mahatma to share his master's belief in the capacity of Will, when based on truth and justice, to prevail against oppression, however tyrannous, however powerful. 'I am convinced,' wrote Gandhi in November 1938, 'that if someone with courage and vision can arise among them to lead them in non-violent action, the winter of their despair can in the twinkling of an eye be turned into the summer of hope.'[5] He is writing not of his fellow Indians but – alas! – of the Jews of Europe. Here was voluntarism with a vengeance.

Some of it, of course, rubbed off on Nehru. 'Long years ago we made a tryst with destiny,' he told the Constituent Assembly on the eve of independence, 'and now the time comes when we shall redeem our pledge ... At the

3 *Memoirs*, I, pt I, *The Call to Honour* (Collins, London 1955), 83
4 Quoted in W.W. Kulski, *De Gaulle and the World* (Syracuse University Press, Syracuse 1966), 368
5 'The Jews,' in M.K. Gandhi, *Non-Violent Resistance* (Schocken Books, New York 1961), 349

stroke of the midnight hour, when the world sleeps, India will awake to life and freedom.'[6] Who but a voluntarist in politics could hope, as Nehru hoped, to push such a country, with its millstone masses, its deadweight customs, its fierce antagonisms, its desperate poverty, into the modern states system? Who but a voluntarist in foreign policy could hope, as Nehru hoped, not merely to enter that system but to convert it?

In the end, modernization and messianism proved too daunting, the burdens of leadership too heavy, the voluntarist impulse too feeble. Co-existing uneasily with Nehru's Gandhian inheritance was the very different legacy of his English up-bringing – pragmatic, doubting, world-weary, and worldly-wise. By so supple and flexible a mind the simple verities of the Mahatma could hardly be taken seriously. Nor were they. As early as 1944 he had begun to question them. 'The events of the past few years,' he wrote, 'have been confusing, upsetting and distressing, and the future has become vague and shadowy and has lost that clearness of outline which it once possessed in my mind.' And again: 'Life is too complicated and, as far as we can understand it ... too illogical.' And yet again: 'I am not prepared to deny many things. I just don't know! The most correct attitude, if I may say so, is that of the Buddha who didn't deny it and didn't assert it.'[7] With the years these thoughts took deeper hold. His biographer writes of the caution and conservatism, the pragmatic adjustment to circumstances and problems, by which Nehru's rule was marked. These are nowhere more clearly evident than in the speech which he delivered to the conference of twenty-four non-aligned nations which met at Belgrade in September 1961. He told them not to over-estimate their own importance in the scheme of things:

After all, we do not control the strings of the world, not only in the military sense but in other senses also ... Numbers do not create a force. They may create moral pressure, but not a force. It will not make the slightest difference to the great military powers of today if the militarily weak countries band themselves together ...[8]

Nehru reminded them of Fate. Nkrumah spoke to them of Will. 'Let us utilize our power and influence,' he told them, 'to provide a fresh and vigorous outlook ... We have come here to interpose our influence between the two existing power blocs, for we believe that the time has come when the fate

6 Quoted in Michael Brecher, *Nehru: A Political Biography* (Oxford University Press, London, New York, Bombay & Toronto 1959), 355
7 Quoted in ibid., 599, 600, 607
8 Quoted in D.C. Watt, ed., *Documents on International Affairs, 1961* (Oxford University Press, London, New York & Toronto 1965), 618

and destiny of mankind should cease to hang so dangerously on the desires and ambitions of the Great Powers.'[9] That was more like it. That was what they'd come to hear – a panegyric to voluntarism, not a determinist's dirge. And who more qualified to deliver it than a man whose statue stood upon a marble pedestal on which had been inscribed at his direction: 'Seek ye first the Political Kingdom and all other things shall be added unto it'? Or the man whose autobiography ends with the following paragraph:

As a ship that has been freshly launched we face the hazards of the high seas alone. We must rely on our own men, on the captain, and on his navigation. And, as I proudly stand on the bridge of that lone vessel as she confidently sets sail, I raise a hand to shade my eyes from the glaring African sun, and scan the horizon. There is so much more beyond.[10]

Indeed there was. Within a decade the statue lay shattered in the dust, and the captain stripped of his command – a victim of mutiny, and of a voluntarism too extreme, too over-reaching, even for newly independent Africa.

Nehru is dead; Nkrumah deposed; Nasser survives. His survival owes much to the distinction between Nasser and Nasserism, of which the Egyptian leader has been well aware even if others have not. In September 1956, following their futile confrontation in Cairo, Sir Robert Menzies sketched a profile of his adversary. 'So far from being charming,' he wrote, 'he is rather *gauche,* with some irritating mannerisms, such as rolling his eyes up to the ceiling when he is talking to you and producing a quick, quite evanescent grin when he can think of nothing else to do.'[11] This unflattering portrait reinforced Eden's impression of Nasser as a cardboard dictator, a paper tyrant, whom the first gusts of popular unrest whipped up by the approaching paratroopers would blow into oblivion. But the intelligence was as faulty as the conclusion Eden drew from it.

Nasser was no light-weight, no idiot in diplomacy. For all his inexperience he knew what he was doing. The fait accompli of 26 July 1956 was far from an unthinking reflex prompted by picque and the desire for revenge. The Cairo newspaper *Al Ahram* has disclosed, ten years after Suez, how, well in advance of the move against the Canal Company, Nasser's agents,

working secretly in Cyprus, Malta and Aden, had obtained information about British military dispositions [which] convinced him that a swift and success-ful British strike was not possible.

9 Quoted in ibid., 605
10 *Ghana: The Autobiography of Kwame Nkrumah* (Nelson, New York 1957), 302
11 Quoted in *Full Circle: The Memoirs of the Rt Hon Sir Anthony Eden* (Cassell, London 1960), 471

Before nationalizing the Canal, President Nasser wrote two papers. The first evaluated the situation from the Egyptian point of view, and the second from the Western one. In the second document the President put to himself such questions as "What will Sir Anthony Eden do? What will Guy Mollet do? What will Mr Dulles do?"[12]

Had the Prime Minister of Britain imposed upon himself a comparable intellectual exercise, his invasion fleet would never have been assembled, let alone set sail.

Nasser is a voluntarist in foreign policy, more so than was Nehru, less so than was Nkrumah. His actions are more temperate than his words: these, reflecting the conventions of Arab rhetoric, are less alarming than they sometimes sound. On 9 January 1960, on the occasion of the completion of the first stage of the Aswan High Dam, he told his countrymen: 'Brother citizens, you have laid down a new principle in the twentieth century. This principle is that the small nations cannot in any way relinquish their free will.' Did he believe it then? Perhaps. Does he believe it now? Most likely not. An interviewer finds that the years of power have left their mark, transforming 'the physically powerful, ebullient young man ... into a calmer, slower figure ... He gives the impression of a man seeking tranquility and a way out of endless problems rather than of a revolutionary setting out to blaze new trails.'[13] His belief in Will has waned. He has given himself over to Fate. Such are the ways of statecraft. Such is the syndrome of the statesman.

[December 1966]

12 *The Times* (London), 8 Oct. 1966, 'Egypt's Agents Gave Reports on Suez'
13 Robert Stevens and Patrick Seale, 'Nasser: We Want to be Friends with Britain,' *The Observer,* 5 July 1964

2

The vital centre

Within the British foreign policy tradition, two men are often thought to personify the roles of Will and Fate in foreign policy. Winston Churchill, summoning in his finest hour his people to their finest hour, is naturally revered as the personification of the voluntarist leader inspired by faith in himself and in his country to stand against overwhelming material might, and to prevail. This is the quality in Churchill that appealed to de Gaulle, drawing from him a reluctant tribute: 'On top of everything, he was fitted by his character to act, take risks, play the part out and out.'[1]

So he was. Yet Churchill, for all his daring and defiance, never succumbed, as foreign ministers of the right so often succumb, to the temptation to identify himself with destiny, with his country, even with his countrymen. He had been called upon to give the roar: the lion's heart, as he generously conceded, belonged to the people. Nor was that all. Underneath the great summons to arms and asseveration of Will – 'We shall defend our island, whatever the cost may be, we shall fight on the beaches, we shall fight on the landing grounds' – surely the most magnificent battle-cry in the long annals of war – there lay a realist's calculation of the odds, a sane appreciation of the facts, marshalled by one who, well aware of Fate, was not abashed by her. On 16 June 1940, Mr Churchill composed a despatch to lessen the shock of the fall of France for the prime ministers and peoples of the overseas Dominions. He explained to them that Britain's resolve to fight on alone was 'not based upon mere obstinacy or desperation,' but upon an assessment of 'the real strength of our position,' which he proceeded to detail. Writing years later, as his own historian, Churchill was able to comment justly: 'All came true.'

1   Charles de Gaulle, *Memoirs,* I, pt I, *The Call to Honour* (Collins, London 1955), 57

'Churchillian' has become an adjective; most find it complimentary. Yet you would compliment no one by calling him 'Attleean,' not least because there's no such word. Clement Attlee is too complex a character, his qualities of leadership too elusive, his style in politics too subtle, for his name to have entered the language as a synonym for anything.

Still, Attlee often is compared to Churchill: sometimes disparagingly, sometimes not, always in contrast to him. If from the panorama of their careers one had to choose a typifying frame, the contrast does seem sharp. There is Churchill: man against the storm, bracing Britain for battle, defying the inevitable. And there is Attlee: driven by the storm, ridding Britain of India, giving in to the inevitable. With Churchill, there is no surrender. With Attlee, there is strategic surrender.

Thus juxtaposed, the contrast is too sharp. Just as in Churchill's policy there are elements of calculation and pragmatism which myth has all but obscured, so in Attlee's there are elements of daring and determination which seem oddly out of character. The nonchalance with which Lord Attlee recalls, fifteen years later, the considerations which led him to his decision should not cause us to forget the momentous nature of that decision – the immensity of the forces being tampered with, the severity with which he would have been judged by contemporaries and by history had things turned out differently:

I decided that the only thing to do was to set a time-limit and say: "Whatever happens, our rule is ending on that date" ... Winston was very strongly opposed ... The argument always is of course: "Go slow and things will get better." But there are occasions when if you hesitate and go slow things get not better but worse ... Broadly speaking the thing went off well, I think ...[2]

Churchill and Attlee, each in his own, very different way, personify the heroic tradition in British foreign policy. But the heroic tradition is the exceptional tradition. The British public no longer expects its leaders to conquer the world. It is enough that they cope with it.

The verb 'to cope' is a very British verb, and the act of coping a very British act. The dictionary definition coming closest to our context is 'to have to do with' something or somebody. If this supplies the requisite connotation of reluctance, it will suffice. To cope with a situation is not to fall to with a will; still less is it to exhibit zeal, enthusiasm, or any sort of joy through work. To cope with a situation is to wish it were not there at all; since it is there – through no fault of one's own, and no desire of one's own – the next best thing is to try to make life bearable. Such is the spirit in which the harassed

2 Quoted in Francis Williams, *A Prime Minister Remembers* (Hutchison, London 1962), 209-12

housewife copes with her nagging brood, the besieged storekeeper with his clamant customers, the harried statesman with his impacable agenda. Life is hard and art is fleeting. It is enough to hang on. 'What did you do in the Thirty Years' War?' 'What did you do in the Second World War?' The coper answers: 'I survived.' He thinks it a considerable achievement; and perhaps it is.

Situation-coping – as distinct from problem-solving – comes easily to the career diplomatist. It fits snugly into his prevailing ethos. The experienced foreign service officer, George Kennan has testified, 'sees the task of diplomacy as essentially a menial one, consisting of hovering around the fringes of a process one is powerless to control, tidying up the messes other people have made.'[3] Such a man, with such a view, can only be scornful of Will's chances in any fight with Fate. He is among the 40:60 men – the perennial pessimists of diplomacy. Or else he is among the 20:80 men – the hard-time Charlies of diplomacy.

The coping style in foreign policy, characteristically British, characteristically Foreign Office – where should one look to find it? One should look at the record of a British foreign secretary whose apprenticeship was served in career diplomacy. One should look at the record of Sir Anthony Eden.

Several times in his memoirs Lord Avon extols what the Japanese quaintly call 'high posture policy' – a policy of bold initiatives and firm resolve conducted by men whose self-confidence is matched only by their competence. Such men, Eden reflected in 1934, after visiting Berlin, Rome, and Paris – in that order – are more often found in charge of dictatorships than of democracies; thirty years later he wishes it were otherwise:

It remains true today that if the Western democracies are to make headway against communist and other like-minded dictatorships, they must find men who have the capacity, courage and experience, and give them the time to know their subjects as the dictators know it ... Then they may determine events, instead of confusedly pursuing them.[4]

Of his work in aligning Anglo-American policies in the middle east, following the seizure of the refinery at Abadan, he wrote (slightly misquoting the phrase Churchill had used in *The Gathering Storm*): 'I felt that we had made a beginning which might check the "long, dismal, drawling tides of drift and surren-

---

3 George Kennan, 'History and Diplomacy as Viewed by a Diplomatist,' in Stephen D. Kertesz and M.A. Fitzsimons, eds, *Diplomacy in a Changing World* (University of Notre Dame Press, Notre Dame 1959), 107
4 *The Eden Memoirs: Facing the Dictators* (Cassell, London 1962), 83

der.""[5] And of his Adriatic diplomacy from 1952 to 1954: 'Peace is not just
something that happens. At times it is necessary to take risks and even to increase the immediate danger to win a lasting agreement.'[6]

This is Eden in heroic vein. But there is this other Eden. He is a diplomatist of the old school, who seeks to cope, not conquer. He is the Eden who
writes (apropos of negotiating with the Russians): 'The best diplomacy is that
which gets its own way, but leaves the other side reasonably satisfied. It is often
good diplomacy to resist a score.'[7] Or (apropos of the Geneva Conference on
Indochina): 'It was important that I should not overplay my hand about the
dangers of world war. If I were to cry 'Wolf! Wolf!' too frequently and too
loudly, I would suffer the fate of all alarmists in diplomacy and not be believed.'[8] Or (apropos of arms control): 'One step at a time remains a good
maxim in world affairs; we should try again.'[9]

Throughout his long career as foreign minister and his short career as
prime minister, these competing conceptions of diplomacy fought for ascendancy – high-posture vs low-posture, the headstrong and the cautious, the bold
stroke and the one step at a time, the wilful and the fateful. Will won out.
Casting aside the precepts of a lifetime, Eden plunged into his reckless and
disastrous duel with the president of Egypt. He wanted, on his own admission,
'to knock Nasser off his perch.' He sent in tanks, he sent in bombers, the best
part of a division. In vain. They were not allowed to finish their job. Eden neg-
lected to heed his own advice. He tried to conquer Nasser. He should have
coped with him.

Coping with their situations is far from what the American public has been
brought up to expect of its leaders. In the United States, statesmanship is a
form of salesmanship. The statesman, like the salesman, is expected to deliver
the goods, lug the samples, flog the wares, and do whatever else is implied by
those advertisements for 'aggressive, productive young men: car essential'
which festoon the pages of evening newspapers. The foreign minister, like the
sales manager, is expected to show a profit for his pains: his efforts to prevent
a loss greater than last year's may be prodigious; they may even be successful;
but they will not be appreciated. Foreign policy, like sales policy, is judged
for results, and for certain kinds of results – tangible, measurable, accountable,

5 *Full Circle: The Memoirs of the Rt Hon Sir Anthony Eden* (Cassell, London 1960),
   203
6 Ibid., 188
7 Ibid., 357
8 Ibid., 124
9 Ibid., 379

ascertainable. Ask any secretary of state. Oh, he may tell you, with fine delicacy of feeling, that the most exquisite sensations of pleasure are to be derived
from the subtlest manipulation of the balance of power, a manipulation so
subtle that none but the cognoscenti will know that it has occurred. But he
will add at once, if he is honest with you, that the American democracy allows
this impulse little if any gratification. It is not enough that foreign policy be
done. It must appear to be done. And that is why the statistics of American
statecraft break all the records in *The Statesman's Yearbook*. It is not just
that the United States is the greatest power in the world: if she were all that
powerful, why collect forty-two allies? It is, rather, that alliances, treaties, and
the rest are the statesman's certificate of sale. With them, he gets his commission; without them, he gets fired.

What has been called 'the illusion of American omnipotence' is thus more
complicated than many who have talked and written on this theme have cared
to concede. For if foreign policy is sales policy, and the statesman essentially
a salesman, then foreign ministers will know the agonies of salesmen approaching death. Behind and beyond the most brilliant career lurches the pathetic
figure of Willy Loman, pushing his suitcases along the floor. There have been
plenty of Willy Lomans in diplomacy, even – I do not say especially – in
American diplomacy. But a diplomacy which believes itself to be omnipotent
cannot bring itself to believe in its tragic failures, and doesn't.

American statesmanship is only partly salesmanship. It is also engineering.
For the salesman, failure is ineluctable. For the engineer, failure is unthinkable.
The salesman knows there'll come a day when he can't carry the sample case
any more. No stresses-and-strains technician plans to retire the day his first
bridge collapses, no hydraulics expert calculates his pension from the day his
dam caves in. It's not that they're indifferent to failure; it's that they don't
anticipate failure. A good engineer never needs to.

The engineering approach to foreign policy has a number of readily identifiable characteristics, all strongly voluntarist in nature. Chief among them is
the certain expectation of success, which is the obverse of that unthinkability
of failure I have just referred to. Related to that is reliance upon mechanisms
requiring for their rational deployment belief in the certainties of success –
complicated weapons systems, computerized gadgetry, mechanized gimmickry:
the whole fail-safe syndrome in its infinite variety. And related to that is the
belief that some swift and spectacular stroke may solve problems once and for
all. Hence the fondness for the 'one-shot solution,' for the 'crash-programme'
and the big push and their hoped-for break-through, for crisis management, for
the notion that injuries to international society may be healed by surgical ex-
cision, or by the replacement of worn-out parts, or by the insertion of some
catalytic agent – a pace-maker for peace-makers.

The engineering approach to foreign policy is the United States' approach to foreign policy. That is hardly a cause for surprise. It is in the United States that the engineer has made his most spectacular contributions. Why shouldn't the mind devising the biggest dams, the tallest buildings, the longest bridges, the Manhattan Project and Salk vaccine, Radio City and Willow Run, the Model T and the Thunderbird, be capable of devising solutions to America's problems overseas? Such was President Kennedy's thought in appointing the head of the Ford Motor Company as head of the American defence establishment. (We are told that, had he lived, Kennedy would have appointed him Secretary of State.) We see McNamara in our living rooms, making his customary televised chalk-talk exposition of the latest military enterprise – with his maps, his charts, his pointer, his rapid-fire, dead-sure delivery, he looks every bit the model of the model crisis manager. And perhaps he is.

Much of America's foreign policy, and all of America's defence policy, bears his trade-mark. What but an engineering cast of mind would propose, as a solution for Europe's agonizing over nuclear weapons, the creation of a sea-based fleet of missile-firing ships manned by crews of several countries? Or propose, as a solution for Panamanian nationalism's threat to the Panama Canal, the building of another canal through Nicaragua? Or approach the problems of arms control as if they were problems of earthquake control? Or the problems of Vietnam as if they were problems of pest control? *C'est magnifique, mais ce n'est pas la diplomatie.*

McNamarian voluntarism may be contrasted with Ruskian determinism. It was not for a deterministic outlook on foreign affairs that John Kennedy picked Dean Rusk as his Secretary of State. In April 1960, Rusk, not then in government service, had published an article called, simply, 'The President,' which began with a ringing affirmation of the voluntarist creed:

The United States, in this second half of the twentieth century, is not a raft tossed by the winds and waves of historical forces over which it has little control. Its dynamic power, physical and ideological, generates historical forces; what it does or does not do makes a great deal of difference to the history of man in this epoch. If realism requires us to avoid illusions of omnipotence, it is just as important that we not underestimate the opportunity and the responsibility which flow from our capacity to act and to influence and shape the course of events.

And he went on to say that when in the great debate between Fate and Will 'the emphasis of discussion falls too heavily for my taste upon the limitations on policy, I recall from early childhood the admonition of the circuit preacher: "Pray as if it were up to God; work as if it were up to you." '[10] Kennedy, when

10 *Foreign Affairs*, XXXVIII, no 3, Apr. 1960, 353

president-elect, read the article, liked what he read, and summoned its author (whom he had never met) to Washington. After a single meeting, he offered Rusk the position of Secretary of State in his Administration.

A White House witness who should know says Kennedy came quickly to regret his appointment of Rusk to what he conceived as potentially the most important position in the government next to his own. The metamorphosis from activist to determinist, from plunger to stonewaller, from voluntarist to fatalist – a metamorphosis which, as I have argued, all statesmen undergo to some degree, at some time – was, in Rusk, unusually rapid and complete. He seemed burnt out before he began. Arthur Schlesinger, then special assistant to the President, provides a portrait of the Secretary of State as vivid as it is savage:

Unlike McNamara, his organizational instinct was for service, not for mastery. Nurtured in the successive bosoms of the university, the Army, the government department, the foundation, he drew reassurance from the solidity of the structure, the regularity of the procedures, the familiarity of the vocabulary. His mind, for all its strength and clarity, was irrevocably conventional. He mistrusted what he called "the flashy or sensational" and rejoiced in the role of "tedium" in diplomacy ...

He seemed actually to prefer stale to fresh ways of saying things. One felt that he regarded novelty as an effort to shock or make mischief ... The stereotypes of diplomacy were his native tongue. At times one wondered whether the harshness of life – the seething planet of revolutionary violence, ferocity and hate, shadowed by nuclear holocaust – ever penetrated the screen of clichés, ever shook that imperturbable blandness ...

He had authority but not command ... Where McNamara ... would forcefully and articulately assert the interests of [his] department in impending foreign policy decisions, Rusk would sit quietly by, with his Buddha-like face and half-smile, often leaving it ... to the President himself to assert the diplomatic interest. If the problem were an old one, he was generally in favor of continuing what Herter or Dulles or Acheson had done before him. If the problem were new, it was generally impossible to know what he thought ...

Kennedy was always impressed by Rusk's capacity to define but grew increasingly depressed by his reluctance to decide ... He wanted someone who could not only mass the State Department but be a constant source of definite recommendations and fresh ideas ... The Secretary, he would say, "never gives me anything to chew on ... You never know what he is thinking."[11]

11   Arthur M. Schlesinger, Jr, *A Thousand Days: John F. Kennedy at the White House* (Houghton Mifflin, Boston 1965), 434-6

He must have thought of firing him; but, when a confidant suggested this solution, Kennedy replied: 'I can't do that to Rusk; he is such a *nice* man.'

There are as yet no informers at large to spill the secrets of the Johnson presidency; and, until there are, we will not know what qualities of Dean Rusk's mind and heart so appeal to the President as to enable Rusk to enter upon his seventh consecutive year as Secretary of State. But it cannot be the quality of Will. In that, the Secretary has demonstrated himself to be increasingly deficient, nowhere more so than in his testimony on the Vietnam War before the Senate Foreign Relations Committee in February 1966. He was asked by a member of the committee if he saw any end to the 'corridor we are following.' Here is his answer: 'No; I would be misleading you if I told you that I thought that I know where, when, and how this matter will be resolved.' And he added: 'The nature of a struggle of this sort ... is, of course, substantially determined by the other side.'[12]

But it's not the Secretary of Defense or the Secretary of State who makes the foreign policy of the United States. The President makes foreign policy. That, as Dean Rusk himself once remarked, 'is not the whole story, [but] it serves very well if one wishes to deal with the matter in five words.' To say this is to say nothing of the President's readiness to bear the burden thrust upon him by the Constitution and by the situation. Some, like Truman and Kennedy, have been eager to exploit the opportunity. Others, like Eisenhower, have been content to delegate it to some trusted lieutenant. Here I will speak only of Truman and Kennedy.

Commenting upon the reluctance of certain chief executives to enter fully upon the responsibilities of office, Dean Acheson has said: 'If a President will make decisions, you're in luck.' He added: 'And if he makes correct decisions, you're in clover.' Under President Truman, the American people were at least in luck. For Truman never shirked decision-making. On the contrary, he revelled in decision-making. He calls the first volume of his memoirs of his presidency 'Year of Decisions,' and there is nothing vainglorious in the title. Problems came at him in waves to swamp the most industrious sorcerer's apprentice, but Truman neither flinched nor panicked. 'I have to take things as they come,' he wrote to his mother and sister – 'Mama and Mary' – after about six weeks on the job, 'and make every decision on the basis of the facts as I have them and then go on from there; then forget that one and take the next.' 'Every day,' he wrote again to 'Mama and Mary' on 16 June 1945, 'I see some notable of some sort, pin medals on heroes and make world shaking decisions. It seems

12 Hearings before the Committee on Foreign Relations, US Senate, 28 Jan. 1966 (US Government Printing Office, Washington 1966), 32

to agree with me for I've gained twelve pounds since last January.'[13] It was just as well it did. For ahead of him lay the most momentous decisions of history: to explode atomic bombs over Japanese cities; to rebuild Europe; to check communism in Greece; to run the blockade of Berlin; to resist aggression in Korea; to build, test, and stockpile thermonuclear weapons. His attitude throughout was one of unruffled calm. Never has greater power been deployed with more serenity of spirit.

John Kennedy, when president, also displayed these Roman qualities to good advantage. Yet, while no less calm, no less serene, in the exercise of even greater power in situations no less testing, Kennedy lacked his predecessor's unshakeable faith in the ability of Will to see things through. In the beginning he is as optimistic as anyone. The inaugural address – his first statement on foreign policy at the outset of his presidency – reflects, in its sonorous Sorensen cadences, the voluntarist appraoch:

Let both sides, for the first time, formulate serious and precise proposals for the inspection and control of arms – and bring the absolute power to destroy other nations under the absolute control of all nations ... Let us never negotiate out of fear, but let us never fear to negotiate ...

Rarely, if ever, has a public figure generated greater expectations in more lofty language. But, two years later, the initial confidence had been displaced by puzzlement, optimism by pessimism. Asked by some journalists what he considered to be the most valuable lessons of his experience in the presidency thus far, John Kennedy replied:

The problems are more difficult than I had imagined they were ... President Eisenhower said to me on January 19th ...: "There are no easy matters that will ever come to you as President. If they are easy, they will be settled at a lower level." So that the matters that come to you as President are always the difficult matters, and matters that carry with them large implications. So this contributes to some of the burdens of the office ...

Secondly, there is a limitation upon the ability of the United States to solve these problems ... The responsibilities placed on the United States are greater than I imagined them to be, and there are greater limitations upon our ability to bring about a favorable result than I had imagined them to be ... It is much easier to make the speeches than it is to finally make the judgments ...[14]

13 Harry S. Truman, *Memoirs*, I, *Year of Decisions* (New American Library, New York 1955), 293, 294
14 *The New York Times*, 19 Dec. 1962

As Kennedy's term of office drew towards its tragic close, he shed much of his earlier optimism about the ability of the United States to make its way in the world and to make over the world to its liking. In conversation with his confidants, and in those extraordinarily candid and introspective musings in public, such as the one from which I've just quoted, the President disclosed not so much disillusionment, certainly not disenchantment, but a kind of quiet fatalism. He worked as if it were up to him, no doubt he prayed as if it were up to God; but he seemed increasingly sceptical that the exertions of either would make much difference in the end. 'He talked more and more,' Theodore Sorensen has testified, 'about the limitations of power. "Every President," he wrote, "must endure a gap between what he would like and what is possible." And he quoted Roosevelt's statement that "Lincoln was a sad man because he couldn't get it all at once. And nobody can."'[15]

[December 1966]

15 Theodore C. Sorensen, *Kennedy* (Harper & Row, New York 1965), 391

3
Ignorance and knowledge

In that passage in *The Prince* where Machiavelli allows, more optimistically than some of whom I have been writing, that Fate disposes of about half of human affairs, Will disposing the rest, he reflects as well upon the measures that may be taken to assure that Fate remains content with her fair share. 'I would compare her,' he writes, 'to an impetuous river that, when turbulent, inundates the plains, casts down trees and buildings, removes earth from this side and places it on the other; every one flees before it, and everything yields to its fury without being able to oppose it; and yet though it is of such a kind, still when it is quiet men can make provisions against it ... So it is,' he concludes, 'with fortune, which shows her power where no measures have been taken to resist her, and directs her fury where she knows that no dykes or barriers have been made to hold her.'[1] In this section and in my next, I shall discuss two of the ways by which the statesman may protect himself from the hammer-blows of Fate, and so assert his Will.

First he must fortify himself with knowledge.

To be ignorant is to deliver oneself entirely over to Fate's charge, which often is unkind. Hence the acquisition of intelligence – the gathering and assessment of information about the international environment – is not only logically the first step in the foreign policy process; it is also the most important step. Where knowledge is power, 'tis folly to be ignorant.

---

1 'How Much Fortune Can Do in Human Affairs and How It May Be Opposed,' ch. 25 (Mentor Books, New York 1952), 131

Some statesmen, it seems, indulge that folly. Holding that it is best to act first and think later, and then only with one's blood, Hitler professed the utmost scorn for his advisers, believing his intuition superior to any intelligence agency. But even a fascist foreign minister cannot, and does not, dispense with knowledge. What happens in his case is that his knowledge of the international environment, blinkered by his prejudice, is erratic and erroneous. Fate has her revenge. Prey to conspiratorial theories of history, victim of paranoia, the fascist totalitarian purges all dissent, sends imaginary troops to battle with imaginary enemies, and soon is buried in the shambles of his state. No regime may dispense with intelligence. But some regimes acquire, because of their ideology, faulty intelligence.

Acquiring knowledge is not only logically the first step, and practically the most important step, in the foreign policy process: it is also an inescapable step. All governments must collect intelligence, just as all individuals must breathe air. But it is possible to avoid collecting certain kinds of intelligence – particularly the kind which disturbs too rudely your image of the world. Here is a prime occupational hazard of the statesman. I will return to it.

Collecting intelligence involves gathering and assessing information. One can make a theoretical distinction between the act of gathering and the act of assessing: practically, the two coalesce into a single and inseparable activity. You do not gather information in the absence of assessment. The data of intelligence isn't collected as children pick blueberries, or squirrels hoard acorns, indiscriminately and at random. You have to start somewhere: but where you start depends on your assessment of what's significant, and what isn't.

A few centuries ago, when government was less complex and policy less esoteric than they have since become, when technology was primitive and statecraft personal, the really significant data of intelligence concerned the humour of the prince and the intrigues of his court. The ideal intelligence operative was thus a close student of human nature. He did not have to be a physicist, he did not have to be a metallurgist, he did not have to be a content analyst. From the age of Lorenzo the Magnificent through the age of Frederick the Great, a country's intelligence needs might adequately be served by its ambassador in foreign parts, if he were a worldly man, and wise. Such a man was Sir James Harris, British ambassador to Russia during the reign of the Empress Catherine. Here is an extract from one of his despatches, dated 1779:

On Monday, at the masquerade given at the Grand-Duchess' birthday, some time after Her Imperial Majesty's card party, at which I had assisted, was finished, M. Korsakoff came up to me and, desiring me to follow him, conducted me a back way into the Empress' private dressing room, and, on introducing me, immediately retired. The Empress, after making me sit down, began by saying that, after her own affairs, ours were those which she had most at heart, and she would be happy if I could obviate the obstacles which ever presented themselves to her mind in every plan she had formed to be useful to us.[2]

Harris remained in the empress' chamber for more than an hour, after which, as he relates, 'she dismissed me, and, it being quite dark, it was with some difficulty that I found my way back through the intricate passages to the ballroom.' Bliss was it in that dawn to be alive, but to be an intelligence operative was very Heaven.

Since those halcyon days the craft of intelligence has become steadily more specialized, steadily more crowded. The ambassador abroad, traditionally the sole purveyor of knowledge of foreign parts to government, has had to yield his monopoly to a host of others, some inside his embassy, some not, but all enjoying (or claiming) diplomatic status, stuffing the pouches with their reports, making the traditional diplomatic life less like what it used to be. Jostled and hemmed in by specialists, the foreign service officer may well wonder what is left for him to say once the commercial, the military, the press, the labour, the financial, the agricultural, the technical assistance, the scientific attachés have had their say; or, if something in his own despatches has escaped their notice, wonder whether his government can possibly find time to read it.

Nowhere has the intelligence community proliferated as it has in the United States. The State Department alone receives 2000 telegrams a day: since seventy copies are made of each, the average daily harvest from this single source comprises 140,000 pieces of paper. Intake at the Pentagon is classified: it can't be any less, it probably is much more. And these are just the field hands. The threshers work back home: 10,000 people at the Central Intelligence Agency headquarters, paid from a budget not accountable to Congress and said to be in billions. At the State Department, 200 analysts sift 100,000 documents a month, winnowing from this chaff enough to fill 600 cubic feet of file drawers a year.

Is it possible to collect too much intelligence? Most foreign offices need more knowledge than would fill a book, but most couldn't use as much as may be stored by a computer. You could jam into their archives data on every statistically identifiable creature in the states system, justifying the effort and expense involved on the grounds that, well, you never know. On occasion these could be justified. On the morning of 23 November 1963 a government so

2 Quoted in Harold Nicolson, *Diplomacy*, 3rd ed. (Oxford University Press, London 1963), 62

equipped could call for the file on Lee Harvey Oswald. But most of the time
it wouldn't be worth it. Even then it wouldn't be worth it. The evening papers
would have it all.

How much, then, is enough? The question's as hard to answer in the context of intelligence communities as it is in the context of military establishments. No general ever has enough troops, no air marshal enough aircraft, no
admiral an adequate fleet. But statesmen often have more than enough military equipment to help them in their statecraft. In the same way, no director
of intelligence ever has enough operatives in the field, enough analysts at headquarters, enough facts in the files. But statesmen often have more than enough
intelligence to help them in their statecraft. 'Few if any of the recent crises of
US policy,' Henry Kissinger has written, 'have been caused by the unavailability of data. Our policy-makers do not lack [information] ; they are in many
respects overwhelmed by it. They do lack criteria on which to base judgments.'[3] That is something else again.

To help keep Fate at bay, the statesman needs a book of knowledge, logarith-
mic tables of the states system with which to calculate the ratios of power
with the minimum margin for error. His margin may be minimal, but it is often
very wide. It must shatter a voluntarist's complacency, as it affords consolation
to determinists, to learn how frequently statecraft miscarries through miscalcu-
lation due to ignorance, how many times the statesman is taken unawares. His
life is full of surprises, usually unpleasant.

No statesman expected an end to the century of peace in 1914: the Great
War surprised them all by breaking out, and in not being quickly won or lost.
Bolshevism surprised them by sweeping Russia, and surprised them again by
failing to sweep elsewhere. Keynes and Smuts stood alone in believing the
Versailles settlement too harsh for a precarious German democracy. Hitler
attracted some slight notoriety, but after the early 1920s no foreign office
thought his career worth much attention. Statesmen of the 1930s hopelessly
misconstrued the intentions of the Nazis and the nature of National Socialism.
No government foresaw the Great Depression or could extricate itself when in
its grip. American statesmen, though fearful of Japan, never dreamed the war
would open by surprise attack upon their Pacific fleet. The Soviet government
did not reckon with a German attack in June 1941, despite – perhaps because
of – Churchill's warnings of its impending time and place. Few foresaw the
Cold War, the reconstruction of Europe, the recovery of Japan, the rearming
of Germany, communism in China, Nasser's seizure of Suez, the downfall of

3   *The Necessity for Choice* (Harper & Row, New York 1960), 351

Khrushchev. The list is endless: each item on it a monument to intelligence failure.

From this sorry inventory an inappropriate conclusion is sometimes drawn. It is that intelligence failure is unavoidable. This tends to be the statesman's view. Naturally so: if he persuades us, he is off the hook. '"The vast external realm,"' Dean Acheson has written,

is so complex, so complicated, and so voluminous that we cannot currently comprehend it; nor, until too much time has elapsed, grasp its full significance. This is not wholly, or even principally, because of man-made impediments to knowledge – iron curtains, censorship, etc. – but because of the obscurity and complexity of the molecular changes which combine to bring about the growth or decay of power, will and purpose in foreign lands.[4]

And Arthur Schlesinger, writing not as an historian but as an apologist for his own brief career in statecraft, would have us believe that no statesman, however well fortified by knowledge, should expect 'to penetrate a process so cunningly compounded not only of necessity but of contingency, fortuity, ignorance, stupidity and chance.'[5]

I shall contend that Will, fortified by knowledge, is capable of doing better.

There are three causes of intelligence failure. The first is the alleged unpredictability of certain kinds of phenomena, certain types of situation, which alter the course of history. Who knows when some natural disaster – earthquake or famine, plague or flood – may lay waste a countryside, turn the current Five-Year Plan into so many worthless pieces of paper, drop a once-powerful nation into the ranks of oblivion like a counter in a game of snakes-and-ladders? Who can tell when technical malfunction – a defect in a firing mechanism, a breakdown in a communications-system – may wreak a holocaust on earth, no less terrible for being inadvertent? Who can predict personal misfortune – the assassination of a president, the illness of a premier – bringing chaos in its wake and incompetence to power? 'Do you honestly expect us,' the statesman asks reproachfully, 'to know when and where these things will happen?' It is a rhetorical question, for we are to answer in the negative. To answer positively, we should require access to intelligence of the occult. It is the kind of knowledge furnished only by the Old Farmer's Almanac, or the crystal ball, or fortune cookies – and about as reliable.

4 'The President and the Secretary of State,' in Don K. Price, ed., *The Secretary of State* (Prentice-Hall, Englewood Cliffs 1960), 35-6
5 'On the Inscrutability of History,' *Encounter*, Nov. 1966, 16

This is not so at all. Consider the phenomena of personal misfortune, by which the world is often changed. King Alexander of Greece died in the autumn of 1920 from a bite of his pet monkey, which happened to be rabid: his untimely death touched off a train of events which led Winston Churchill to remark that 'a quarter of a million persons died of that monkey's bite.' In 1923 Trotsky went duck-hunting: the long wait in the marshes caused him to contract a fever, thus putting him *hors de combat* at a critical stage of his struggle for power, from which he emerged the loser. Trotsky comments retrospectively: 'One can foresee a revolution or a war, but it is impossible to foresee the consequences of an autumn shooting trip for wild duck.'[6] Who could have known that Sir Anthony Eden would succumb to mental breakdown at the height of the Suez crisis, causing him to call off the war? Or that John Kennedy would be struck down by an assassin's bullet?

Each of these events is said to have been unpredictable. But that does not mean that knowledge, relevantly assessed and properly applied, cannot illuminate the scene. We know, for example, that American presidents are prone to be assassinated. We know that the political climate in the American southwest at the time of the visit to Dallas of President Kennedy was violent and ugly, irrational and hostile. We know that such climates may stimulate unstable individuals to commit terrible crimes. With such knowledge at his disposal, no one could have been surprised by what happened. Shocked, grieved, desolated, even momentarily unhinged: but not surprised. What happened at Dallas, so far from being beyond the power of relevant knowledge to anticipate, was indeed anticipated at the time. A month before the fatal shooting, Adlai Stevenson, who was jostled and spat upon by a Dallas mob, telephoned to Arthur Schlesinger: 'I talked with some of the leading people,' he told him. 'They wondered whether the President should go to Dallas, and so do I.'

Disasters, malfunctions, misfortunes cannot individually be brought to the attention of the policy-maker in advance of their occurrence. Trends, tendencies, and dispositions may be.

If the statesman is unaware of trends, of tendencies, of dispositions, it is not because these lie beyond the zone of awareness. But it may be because of stupidity – other peoples', or his own, or both. Here is the second cause of intelligence failure.[7]

People make mistakes, even those who should know better. Airline pilots attempt landings with their wheels up. ('One pilot who did this recently,'

---

6 Quoted in E.H. Carr, *What is History?* (Macmillan, London 1961), 92
7 See also below, 'Stupidity and Power,' 156-62

according to *The New York Times,* 'said he had been unable to hear the control tower warnings for the "honking" in the cockpit. The "honking" he heard was warning that something was wrong.') Surgeons leave sponges in the vitals of their patients. Generals send their troops to ambush. Mariners run their ships on rocks. Statesmen bring their states to ruin.

It is common to think subordinates stupid, holding superiors to be blameless. But stupidity is no less common on the commanding heights than down below; it only seems to be. This for two reasons. The commanding heights invest their occupants with a kind of charisma, which ordinary mortals are both loath and fearful to disturb.

> There's such divinity doth hedge a king,
> That treason can but peep to what it would.

And not kings only, but presidents and premiers. Secondly, the commanding heights, because they are commanding, enable their occupants to deploy a myriad of elaborate devices to deflect criticism and blame, as a decoy draws off counter-fire. The memoirs of President Eisenhower are remarkable in this respect — and in this respect alone. The blunders of his presidency were legion, but — so Ike assures us — it was never his fault, ever. Such inordinate self-justification, such shameless sloughing of responsibility, is typical of statesmen. John Kennedy is an honourable exception. On 22 April 1961, his Cuban intervention already a fiasco, the President met the press. 'Victory has a hundred fathers,' he said, 'defeat is an orphan.' But not on this occasion, for the President fiercely insisted upon his paternity. It does not happen often.

All leaders acquire some immunity to blame, leaders of government more than most. But they are not entitled to it. 'The state,' Charles Burton Marshall comments wisely,

is only man. It is not superman. The institutions of political life do not add to the dimensions of the human mind. They have no insights denied to individuals. They produce no wisdom beyond the compass of man's mind. The intelligence operating in the lines of decision and execution is but human intelligence. It has the inherent attributes of contingency, fallibility, and subjectivity. Service to the state does not bring to the minds of the servants any additional endowments for perceiving the future.[8]

Or even the present.

Indeed it does not. So far from that, service to the state may constitute a handicap in the acquisition of relevant knowledge. There are certain occupa-

8 *The Limits of Foreign Policy* (Henry Holt, New York 1954), 14-15

tional hazards involved in the craft of intelligence. These constitute together the third cause of intelligence failure.

None of these occupational hazards is more conducive to disaster than wishful thinking. To think wishfully means, in the context of intelligence, hearing what one wants to hear, seeing what one wants to see, believing what one would like to be true. Wishful thinking is not the same thing as stupid acting, though it often leads to stupid acts.

Wishful thinking is found among both parts of the intelligence community – among the agents in the field, charged primarily with the collection of data; and among those at headquarters, charged primarily with its assessment.

Wishful thinking in the field is caused most commonly by the natural desire of the accredited representative to want to like, and be liked by, the government and people of his country of accreditation. Only a misanthrope enjoys being persona non grata; the career diplomatist, with all his faults, is rarely misanthropic. He studies the history and culture of his posting with sympathetic understanding: why would he do it any other way? He has to spend the next three years or so in a distant and unfamiliar land; the natural inclination is to look for the brighter side, just as the natural inclination, on moving into a strange and gloomy house, is to paint it cheery colours and install your own furniture. The grimmer the environment, the stronger the tendency. Then there are the leaders of the government, who are in a sense one's hosts. Again the inclination is to make the best of it, or them. Politicians having international reputations as butchers and carvers turn out, on close inspection, to be intriguing personalities with diverting characteristics, good fellows with a bad press. They dispense hospitality with gusto; their ladies are pleasant and perhaps pretty; as Old Owl said, reading his recipes for squirrel stew, 'It all seems so inviting.' And the despatches are mines of bias and misinformation.

To think wishfully about a foreign country is not necessarily to think well of it. The reports of Nazi diplomatists stationed in the United States before the war breathe contempt for the American people – for their cloddish materialism, their ignorance of Europe, their susceptibility to propaganda. At the same time the strength of isolationist sentiment was persistently exaggerated. 'More and more pictures are appearing in the newspapers showing the Führer in the field,' the German military attaché cabled from Washington in the summer of 1940. 'The opinion of Senator Pitman, who has described the Führer as a genius, is everywhere gaining ground.'[9] None of this was true. Nor was it in the Nazi interest to believe it to be true.

9   Quoted in Gordon A. Craig, *From Bismarck to Adenauer* (Johns Hopkins Press, Baltimore 1958), 121

Erroneous intelligence may result as well from the desire of its supplier to gratify and curry favour with its recipient. To this end he transmits what he thinks the statesman will want to hear, withholding that which he thinks will cause him displeasure. Many of the reports reaching Washington about conditions in Vietnam are only comprehensible as attempts to gratify the President. It is said that after listening to two widely differing accounts of a mission to Vietnam, one furnished by an optimistic general, the other by a pessimistic foreign service officer, President Kennedy asked them: 'Are you sure that you gentlemen visited the same country?' Literally, yes; figuratively, no.

Wishful thinking at headquarters can be just as harmful to statecraft as wishful thinking in the field. The best intelligence is useless when unduly disregarded. The totalitarian statesman suffers most acutely this occupational hazard, for his knowledge of the world has to conform to the requirements of the local ideology. Sometimes it doesn't fit, and policy goes astray. In 1946, the Polish military attaché in Washington reported to his communist superiors that in his first-hand observation the United States did not appear headed for that catastrophic economic collapse predicted by doctrine and the party line, and warned that it would be unwise for Soviet policy-makers to predicate their actions on the basis of such an assumption. For this helpful advice he received the following reply:

The method of the thematic treatment of the problems touched upon in your reports shows that you are falling under the influence of your environment, losing to a considerable extent the feeling of objectivity in the realistic evaluation of the situation and intentions of American policy. It would be from all points of view a desirable thing that you analyse events, getting at their source, rationally, critically, and free from the thinking habits of the big capitalist world. Then your material will give a true insight into the problems of interest to us.[10]

Being a prudent man, General Modelski, on reading this disconcerting message, promptly defected to the west – which is how we come to know of the exchange. Doubtless the files of the Soviet and Chinese foreign offices are full of similar examples.

In western foreign offices they are – one hopes – more rare. But they are not unknown. John Paton Davies was once an American diplomatist. When stationed in China in 1944, he reported the likelihood of a communist victory in the civil war, and suggested that the United States would do well to prepare

10 Quoted in Zbigniew K. Brzezinski, *The Permanent Purge* (Harvard University Press, Cambridge 1956), 202n3

herself for this impending massive shift in the world balance of power. For this service to his country Davies was dismissed from the service of his country. A board upholding his dismissal stated that his intelligence reports 'were not in accordance with the standard required of foreign service officers and show a definite lack of judgment, discretion and reliability.' Few of Davies' peers and colleagues shared that evaluation – none were represented on the board – but, notwithstanding their protests, he was compelled to resign, a victim of the paranoid style of American politics. It can happen there, and has. It could even happen here.

What, then, are we to say to those who still insist that the international environment is inscrutable and that statesmen, accordingly, are doomed by Fate to toil in a twilight zone between day and night, illumination and darkness, knowledge and ignorance? We may say to them that they are misinformed. Of course there is no perfect knowledge. We need no wise owls to tell us that. But there is sufficient knowledge for successful foreign policy. And it is available to any statesman who is alert to the trends and tendencies of his times, who trains himself and his subordinates not to make careless and stupid mistakes, who, aware of the occupational hazards of his craft, tries diligently to avoid them. A statesman whose statecraft goes awry through ignorance has no business pleading the inscrutability of history or the impermeability of events. He does better to pass upon himself the verdict once uttered by Senator Fulbright on taking what he came to regard as a mistaken course: 'I have only myself to blame for it because I should have been more intelligent, more far-seeing, more suspicious.'[11]

[December 1966]

---

11 *The New York Times,* 24 Nov. 1966, 'Record of '64 Senate Hearing on Tonkin Gulf'

4

Blindness and prevision

The making of plans, like the acquiring of knowledge, is an inescapable consequence of living in society. Someone once gave to a book the title *Plan or No
Plan?* It is a foolish title, for the question it poses is a spurious question, the
alternatives offered are false alternatives. The choice is not between plan or
no plan, between whether or not to make provision for the future. The choice
is among various types of planning (partial or comprehensive); among various
methods of planning (indicative or directive); among various ranges of planning
(short-range or long); and among various expectancies of planning (sceptical or
confident, dubious or trusting).

So whoever first said 'We are all planners nowadays' was right, but he
didn't say anything profound. Men were planners in the Stone Age. Neander-
thal Man made preparations only for the morning's breakfast, whereas modern
man – American Man – is so preoccupied with the day after the day after tomorrow that he might well be called Pension Plan Man. But the difference is
only of degree. Man is by nature a planning animal, as he is by nature a political animal. Politics is planning. Policy is planning. The expression 'policy-plan-
ning' is a tautological expression. You have to plan policy: there's just no other
way to do it. You can't make policy on the cables, whatever the diplomats may
say: you can't make it up as you go along. What distinguishes policy planning
councils from the other parts of foreign offices is not the activity of planning
as such, but the time they spend at it, the range they work to with it, the faith
they have in it.

The purpose of planning is to improve performance. If one knew, or
thought one knew, that planning would degrade performance, one ought to
try to do as little of it as possible. You cannot do none at all, planning being

a part of living. But you can cut planning to the bone. On certain views of the world this is an appropriate thing to do.

It is appropriate for extreme determinists. In a universe where the planning already has been done for you, in a world whose future is preordained, in an environment whose changes are predetermined, there is logically no point in piling planning on. Planning becomes a waste of time, a pointless activity in a totally planned creation.

Such an attitude to life often seems justified by life: philosophers as well as theologians may accept it. But their acceptance is mostly theoretical. As a life style it's a hard line to practise. Does Calvinism ever if at all lead Calvinists, believers in predestination, to live a life without purpose or direction? Does Marxism ever if at all lead Marxists, believers in determinism, to let the dialectic do it all? Neither Calvinists nor Marxists do anything of the sort.

Minimal planning is also appropriate for apostles of the irrational and the absurd. If you believe that the world is ruled by chance, that coincidence is king, that events occur at random, that history is all happenstance and circumstance, then not only is there no point in planning for the future, there is point in not planning for the future. By not planning you are likely to land on your feet at least some of the time; by meddling in so muddled an order you will only reduce your chances of success. If night doesn't follow day, if the sun sets in the east, if birds don't sing in the morning, if rivers run uphill, if money brings no interest and power brings no reward, then planning is a waste of time, a pointless activity in a pointless landscape.

Once again, such an attitude to life often seems justified by life: philosophers as well as drifters may accept it. But it is not a customary stance among policy-makers. These may be sceptical; they often are sceptical; but they are rarely that sceptical. Dean Acheson, in whom scepticism is more highly developed than in most statesmen, describes as 'heartening and wise advice' the homily that 'the future comes one day at a time' and, even so, 'may take us by surprise.' But he recoils, all the same, from that course of aimless drifting to which so negative and nihilist an outlook ought logically to lead. 'While it is true,' he writes, 'that the problems of the voyage come to the mariner day by day, it is essential to his success, and perhaps [to his] survival, that he ... prepare, as best he may, for what lies ahead.'[1] His best may be none too good: it's likely to be rather bad. But in the world of the policy-maker one must do what one can. 'We are never relieved,' Arthur Schlesinger insists, 'despite the limits of our knowledge and the darkness of our understanding, from the ne-

1   'The President and the Secretary of State,' in Don K. Price, ed., *The Secretary of State* (Prentice-Hall, Englewood Cliffs 1960), 36

cessity of meeting our obligations.'[2] The statesman may be a sceptic; he cannot be a beatnik. He may wait to see what happens; he can't wait for Godot.

Planning is inescapable, but that doesn't mean it's popular. Only recently has it attained a vogue. Only very recently has its applicability to foreign policy been conceded by practitioners of foreign policy. And still their concession is grudging and sharply qualified.

So long as the public philosophy is hostile to state intervention in the affairs of society, believing that government best which governs least, planning is bound to be unpopular. Such a conviction, and with it planning's unpopularity, has been steadily eroded since the eighteenth century, when once it held sway. Oh, you may still see automobiles on American highways whose bumpers proudly proclaim their owners' boast: 'I fight poverty – I work.' But the slogan discloses only the prejudice of their owners – that, and their profound ignorance of the role of the state in what they erroneously suppose to be their ruggedly individualistic existence.

Today, when the state in capitalistic societies hardly less than in socialist societies intrudes into the lives of the citizenry in every conceivable way – delivering them, educating them, feeding them, housing them, transporting them, entertaining them, burying them – planning is more and more common in more and more ways in more and more affairs.

In time, even in foreign affairs. But not at once, and not without a struggle. No one disputed the right of the state to conduct foreign policy which, of all the manifold activities of society, seems least appropriately left to the private sector. (In some states, such as the United States, trespassers in the domain of diplomacy are liable to be prosecuted.) No, what was disputed was the propriety of servants of the state trying to plan foreign policy. It was all very well for planners in other fields to strut their stuff. Geologists might project the life of mines and oilfields, demographers plot the growth and composition of populations, economists anticipate gross national products. These were the exact sciences – more or less exact. The quotients precise, the columns even, the conclusions concrete. But foreign policy? International politics? How could one cast the horoscope of states? How could one plan for a future as inscrutable as that awaiting the states system in twenty years', ten years', even five years' time? It couldn't be done. No point pretending it could be done. The gift of prevision – the privilege of the planner in less problematic kinds of policy – is not given to the foreign service officer. His fate is to be handicapped by a form of political astigmatism, blinding him to all phenomena save those

2 'On the Inscrutability of History,' *Encounter,* Nov. 1966, 17

closest to his gaze. To him, as Charles Burton Marshall puts it, 'the long run ... can only be an aggregate of short runs.' If he engages in forward planning, it is 'not because the future is predictable, but because it is not.'[3]

Scepticism for foreign policy planning was earliest and most easily overcome in totalitarian states, particularly those embarked on civilizing missions and wars of liberation. If you are out to conquer the world, you need a certain confidence for the enterprise: it helps to gain confidence by having a plan of attack, a time-table for aggression, a blueprint for occupation. Besides, if you are out to control the future, it is easier to predict it. This is why the most precise and detailed plans for future international action are to be found either in the files of the General Staff or else in the programmes of the dictators.

Leaders whose goal it is to initiate and carry through momentous social and political change – leaders who fancy themselves as civilizing missionaries and conquering heroes – find it easy, indeed find it essential, to think ahead about a future less aggressive folk find difficult to fathom. But what about these less aggressive folk, those who have no grand designs even upon the status quo, let alone upon their neighbours? Are they doomed always to wait and see what others will do first, to react to the actions of their adversaries, to have only a second-strike planning capability? Or can they ever hope to strike out boldly on their own?

The most important of the status quo powers are the United Kingdom and the United States. Neither took readily or kindly to the notion that planning in foreign policy is at once as feasible and as productive as planning in any other kind of policy. They could do it in war, in short bursts for a short time; over the long haul, they felt, it was not for them. The British, particularly, rooted in empiricism, staunchly pragmatic, distrustful of dogma, were loath to espouse planning in foreign policy with any enthusiasm. The famous inaugural lecture given by Michael Oakeshott at the London School of Economics in 1951 expresses their outlook perfectly. 'In political activity men sail a boundless and bottomless sea. There is neither harbour nor shelter nor floor for anchorage, neither starting place nor appointed destination. The enterprise is to keep afloat, on an even keel.'[4] That being the case, as Oakeshott said it was the case, you might need ballast, you would need seamanship. But you didn't need sailing orders to tell you where to head for; you didn't need manifests to say what you were carrying; you didn't need charts to show you

---

3 'The Making of Foreign Policy in the United States,' in Edward H. Buehrig, ed., *Essays in Political Science* (Indiana University Press, Bloomington 1966), 43
4 *Rationalism in Politics and Other Essays* (Methuen, London 1962), 127

how to get there. Drift on, O ship of state. Drift on, O union strong and great. I well remember, as a member of Oakeshott's audience, the ripple of indignation running through the hall as he proceeded to demolish all that Harold Laski, his predecessor in the Chair, had stood for. But, so far as the Foreign Office was concerned, he was preaching to the converted. 'It is well to recognize the limits of human endeavour.' That maxim, a favourite of one of its permanent under secretaries, could well stand as an epitaph for most of the men who have occupied that great post at one time or another.

Eventually, in the United States, even in the United Kingdom, the importance of planning in foreign policy has come to be recognized along with the difficulty of planning in foreign policy.

Three factors have brought about this conversion. The first is that other countries, almost everywhere, have become convinced that planning in every sector of national life is a means to the good national life. This has made it difficult for states with anti-planning attitudes to hold aloof much longer.

The communist example has been particularly compelling in this respect. By the 1950s, communism had become a real competitor of the west, offering glittering prizes of prestige and productivity to those who looked to Moscow, even to Peking, for models and for methods. After the successful launching of the sputnik, it became harder than ever to argue that the achievements of communist technology had come about despite communist techniques rather than because of them. It became fashionable for liberal democrats to draw invidious comparisons between the drift and aimlessness of their society and the stern purposefulness of Soviet society. The point was made – most stridently by people calling themselves moral re-armers but not by them alone – that if the west was to survive it must embrace henceforth something of the public philosophy of its adversary. At the very least, they argued, the west must re-examine its traditional attitudes of hostility or indifference towards the fully planned society. The west, no less than communism, required goals to aim at, timetables to keep to. In the United States, those eastern seaboard Republican internationalists whose forbears had stood four-square against everything their descendants now came to stand for, eagerly responded to the call. Under the leadership of the McLoys, the Rockefellers, the Wristons, task forces were assembled, panels mobilized, inventories made of national assets from ore-bodies to orchestras, national goals formulated, national purposes proclaimed, national interests defined. They acquired a philosopher, of sorts, in Walt Whitman Rostow, whose book, *The Stages of Economic Growth,* sub-titled 'A Non-Communist Manifesto,' they and he regarded as the west's answer to the Marxist way of looking at the world. Certainly it stood alone in the vaulting voluntarism of its recommendations and in the confidence of its analysis. 'The tricks of growth,' Rostow assured the statesmen of the west, 'are not all that difficult; they only seem so, at moments of frustration and confusion.' He appealed to them to 'deal with the challenge implicit in the stages-of-growth ... at the full stretch of our moral commitment, our energy, and our resources.'[5] A year later Professor Rostow became head of the Policy Planning Council at the State Department and there contrived, in due course, the Alliance for Progress.

There was also the example of the so-called new nations. Among the fifty to sixty political communities attaining independence since the Second World War, planning was something of a panacea. Certainly no one scornful of planning could hope to gain their favour; and since gaining their favour was an objective of western policy, western policy-makers were obliged if for no other reason to abandon at least the appearance of scepticism. Nor was that the only reason. States sceptical of planning tended to be wealthy states, sharing their wealth with the poor. To inject large amounts of capital and technical assistance into the fully planned economies of their recipients required a certain amount of planning on the part of the donors. Linked in this way in a continuous transfusion of resources, the donors insensibly acquired some of the characteristics of those whom they were aiding, of which no characteristic was more pronounced than their touching faith in the efficacy of the national plan.

A second factor converting the critics of planning in foreign policy into advocates of planning in foreign policy is the mounting importance in external affairs of their military component. Among the military, planning has always enjoyed a central and unquestioned position. In peacetime, military establishments live their own lives, little influenced or interfered with by the society outside. Within the privacy of the map-room and the mess, the military planned at will, secretly to be sure, but without shame or hindrance. In wartime, they sallied forth to put their plans in practice. If they won their war, they enhanced the reputation of both planning and themselves. But if they lost, it was only their reputation that suffered. Planning itself was unimpaired. What was needed were new plans, better plans. And the military planners would go back to the map-room and the sand-table. In due course new plans would emerge. Perhaps they might be better.

During the Second World War, military planning was immeasurably refined by the application of scientific and mathematical techniques to military problems hitherto left largely to the intuitions of experienced (or inexperienced)

5 (Cambridge University Press, Cambridge & New York 1960), 166-7

officers, which sometimes let you down. Since then the military planner, proudly wearing his new title of 'operations researcher' or 'systems analyst,' has never looked back. His vogue is great, his power enormous, his prestige unchallengeable.

The emergence of the national security planner to these dizzy heights of influence was made possible, and in a sense inevitable, by two post-war developments. The first was the reliance for the nation's security upon the deterrent capacity of nuclear weapons and their delivery systems, both bombers and missiles. The problems raised by the new kind of weaponry – its siting, its targeting, the correct calibration of its various components (the problem of the 'mix'), the relationship of deterrent to operational forces, the doctrines by which these forces were to be deployed, the contrivance of effective systems of command and control – such problems were at once so novel and so baffling, so esoteric and so critical, that anyone who seemed as if he might know the answers was assured a hearing and found his talents at a premium. Likely as not, those who seemed to know the answers were striplings from the academies, sporting as campaign ribbons their doctorates in quantum mechanics or the theory of games. The field in which they professed competence was that of thermonuclear war. Since thermonuclear war knows no practical military experience, one could not tell, at least by the traditional tests, whether the whiz kid planners were letting the side down or not. Only an outbreak of general war could prove them wrong: there was scant satisfaction in that even for their most rabid critics. On the other hand, so long as holocaust remained averted, they could claim without serious fear of refutation to have been right; for in the thermonuclear age the court-martials are mostly posthumous.

The second, and related, development was the fantastic increase in the price of weaponry, which placed a premium upon the talents of the systems analyst and the cost accountant. By the middle 1950s, the United States was spending about $15 billion a year on military equipment largely on the basis of successful lobbying by its manufacturers. There was no planning in procurement, only politics. All that changed in 1961 when Robert S. McNamara came to the Pentagon determined to apply to the national security the same techniques of cost effectiveness which he had learned as an automobile executive. In testimony before a Senate committee, Mr McNamara expressed his philosophy in these words: 'I equate planning and budgeting and consider the terms almost synonymous, the budget being simply a quantitative expression of the operating plan.'[6]

6   Quoted in William W. Kaufmann, *The McNamara Strategy* (Harper & Row, New York, Evanston, & London 1964), 169

The State Department remained sceptical, as state departments will. But even there the reverberations of the McNamara revolution were felt in time. On 19 September 1962 Dean Rusk spoke at the inauguration of the new departmental computer – the first to be installed in any foreign office in the world. 'This innovation in communications technique,' said he guardedly, 'represents an important contribution to management effectiveness and will aid us in the achievement of our foreign policy objectives.' Exactly how, the Secretary didn't disclose. But the patrons of planning could not have been more dramatically vindicated.

The third factor making the planning of foreign policy acceptable to the makers of foreign policy is the improvement in the techniques of prediction. Until quite recently the statesman had but two such techniques at his disposal. He could read history, and reflect upon its lessons. He could consult his own experience, and rely upon its intuitions. These may not sound like much, but they were all he had.

Learning from history and intuiting from experience both involve extrapolating from the past, allowing what has gone before to be your guide to what may lie ahead. Machiavelli preferred the first technique to the second: the wisdom of experience is of no use to the inexperienced, whereas the lessons of history are as varied as the library at one's disposal. 'As to exercise for the mind,' he counselled his Prince,

read history and study the actions of eminent men, see how they acted in warfare, examine the causes of their victories and defeats in order to imitate the former and avoid the latter ... so that when fortune changes she may find [you] prepared to resist her blows, and to prevail in adversity.[7]

From history as a pedagogue one may expect too little or too much. It is to expect too little to believe, with Coleridge, that whatever illumination history provides is but 'a lantern on the stern, which shines only on the waves behind' – useless as a look-out, worse than useless as a radar. Or to believe, with Hegel, that Minerva's owl takes flight only in the gathering dusk. These verdicts are too severe. Perhaps Clio, history's muse, is unfit to conduct a seminar for statesmen. But she is competent enough in kindergarten. 'The assertion that men learn nothing from history,' E.H. Carr has written, 'is contradicted by a multitude of observable facts. No experience is more common.'[8]

But, pressed too hard for much too much, history will let you down. And it is the way with statesmen to ask of history more than she is in the position

7   *The Prince* (Mentor Books, New York 1952), 91
8   *What is History?* (Macmillan, London 1961), 61

to provide. For more details of the future than the record can foretell; for more certainty about the future than the record may justify. In its extreme form this importuning of history results in the elaboration of pseudo-historical theories of the rise and fall of empires and civilizations; or in affirmation of infallible analogies; or in postulation of false alternatives. But these are not the faults of history. They are the faults of the charlatans who, speaking in history's name, abuse her confidence and misapply her methods.

Distinct from the tuition of history is the intuition of experience. Its value as a tool of prediction depends partly on the experience, partly on the 'flair' (as Delcassé put it) with which the statesman interprets his experience. These have nowhere been better blended than in the mind of Winston Churchill, who was also a star pupil of history. Churchill possessed in consequence truly phenomenal powers of prevision. As well as predicting epochal events – the coming of war, the slaughter in India – he was capable of curiously exact premonitions on a smaller scale. In August 1939, informed of regulations to shoot animals let loose from the zoo by air-raids, he remarked as follows: 'Imagine a great air raid over London ... The corpses lying about in the smoking ashes – the lions and tigers roaming the ruins in search of the corpses. And you're going to shoot them. What a pity!' Now look at his war history. In its third volume, written ten years later, occurs the following description of the first German air attack on Belgrade:

When silence came at last ... over 17,000 citizens ... lay dead in the streets or under the debris. Out of the nightmare of smoke and fire came the maddened animals released from their shattered cages in the zoological gardens. A stricken stork hobbled past the main hotel, which was a mass of flames. A bear, dazed and uncomprehending, shuffled through the inferno with slow and awkward gait towards the Danube ...[9]

The correspondent[10] drawing the attention of readers of *The Times* to this striking parallel was then a member of the Policy Planning Council: his comment betrays professional admiration, slightly tinged by envy: 'As on larger matters, Mr Churchill's vision was fulfilled and he was able to describe reality in the same terms that he used to foresee it.' This is the sort of quality claimed by C.P. Snow for scientists – men who have the future in their bones. There aren't many of them around.

9   *The Second World War,* III, *The Grand Alliance* (Houghton Mifflin, Boston 1950), 175
10   Mr Henry Owen

To avoid blindness and attain prevision, the modern statesman need not rely solely upon extrapolation from the past. He may fortify himself with the technique of the scenario, and with the technique of simulation.

The trouble with history is that while historians may repeat each other, history never repeats itself. Not, at any rate, exactly. (When Mark Twain declared 'History does not repeat itself, but it rhymes,' he went about as far as he could go.) Even the closest historical parallels are only analogues; they are never identical. Frequently they aren't even analogous: they are more like metaphors. And often you can search history from the beginning to the present without encountering any sort of experience relevant to the problem at hand. As, for example, the problem of waging and surviving nuclear war.

Here's where the scenario can help. The writing of scenarios involves the controlled use of the imagination to invoke fictitiously the shape of things to come. The object of the exercise is to reduce the incidence of unpleasant surprise. By imagining previously unimagined situations, by thinking about the unthinkable, by postulating the impossible, by pondering the imponderable, the scenarian helps the statesman to choose his course more surely.

Simulation has only recently been taken up by statesmen, but it has long been known to soldiers. Military manoeuvres are a classic way of simulating warfare. They are also cumbersome and costly: when time is fleeting and money short, the military make do with mock manoeuvres, deploying toy soldiers and model tanks across a miniature landscape, so attaining, in a game of double make-believe, a simulation of a simulated war.

Since 1945, the step from war gaming to cold war gaming, from military simulations to strategic simulations, from *kriegspiel* to *staatspiel,* has been slight and irresistible. Once the traditional distinction between peace and war had broken down, once governments relied on weapons and doctrines for which there was no previous operational experience, once civilians displaced soldiers in the making of grand strategy, it was inevitable that the techniques of simulation should find a wider application. They moved out briskly, from the war colleges to the universities, from the Defense Department to the State Department. There they were not always well received. Those who relied primarily upon their intuitions and experience for such glimpses of the future as they might be privileged to see were highly sceptical of what seemed at best a diverting pastime and at worst an untrustworthy guide to policy. One such sceptic, a former member of the Policy Planning Council, recalls his experience in terms which suggest that while he found it enjoyable, he found it anything but profitable:

On the occasion in question I was one-fifth of a United States notional government. An admired and scholarly friend was the simulated President. We were pitted against wily and determined adversaries in a putative confrontation growing out of an infiltration scrape involving a far country. We smote them hip and thigh and came off with a considerable diplomatic success. I wish the nation might always do as well in real life ...[11]

Though there is reason to be sceptical, there is none to be scornful. A simulation is neither occult nor foolish. A simulation is a model of a system, in this case the international system. You can represent international politics mathematically (as in the theory of games) or verbally (as in the scenario): the simulated model differs from these in that the model is in motion. You choose up sides; you lay down rules; then you let the players play at statecraft, observing, recording, and interpreting the results in the hope of finding something out about the system that could hardly be found in any other way. Simulation, as even its defenders concede, is a crude and primitive technique of prediction. But then the simulated system – international politics – is also crude and primitive.

The scenario and the simulation are the newest instruments in the kit-bag of policy prediction. Like any instrument they may be used or abused. They are abused if the policy planner mistakes the scenario for the future, the simulation for reality – if he becomes so enamoured with his own constructed sequence of events, or with his postulated outcome, as to be oblivious to all the other possible sequences and all other possible outcomes. But they serve their purpose if, in the words of T.C. Schelling, they awaken planners 'to certain contingencies that might not otherwise have been taken seriously, and acquaint decision-makers in advance with some of the options that may be available to them and with situations that arise.'[12] A modern Machiavelli may prudently commend scenarios and simulations to his Prince, not as an infallible method of putting Fate to flight, but rather to prepare him to resist her blows.

[December 1966]

11 Charles Burton Marshall, *The Limits of Foreign Policy* (Henry Holt, New York 1954), 40
12 'Comment,' in Klaus Knorr and Thornton Read, eds., *Limited Strategic War* (Praeger, New York 1962), 256

5

Inertia and innovation

Not least among the obstacles confronting the statesman determined to make events conform to Will is the caution of his professional advisers. Pressing against the innovating tendencies of foreign ministers, especially fledgling foreign ministers, are the inertial masses of bureaucracy. All too often inertia prevails and innovation loses.

All bureaucracy's conservative, but the conservatism of diplomatic bureaucracy is in a class by itself. The normal reaction of a foreign office to some new foreign policy idea or some fresh foreign policy approach is to want to make it go away. The ethos of diplomacy is an ethos of suspicion – suspicion tempered by scepticism, snow tempered by ice. The foreign service officer is a nay-sayer in statecraft, the abominable no-man of diplomacy. His mission in life is to preserve the status quo from those who propose to alter it. Where the new idea or the fresh approach cannot be banished, his impulse is to denature them. Where he cannot avoid change, he seeks to slow it down. He is capable of performing quite unscrupulous acts in the interests of delay. He moves at the pace of snails. He measures his progress in inches. He employs the tactic of Prufrockian deliberation, taking one thing at a time and much time over that one thing:

> Time for you and time for me,
> And time yet for a hundred indecisions,
> And for a hundred visions and revisions,
> Before the taking of a toast and tea.

I must take a moment to stress that this is not an exaggerated description. My portrait of the foreign service officer may be slightly overdrawn, so as to bring out his essential feature; it is not a caricature. This is how he really is; this is what he's really like. There's evidence to prove it. There's the evidence of his critics – critics such as Churchill, who once remarked that all he ever got from his advisers was the sum-total of their fears. There's the evidence of his defenders – defenders such as the official historian of the British Foreign Office during the Second World War who remarks with approbation of the 'habits of caution and understatement' by which the style of the Office was marked even during wartime, and of how 'a good deal of the time and energy of ... the Permanent Under-Secretary and the Staff of the Office was taken up in efforts to persuade [Churchill] that not all his proposals were suited to British interests, or adequate to meet the many important factors in a situation.'[1]

And there's the evidence of the diplomatist himself, provided in his memoirs. Diplomatic memoirs are replete with grievances, among which none recurs more often than the complaint of the diplomatist that his political master acts too precipitately, acts too boldly, indeed, that he acts at all. Historians deal kindly with this literature – too kindly – perhaps because their sympathies in the struggle between foreign minister and foreign service lie more with the foreign service than with the foreign minister. One of their number writes disparagingly of 'the evils of abrupt and inexpert intervention by [those] whose experience has been confined to the domestic field'; another, no less distinguished, writes of the loneliness and self-discipline of the foreign service officer, who

knows that he could win much greater approval and popularity, at any given moment, by a liberal measure of charlatanism: by abusing the responsibilities he bears, by exploiting the ignorance and prejudice of others, by inflaming rather than assuaging the passions of men and then making himself the mouthpiece of those passions –[2]

by, to put it shortly, acting more like a politician than a diplomatist.

The time has come, I think, for the historians to reduce their bias and regain their balance on this issue. If we reproach the political practitioner of foreign policy for his characteristic vices, we should not lose sight of the characteristic vices of the professional practitioner of foreign policy. Those of the politician – his rashness, his impetuosity, his fondness for the unortho-

1 Sir Llewellyn Woodward, *British Foreign Policy in the Second World War* (Her Majesty's Stationery Office, London 1962), xxvi, xliii
2 George F. Kennan, 'History and Diplomacy as Viewed by a Diplomatist,' in Stephen D. Kertesz and M.A. Fitzsimons, eds., *Diplomacy in a Changing World* (University of Notre Dame Press, Notre Dame 1959), 108

dox solution and the direct approach – are known well enough. Those of the professional deserve to be known better. It is my purpose in this section to see to it that they are.

What may the political practitioner of foreign policy do to prevent this enthusiasm from being dampened and his initiatives from being stifled by the caution of his professional advisers? What measures may a foreign minister take to ensure that his plans and projects are not lost in the labyrinths of officialdom or doomed to moulder in the files?

There are three courses open to him. He may take the apparatus as he finds it, hoping to make it responsive to his bidding by the vigour of his advocacy and the force of his leadership. Or he may attempt to reform the apparatus, hoping by some structural change or institutional alteration to produce a bureaucracy more cordial to change and receptive of innovation. Or, finally, he may bypass the bureaucracy altogether, hoping to tap other outside sources for that flow of fresh ideas without which policy remains infertile and progress can't be made.

The line of least resistance is to take the apparatus as you find it, hoping it can be made to serve you better than it may have served your predecessors. This is the line followed most frequently by British foreign ministers, not because they are any more craven or more lazy than the foreign ministers of other countries, but because the British system of government sedulously protects the public service from politicians who might want to tinker with it.

A pioneering attempt to fashion the Foreign Office to his liking was that of the Foreign Secretary in the Labour government elected in 1929. It was Arthur Henderson's notion that the government should actually keep its election promises in foreign policy, particularly its promise to sign the Optional Clause of the World Court, so committing the United Kingdom to the compulsory jurisdiction of its international disputes. Knowing well that so radical a break with tradition would find little favour with the Foreign Office, Henderson soon summoned a meeting of its legal advisers. 'He sat in his chair with a stubborn look,' an eye-witness recalls,

and declared that the Government was in favour of signing the Clause with the least possible delay. He did not wish to hear "a lot of legal arguments" about reservations. He, in his speeches during the campaign, had not spoken about reservations. He had spoken about signing the Clause. If there were any real difficulties which they could put up, he was willing to consider them. But he expected that, when they put them up, they would also suggest ways of overcoming them. All this produced a rather shattering effect, and after the meeting Henderson said to me: "Don't these chaps know what our policy is?"[3]

But, as it turned out, Henderson, not 'those chaps,' didn't know what his policy was, or was to be. The government signed the clause: but the Foreign Office smuggled so many reservations into the fine print as to make the signature a meaningless gesture. Did Henderson resign in protest? Not at all. By then he didn't notice; or he simply didn't care.

Ernest Bevin likewise came to the job determined to deal firmly with his diplomatic advisers; and once again it was the diplomatic advisers who dealt firmly with him. And of course they loved him for it. 'For a month or two after he first arrived,' a senior Foreign Office official recalls, 'he was not very sure about us; but this period of hesitation soon passed ... There grew up between Bevin and his officials, both at home and abroad, a relationship of mutual confidence and esteem which had the happiest effect upon the work of the Service.'[4] The Service had reason to be happy. They enjoyed what was from their point of view the ideal division of labour. The Foreign Secretary controlled the style of policy, the Foreign Office controlled its substance. Watching Ernie Bevin arrive at Potsdam, tunelessly humming the 'Red Flag,' or listening to one of his fabled interventions - 'I don't like it. I don't like it. When you open that Pandora's box, you will find it full of Trojan 'orses' - one might have supposed that, at long last, a real change was under way. One would have been wrong. The voice was the voice of Jacob, but the hands were the hands of Esau. Jacob was a plain man, as the Bible says, and Esau a cunning hunter; and it was in the cunning hands of Whitehall that British foreign policy remained. There it was kept intact, safe, unaltered. It made so little difference whether Anthony Eden or Ernest Bevin was in charge of the Foreign Office that an opposition critic noted the fact in the House of Commons soon after Bevin took over:

We were told in the election from the platforms of hon. Gentlemen opposite that their return would create a new world ... Well, we have now had a fortnight of the new world and certainly in the new world there are still some familiar speeches. The right hon. Gentleman, the Foreign Secretary, in that splendid speech he made ... which was acclaimed in all parts of the House, made me wonder whether in his spare time ... he had not been dipping into that brilliant old play, "The Importance of Being Anthony."[5]

3 Hugh Dalton, *Memoirs, I, Call Back Yesterday* (Muller, London 1953), 237
4 Lord Strang, *Home and Abroad* (André Deutsch, London 1956), 295
5 Quoted in Sir Anthony Eden, *Full Circle* (Cassell, London 1960), 6. The speaker was Mr Oliver Stanley.

He might just as well. He was reading from a Foreign Office brief.

Finally there is the example, not yet complete, of George Brown. Few men, in the long history of the Foreign Office, have taken charge of it with such evident determination not to be taken captive by it. 'I am the Foreign Secretary,' George Brown declared soon after becoming Foreign Secretary,

but I am an ordinary man, selected to represent them by ordinary people. And I intend to talk and behave about everything in a way that ordinary people can understand. Why should I start wearing striped pants and behaving like a stuffed shirt? There's too much striped pants and stuffed shirt attitude in international relations still, and no good it's doing anybody. Foreign policy is about people, about how people are trying to be happy, trying to avoid being wretched, groping forward to the day when one nation's security isn't being purchased by the subjection of another, when men will live with men as their Maker intended them to live, not as animals in the jungle ...

When I say "striped pants," I've got nothing against men wearing striped pants and black jackets if they want to ... It's the wearing of striped pants in the soul I object to, and having a Homburg hat where your heart ought to be ...[6]

What a splendid creed for a foreign minister! What brave words these are! How long, one wonders, before they have to be forgotten, before they have to be eaten? Or before their author is compelled to retire from the scene? History teaches not too long.[7]

Some foreign ministers, despairing of reform by precept and persuasion, attempt to reform by restructuring the apparatus of foreign policy so as to make it more productive of ideas. This approach has especially commended itself to American practitioners of foreign policy, and finds its clearest manifestation in the creation, in 1947, of the Policy Planning Staff in the State Department.

In every foreign service officer there is a foreign policy planner, struggling to be free. Scratch a liberal, Dicey remarked fifty years ago, and you'll find a socialist: scratch a diplomatist, and you'll find the frustrated artist of some grand design. Talk to him about his work and, if he's at all candid, he'll tell you two contradictory things. The first thing to emerge is his scepticism. There's no such thing as originality in foreign policy, he'll say. There's nothing new under the sun. The enterprise is to keep afloat. What matters most is

---

6 'Why I Am What I Am: George Brown the Foreign Secretary Explains Himself to Kenneth Harris,' *The Observer,* 14 Aug. 1966

7 Fourteen months, as it turned out; George Brown resigned from the Foreign Office on 15 Mar. 1968

the next twenty-four hours. Ideas have their place, but not in his place. Perhaps he'll compare the planner in foreign policy to the boastful pilot who reassures an apprehensive captain that he needn't worry that his ship is moving too fast into port. 'I know every rock in this harbour,' says he, confidently – and just as he says it, there's a tremendous crash as the ship shatters on a reef. 'You see?,' he says – 'there's one of them now.'

But beneath this sceptical veneer, if you can only get at it, is something very different. If the foreign service officer is contemptuous of the ideas of others, he yearns for the opportunity to produce ideas of his own. He yearns for it because in the ordinary course of his duties he has so little time for it. It's all crisis managing and crash-programming, making policy on the cables, making policy at the eleventh hour. The affairs of state are like an emergency ward on a rainy night, statesmen like its harried internes. 'Their principal effort,' Dean Acheson has testified, 'goes into dealing with the overpowering present, the present which, like the Mississippi in full flood, absorbs the whole energy and thought of those who man the levies.' This is how it is, but this is not, as Acheson says, how it ought to be:

The truth is that in foreign affairs manhours spent in thinking and planning on future action are by far the most profitable investment. The thundering present becomes so soon the unchangeable past that seizing it at any moment of its acceleration is as dangerous as mounting a train gathering speed ... Every bird-shooter knows that you must lead your bird and swing with its flight ... The true problem lies in determining the emerging future and the policy appropriate to it.[8]

All this being so, how much more satisfactory it would be if there could somehow be built into the policy machine some haven for reflection, a meditation room for statesmen, a group of gifted foreign service personnel who, liberated from day-to-day chores of operations and housekeeping, could spend their time thinking about foreign affairs in their broadest aspects and in their longest range.

The Policy Planning Council, formerly the Policy Planning Staff, of the American State Department conforms precisely to these specifications. Over its twenty-year history, begun under the chairmanship of George Kennan, it has attracted to its ranks men of luminous intelligence and great ability – Kennan himself, Louis Halle, Paul Nitze, John Paton Davies, Charles Burton Marshall, Walt Rostow, Henry Owen. The Council, according to a former member,

8 'The President and the Secretary of State,' in Don K. Price, ed., *The Secretary of State* (Prentice-Hall, Englewood Cliffs 1960), 47

remains one of the few places where there is a chance to observe and assess the nation's position along the whole front of military and foreign policy – to place what we are doing and trying to do in the long sweep of history ... This job is done in a setting where the members of the Council are each engaged on a few critical issues and do not have to bear the heavy burden of day-to-day operations.[9]

It sounds like a terrific idea. Here is what is wrong with it.

For the Policy Planning Council to be any good, its members have to be extraordinarily good – as on the whole they have been. But good people are in short supply – even in Washington. What happens to the fine minds who are told to repair to the seventh floor of the State Department and there to brood about the future is that they are in extraordinarily keen demand to act about the present. Everything in the policy process conspires to place a premium upon and attach priority to the short run. Let the future take care of itself. Let the future go hang itself. So what happens to the idea man on the seventh floor? His phone rings. That's what happens. It's the Secretary of State on the line, perhaps the President himself. 'There's a meeting in the Oval Room in half an hour,' the gruff voice says authoritatively. Who in such circumstances would dare to say he could not come for any reason, let alone that he had to finish reading Thucydides' account of how Pericles put the case for war against the Peloponnesians? Never mind that the policy planning councillor could hardly find reading more relevant for the defence of the policies of the administration: he may be forgiven for supposing that its chief executive might fail to appreciate its relevance. And so he closes his book and calls for his taxi. A month, six weeks later, he returns to his office and finds Thucydides open before him at page eighty-four. He wonders why.

Secondly, the Policy Planning Council is a committee. A very exalted committee, to be sure, but a committee nonetheless. A committee is no place for innovation. A committee conduces to inertia. It doesn't create ideas: it consumes ideas. 'The ideal committee man,' Henry Kissinger has written, 'does not make his associates uncomfortable. He does not operate with ideas too far outside of what is generally accepted. The thrust of committees is toward a standard of average performance.'[10] If the Policy Planning Council has on occasion succeeded in moving beyond and above that standard, it is in spite of its format, not because of it.

9   W.W. Rostow, 'The Planning of Foreign Policy,' in E.A.J. Johnson, ed., *The Dimensions of Diplomacy* (Johns Hopkins Press, Baltimore 1964), 45
10   *The Necessity for Choice* (Harper & Brothers, New York 1960), 345

Finally, the Policy Planning Council is composed, for the most part, of foreign service officers. Of able and imaginative foreign service officers, to be sure, but foreign service officers nonetheless. Scratch a foreign service officer, as I have said, and you will find beneath the veneer of his scepticism the frustrated artist of a grand design. But this is not to say his grand designs are any good. He may think he has it in him, he may think he's on the ball: chances are he's much mistaken. Intellect grown rusty with disuse, imagination grown torpid with slumber over years, will not suddenly spring up, lambent and alive, to do their owner's bidding. And, after years of toiling in the diplomatic underbrush, intellect and imagination are all too likely to have grown rusty and torpid. 'The training and life of a foreign service officer,' Dean Acheson remarks,

are not apt to produce men well fitted for the task [of innovating policy] ... The bureaucratic routine through which foreign service officers must go produces capable men, knowledgeable about specific parts of the world, and excellent diplomatic operators. But it makes men cautious rather than imaginative ...

And he recalls that the three great innovative achievements of his own tenure as Secretary of State – the Marshall Plan, the Fulbright Program, and Point Four – were conceived and developed by outsiders – 'men whose training and experience were broader than the State Department mill provided.'[11] President Kennedy had a similar experience. 'They never have any ideas over there,' he complained, 'never come up with anything new ... The State Department is a bowl of jelly.'[12]

You can't restructure a bowl of jelly. Such, at any rate, was the conclusion at which John Kennedy arrived after a year or so of vainly attempting to squeeze out of the Policy Planning Council a reasonable quota of ideas. Being incapable of dispensing with ideas, he sought ideas from other sources. The professions had let him down: perhaps the amateurs could help him out. The bureaucracy had failed: perhaps the academy could succeed. For where more natural to look for new ideas, for creativity, for innovation, than to the great universities of America, the powerhouses of its intellect?

The President had but to snap his fingers and the intellectuals came running. From Harvard, mostly, though not from Harvard only. Down they

11 Acheson, 'The President and the Secretary of State,' 48-9
12 Quoted in Arthur M. Schlesinger, Jr, *A Thousand Days: John F. Kennedy in the White House* (Houghton Mifflin, Boston 1965), 406

streamed, the fresh young men of the New Frontier, bright-eyed and bushy-tailed, supremely confident in the ability of their brain-power to get America moving again. Did they get it moving? And to any useful purpose?

It may be still too soon to tell. Those vibrant thousand days, those glittering thousand nights, the radiant company, the vaunted style, are too close to place in historical perspective, too bright in our memory for dispassionate appraisal. But, when the time comes for judgment, I will guess that the experiment will be judged a failure. That the President, instead of putting the intellectuals to work on foreign policy, would have done better to have left them where they were.

The proposition that intellectuals are sources of ideas is plausible enough. Less plausible is the proposition that you will garner intellectuals, and with them their ideas, by scouring the academies. I do not say it is impossible for an intellectual to survive in the environment of the modern university: I only say that it is damnably and increasingly difficult for him to survive. Irving Howe has drawn our attention to the way in which 'the vocabulary of academic statesmanship – the university should be "pluralist" in outlook, "moderate" in tone, "responsible" to the community, "alert" to the national interest – helps to blend the university into the surrounding landscape and thereby to rob it of its reason for existence ... The university becomes a place of mediocre efficiency, a busy middleman of culture, a training school for the professions, a center of usable research.'[13] To turn to such a place for personnel, in preference to existing personnel, is to exchange King Log for King Stork. In fact the trade's less advantageous than that: all you get is the bureaucratic mentality without the bureaucratic experience.

To assume that when the statesman turns to the academic man for help in foreign policy, he turns to the intellectual type of academic man rather than to his own type of academic man, is to assume a great deal and I think too much. Surely what he looks for is his own type – a known quantity, a recognizable quantity, someone whose methods he can understand, someone, therefore, he can trust. Applying these criteria of selection, the statesman recruits to his cause not an intellectual but an operator, not a scholar but an entrepreneur. Having at his disposal the full array of the nation's intellect, President Kennedy picked as the head of his White House staff the dean of arts at Harvard University. McGeorge Bundy was exactly the sort of man he wanted. Kennedy told his friends that Bundy was the second brightest man he had ever known. (Doubtless he would have picked the brightest had David Ormsby-

13 *Steady Work: Essays in the Politics of Democratic Radicalism, 1953-1966* (Harcourt, Brace and World, New York 1966), 109

Gore not already been on the payroll of a foreign power.) 'Bundy possessed dazzling clarity and speed of mind,' a close associate has said of him, 'as well as great distinction of manner and unlimited self-confidence.' It may well be so. Yet none of these qualities, so desirable in a governmental trouble-shooter, are the essential qualities of the intellectual.

But this is only part of the problem. Not only does the statesman prefer a certain type of mind, when he turns to the academies for help; he prefers a mind with a certain point of view. The closer this is to his own, the better it is to his liking. For the typical statesman is less than candid about the kind of help he's looking for. He's not looking for criticism. He's looking for endorsation. He doesn't want the intellectual to tell him what is wrong. He wants him to tell the world that all is right. He wants the imprimatur of intellect, not its condemnation. If he is exceptionally obtuse, he will even deny the intellectual his primary role. 'The responsible intellectual,' President Johnson declared at Princeton University in May 1966, 'who moves between his campus and Washington knows, above all, that his task is, in the language of the current generation, to "cool it."' Now there is news for Socrates. And here is news for President Johnson. The responsible intellectual will not move between his campus and Washington. He will stay on his campus. He will say to those who seek to lure him from it what Archimedes said to the intruding Roman soldier: 'Do not disturb my circles.'[14]

Let us, however, assume that the statesman does seek out the intellectual rather than the operator, and that the intellectual responds to the call. What sort of help is he likely to be to the statesman in his quest for new ideas in foreign policy?

This depends, to begin with, on his terms of employment. If he is engaged half-time, part-time, he's not likely to be much help. The part-time helper cannot be expected to exert, does not in fact exert, that cumulative and unremitting pressure by which alone ideas are transformed into policy. 'You cannot come in and out of government, on a week-end, I'll-write-you-a-letter basis,' McGeorge Bundy has testified, 'and expect your opinions to have the kind of impact which in your sense of virtue and of rightness you think they deserve to have upon the process of government ... Nobody ever made a lasting contribution to government by one visit to Washington.'[15] Or, indeed, to Ottawa.

For the intellectual this is bad news. He does not, of course, expect – if he has any worldly wisdom at all – that the policy community will fall all over

14 A rejoinder first suggested by Hans J. Morgenthau; see his essay, 'Truth and Power' in *Truth and Power: Essays of a Decade, 1960-1970* (Praeger, New York 1970), 15
15 'The Scientist and National Policy,' in Sanford A. Lakoff, ed., *Knowledge and Power: Essays on Science and Government* (Free Press, New York 1966), 423

itself in admiration of whatever panacea he happens to take out of his brief-
case, or that the business of government will be abandoned so that his own
project will receive top priority. Still, he may well expect that after a week
or two, a month at most, of patient exposition on his part, the key men will
have been convinced, the memoranda circulated, the proper phone calls made
so that, his mission accomplished, he can return in triumph to his laboratory
or library.

But to expect even that much is to expect much too much. 'What really
bends the processes of government' – it is McGeorge Bundy's testimony again
– 'is continuous, sustained, and intensive effort, generally uncertain at the beginning of what its exact final outcome will be, always responsive to the situation as it is, and continuously aware of the need to be on top of *that* situation,
and not of some abstract plan of what it ought to be, or was when one once
knew it, or would be if only the people in Washington had more sense.'[16] Government, it seems, is a kind of inert mass upon which impression may be made
only by constant and unremitting pressure, by the reiteration of ideas, by un-
relenting advocacy, by constant repetition, as in the Chinese water torture.
And for the intellectual nothing could be more distasteful than this mindless
goading of the great beast of bureaucracy. It offends his esthetic. It is alien to
his habits of work. It runs counter to his cast of mind. The intellectual hates
to repeat himself. Repetition bores him. He wants to get on with the job. The
job is to create, not to convert; to innovate, not to instruct. That is why, even
within the native habitat of the academy, the intellectual is often unsatisfactory as a teacher. Outside his native habitat, in the alien jungle of bureaucracy,
he is worse than unsatisfactory. He is hopeless.

It would be hard enough if the mass were merely inert, the dead-weight
merely dead. But bureaucracy is not just passively uncaring of outsiders in its
midst. It is unalterably hostile towards them. Especially the diplomatic bureaucracy. Here is no simple trade union exclusivity. Its baleful resentment of
hands hired from collateral pursuits is more than the normal jealousy of a profession anxious to keep its ranks free from the meddling of triflers and amateurs. It is as if some invading tribe were attempting the destruction of its
totem. Dean Acheson always writes with acerbity, but he saves his special
scorn to pour upon those 'correspondents, legislators, some academicians, and
most New York lawyers over forty' to whom 'foreign affairs are an open book,
though they often differ on the meaning of the text'[17] – implying clearly
enough that the republic would not be gravely imperilled if for some reason

16   Ibid.
17   Acheson, 'The President and the Secretary of State,' 43

the services of these interlopers were no longer available to it. The official history of the British Foreign Office observes disparagingly of Churchill 'that the Prime Minister ... listened too readily to the opinions of a few advisers of whose opportunities for obtaining full evidence the Foreign Office was less sure.'[18]

Confronted by an environment as inhospitable to his presence as it is unyielding before his argument, the wise outsider will quickly conclude that to help part-time is to help not at all. He may return, sadder if not wiser, to the retreat from whence he came, where we need follow him no longer. Or he may decide to commit his intellect full-time. He gets his leave of absence and signs on for the duration.

As full-time help to government he stands a better chance, but still his chances aren't too good. Either he's accepted by the bureaucracy, or not. If he's not accepted, he's no better off than his part-time associate – though he costs the taxpayer more. If he is accepted by the bureaucracy, it's because he's been won over to its ethos, or that he wraps it around him as a form of protective colouration. So the outsider becomes an insider, the would-be fount of innovation part of the apparatus of inertia. He came to stir things up; he stays to calm things down. There may be new ideas in foreign policy, but they will not come from him.

So the statesman is unlikely to make bureaucracy as he finds it into a cockpit for innovation, or to be able to make it over for that purpose. He is unlikely, too, to draw new ideas from outside help. Then where on earth are his ideas to come from?

The answer is simple. They are to come from his own mind. He has to think them up himself. A statesman incapable of innovation on his own is incapable of statecraft on his own. A statesman incapable of statecraft should find himself another job.

[January 1967]

18   Woodward, *British Foreign Policy in the Second World War,* xliv

6

Force and impotence

Foreign ministers can make their own foreign policies, even if they say they can't. There, in a sentence, is my argument thus far. If foreign ministers are ignorant, they can always acquire knowledge. If they can't foresee the future, they can always plan for its contingencies. If they can't extract ideas from their bureaucracies, they can at least think for themselves.

Now I must face a further difficulty. Suppose our foreign minister to be as knowledgeable, as far-sighted, as imaginative, as it is possible for anyone to be. But suppose that the country for whose foreign affairs he is responsible is a weak country. Suppose that the resources of his community are insufficient to sustain the sorts of policies he would like to initiate on its behalf. Suppose its ore-reserves exhausted, its gold reserves depleted, its industry inefficient, its army ineffective; suppose its institutions are in disarray and its people no longer care. What then may a foreign minister do to save his country and his reputation?

We may as well concede at once that he can't do as much from positions of extreme weakness as he might from positions of great strength. The exercise of sovereignty's a costly exercise. There's no point pretending it isn't so.

There was once a time - and it wasn't long ago - when the paraphernalia of statecraft were few and didn't cost you very much. France paid Rousseau a few francs weekly to represent her in Venice - and, to judge by what he says in his *Confessions,* he overcharged at that. Today, several hundred millions a year - francs, roubles, dollars, pounds - hardly begin to pay for the equipment.

For a start you need an intelligence network. It need not be as elaborate as the Central Intelligence Agency. But it should be large enough to be able to report upon goings-on in those parts of the world of interest to you. And this costs money, which most governments can ill afford to spend. Some spend it all the same - often, it must be admitted, more to buy prestige than to buy intelligence. A few - a very few - buy what intelligence they think they can afford. The government of Ghana has just decided it can no longer afford to maintain about half of its missions abroad and has accordingly closed down its embassies and legations in twenty different countries, including China, Cuba, Zambia, and North Vietnam. Even wealthy countries will hesitate, on account of the cost, to exercise their right of legation as fully as their foreign ministers would like them to. In 1960, the Canadian foreign minister was asked in parliament whether there was 'any likelihood of any mission being established in Baghdad.' Mr Howard Green replied: 'This is a mission I would like very much to have established, and there are others too I would like to have established, but in getting these wishes carried out, I always run foul of the Treasury Board.'[1]

Then there is the bill for propaganda. This is also steep. Even a weekly news-letter, ground out on the embassy duplicator and sent out by second-class mail, costs something over the years. But few countries are content with so modest a programme. The more ramshackle their economy, it sometimes seems, the more elaborate their public relations, as if to conceal the extent of their dilapidation from the rest of the world. And where the object is to sub-vert one's neighbours, rather than to keep up with one's neighbours, the bill is really steep. Public relations becomes psychological warfare. All too easily governments become embroiled in a kind of arms race of the airwaves, in which the weapons are shortwave transmitters and the apparatus, hardly less expensive, for jamming shortwave transmissions. It would be instructive to know how much the government of the United Arab Republic spends on radio propaganda.

Economic warfare is costlier still. In economic warfare, you try to fortify your foreign policy by economic manipulations - manipulations intended to confound the politics and frustrate the knavish tricks of enemies and rivals. And so you hoard currency, in the hope of being able to dump it on the market for foreign exchange at a moment calculated to embarrass and dismay. You hoist your tariff and raise your quota. You refuse to buy and you refuse to sell. You give foreign aid, and you withhold foreign aid. This is all very expensive. Too expensive for the weak. The first foreign policy decision of the newly independent state of Lesotho (formerly Basutoland) was to refuse to join in the sanctions against Rhodesia. 'We cannot expose [our] precarious

1 Canada, *House of Commons Debates,* 15 July 1960, 6377-8

economy,' Chief Jonathan explained to Harold Wilson, 'to the dangers of economic sanctions.' There are those who contend that the British economy itself is too precarious to expose to the dangers of economic sanctions. And it may be still too soon to say that they are wrong.

Finally, we come to the far end of the spectrum of coercion, to the military underpinning of diplomacy, to the region where arms and influence interact. Here is a region which not even the humblest member of the states system has been able to leave alone. And of course the deployment of force, even when the scale is token and the purpose ceremonial, is a charge upon the national purse, a drain upon the national economy. Mount a guard of honour: there will be bills for dry cleaning and for pensions. Maintain, for the same purpose, a nuclear capability – the warheads, the delivery systems, all the accessories of atomic armament which come optional at extra cost: the bill will be in billions. Ask any British taxpayer.

It is by deploying these various instruments of statecraft without wincing at the effort or folding in the attempt that states acquire the name and reputation of great powers. It is by deploying them without counting the cost, or seeming to – in the spirit of J.P. Morgan who, asked by an envious friend about the upkeep of his yacht, replied that if one had to ask about it one couldn't afford it – that great powers acquire the name and reputation of super-powers.

The super-power club is an exclusive club. Its prospective membership is more than a hundred. Its actual membership is two. And even two stretches it a bit. Only the United States pays the dues with the requisite degree of nonchalance. The Soviet Union pays like a navvy in a night club. Oh, he'll meet the tab alright. He'll show the toffs he's got the wad. So he pays in cash and over-tips. It costs him a month's wages. It leaves him red of face and breathing hard. Still, he does pay – and plenty. The Soviet defence bill is $16 billion this year. (The United States' is $70 billion.)

Now we come to a paradox. The paradox consists in the fact that it is precisely the United States and the Soviet Union – the big-time spenders of international society – that seem to be experiencing the most difficulty attaining their respective national purposes, achieving their respective national goals. For all their power, the great powers seem incapable of making their way in the world as they would like to do. For all their superiority, the super-powers seem incapable of making over the world as they would like it to be.

Suppose you were in the position of Mr Kosygin, or of Mr Bhreznev, or of whatever member of the collectivity of leadership is currently decisive in the making of Soviet foreign policy. For what immediate achievement would you wish to be gratefully remembered by the Russian people? I would think as the man who, after twenty years of failure, finally destroyed the spectre of a remilitarized Reich ready once again to lunge at the east, this time with atomic weapons. Why then would you not sign a treaty prohibiting the proliferation of nuclear weapons, as at least a first step towards a secure and peaceful Europe? Surely this is as much a goal of Soviet policy as it is of any policy. And yet no Soviet foreign minister has so far seemed able to take that step. Conversely, what above everything else would you labour to prevent if not the prospect - the incredible, almost bizarre prospect - of a shooting war with the other great member of the communist camp? Yet, in 1967, less than twenty years after the signing of the Sino-Soviet Treaty of Friendship, Alliance and Mutual Assistance, Communist China and Soviet Russia are virtually at war.

Nor is the recent record of the United States any better than this. Whatever American foreign policy may have been, it was not designed to bring about the communist take-over on Cuba, the destruction of North Atlantic unity, least of all that bitter, brutal, detested confrontation on the rimland of Asia against which every strategist, hawk or dove, has warned every administration, Republican or Democratic. Certainly President Johnson and his advisers, as they view with ill-concealed dismay the wreckage of a policy which, after two years of air bombardment and the deployment of a land army of more than 300,000 men, has not yet been able to bring a tiny Asian nation to surrender, may with reason be tempted to believe, with Machiavelli, 'that worldly events are so governed by fortune that men cannot by their prudence change them,' and so 'judge it to be useless to toil much about them.'

What is it, then, condemning these great powers - powers judged great by every index save that of achievement itself - to so sorry a record of failure and frustration? Before trying to answer that question I must first say something of the nature of power.

Adam Smith once wrote a book, which he called *The Wealth of Nations.* And there is nothing wrong with that. The wealth of nations, like the wealth of individuals, may be ascertained by any qualified accountant. Wealthy states, like wealthy individuals, are rich by virtue of having in their possession certain assets - negotiable securities, marketable currencies, saleable commodities, exploitable potentialities - greatly in excess of the per capita average in their respective societies. So it becomes possible to rank states on the basis of their wealth. At one end of the scale you have the Jukes families of the international system - the problem poor, seemingly always with us. At the other end are its Rockefellers and its Gettys, its Lady Dockers and its Lady Eatons.

We know of these individuals that, unquestionably wealthy as they are, they are not necessarily powerful. Wealth may be a means to power; it is no guarantee of power. It may be so among the Kwakiutl Indians, but it is not so among us. Nor is it so among the members of the international system.

This simple perception has for too long been obscured by the notions of geopolitics. The geopolitical interpretations of international society are varied; but they all hold one syllogism to be self-evident. The power of states, so the geopoliticians insist, is a function of their physical strength. Physical strength could be measured, more or less exactly, by taking inventories of its various components. Progress in the infant science of international politics therefore consisted in making more refined and exact calculations of the ratios of power.

The early measurements of power were crude affairs, featuring what has been termed the fallacy of the single factor. In the eighteenth century the physiocratic school fastened on the factor of bullion, prescribing the hoarding of gold as the means to power. Voltaire is said to have remarked that God is on the side of the biggest battalions, from which a later generation of strategists derived the proposition that God is on the side of the biggest standing army. Or, as Winston Churchill once thought, on the side of the biggest standing navy. 'For consider these ships,' he wrote of the Royal Navy on the eve of battle in the First World War:

On them ... floated the might, majesty, dominion and power of the British Empire. All our long history built up century after century, all our great affairs in every part of the globe, all the means of our faithful, industrious, active population, depended on them. Open the sea-cocks and let them sink beneath the surface ... and, in a few minutes, half an hour at the most, the whole outlook of the world would be changed.[2]

Geopolitics proper got its name from the identification of power not so much with special sources of wealth or special kinds of weapons systems as with particular regions of the world. Among the earliest geopoliticians – though he would not have recognized the term – we must place Lord Curzon, for his argument that 'as long as we rule India, we are the greatest Power in the world. If we lose it, we shall drop straight away to a third-rate power.' That was perhaps a natural thing for a viceroy of India to say. But Sir Halford Mackinder, who said much the same thing in more pseudo-scientific language, was not so occupationally biased as was Curzon. It was Mackinder who developed and publicized the celebrated doctrine: 'Who rules East Europe commands the Heartland; who rules the Heartland commands the World-Island; who rules the World-Island commands the World.' Heady stuff for would-be conquerors. The line of descent from Mackinder to Hitler, via the German geopolitician Karl Haushofer, is clear and direct. Nor was it Hitler who proved Mackinder wrong. The Red Army proved Hitler wrong.

2 *The World Crisis* (Odhams Press, London 1923), 123-4

So it was that geopolitics, far from discredited by the Second World War, acquired a new lease on life. A new school of geopoliticians – one might call them the neo-geopoliticians – less doctrinaire, less ideological in their approach than their predecessors, tightened their grip upon the theory of the states system. Into the calculation of the might of nations they fed new variables and fresh components. First came the fuels and techniques of the second industrial revolution: to possess pools of petroleum, fields of natural gas, iron ore, and uranium ore, was to possess the ingredients of power. These, and industrial capacity. Above all, industrial capacity. For what had been demonstrated by the Second World War if not that victory had gone to the biggest mass producers rather than to the biggest battalions? The atomic bomb may have defeated Japan, but Hitler's armies had lost to the arsenals of democracy. Not General Montgomery or General Eisenhower, but Henry Ford and Henry Kaiser had really won that war – won it on the battlefields of Willow Run and Gary, Indiana. The power of states, hitherto identified with ore reserves and troop reserves, was now identified with factory floor space, machine tool production, kilowatts generated, engineers graduated. Neo-geopolitics was made in USA more exactly, made in Princeton, with some assistance from the University of Pennsylvania. And for Americans, neo-geopolitics was a comforting doctrine; for, on its reckoning, the 'balance of tomorrow' – to use the title of one of the best known works in its literature[3] – lay securely with the United States. Or so it seemed at the time.

The post-war generation of students of international politics was taught to deal as well in less tangible components of national power. After all, it was told, Germany had produced tanks and aircraft and air-breathing missiles even under the terrible pounding of the Allied air offensive of 1943 and 1944; yet Germany had lost the war. Was there not then something more to the power of states than their capacity to send men into battle and to keep them supplied with food and ammunition? Were not the character of their peoples, the quality of their institutions, the nature of their ideas about society, no less telling ingredients of power than tin or tungsten, heavy industry, ferrous metallurgy? Which, all else being equal, conferred greater power upon a state – democratic government or totalitarian government? Dictators could chop and change – witness the Nazi-Soviet Pact – but democracies (so democrats hopefully supposed) would win out in the end by virtue of their higher political morality and their more sturdy common sense. Did the pragmatic Anglo-Saxons (if they were really more pragmatic) possess more power than the more doctri-

---

3   Robert Strausz-Hupé, *The Balance of Tomorrow* (G.P. Putnam's Sons, New York 1945)

naire Russians (if indeed they were more doctrinaire)? These were the kind of questions to which the post-war generation of students of international politics were encouraged to find the answers. As a member of that generation, I can recall being convinced, along with the rest, that the questions were interesting, that they were relevant, that, if you pondered them long enough and hard enough, you would discover correct answers.

And we were wrong. Hopelessly wrong. For the whole exercise of adding up the components of national power and reckoning the power of states on the basis of which ones got the highest score turned out to be an exercise in futility. It tried to quantify the qualitative, to measure the intangible. It assumed a coefficient of reduction where none could possibly exist. It rested on a simple, yet basic, confusion of language. We thought we were computing the power of nations. What we were really doing was assessing the might of nations. We mistook force for power, the part for the whole. It was a grave mistake. For force is only one of the components of power. It is no longer even the most important, as I shall now try to show.

What do we mean when we say that the United States is a powerful state? We're not talking (if we're at all careful of our terminology) about the resources at the disposal of the United States. What we're talking about is the ability of the United States to have its way with other states. Power consists in having things your way.

To have things your own way, it sometimes helps to be strong. But it doesn't always help. There are other ways of having your way besides pushing people around. Friendly persuasion, for example.

And here's something else. The capacity to push people around is not the same thing as the ability to push people around. A mighty state may hesitate to use its might. Whereas a state deficient in all of the usual components of strength may sometimes get its own way, often in the face of greatly superior force. Power and force, so far from being directly correlated, may even be inversely correlated. It may so happen that to add to your force will diminish your power. It is just this perplexing consideration which, among others, is causing the United States to hesitate before taking a decision to deploy an anti-missile missile system.

That force and power were not the perfect correlates all previous strategy had assumed them to be first became apparent at the turn of the twentieth century. British liberals derided the size of the expeditionary force sent out to crush the Boers in South Africa. It was like crushing a walnut with a sledgehammer. But for a time it seemed as if the walnut was made of iron, and the sledgehammer fatally flawed, as Smuts and his commandos roamed at will throughout Cape Colony, sniping, raiding, retreating, escaping – always escaping. With less and less discrimination the imperial sledgehammer flailed about, laying waste to farms and villages, livestock and crops, in what would today be described as a campaign of defoliation and then – a more candid age than ours – was described as a campaign of barbarism. Smuts in his diary tells graphically of its results:

Last night at Zandspruit. Dams everywhere full of rotting animals; water undrinkable. Veld covered with slaughtered herds of sheep and goats, cattle and horses ... But the saddest sight of all is the large number of little lambs, staggering from hunger and thirst around the corpses of their dead and mangled mothers ... Surely such outrages on man and nature must move to a certain doom.[4]

Smuts was moved by the blood of the lambs. But it must be remembered that the British were guilty of more than mere cruelty to animals. By the time the Boers surrendered, 26,000 of their small civilian population had perished in British concentration camps.

The duel between sledgehammer and walnut turned into a contest between Goliath and David, one to be repeated many times over the next fifty years and during which the going for Goliath got tougher all the time. His clear-cut victories – like those of Stalin over the Baltic states, Khrushchev over Hungary – were obvious mis-matches, bringing little credit to the victor. Often his victories were far from clear-cut – like those of Lloyd George over Ireland, Stalin, again, over Finland. And in recent years, like an aging heavyweight, he has begun to lose. France lost to Algeria, the United States to Cuba. In Vietnam the fight goes on, the outcome still in doubt. But even if, as is by no means certain, the United States should prevail, it will not emerge the victor. Already its reputation for power has suffered, and its reputation for magnanimity has suffered severely. A people emerging from warfare as weaklings and bullies in the eyes of the world can hardly be said to have won their war.

So the Goliaths of our time have sustained shattering and perhaps irremediable reverses of their fortune. What has brought these about? What reasons are there for so drastic a waning in the capacity of might to attain the goals of policy? Whence derives the impotence of force?

It derives, I believe, from three facts of international life in the second half of our century. The first fact, and the foremost, is the dread of the great powers of thermonuclear war.

---

4 Quoted in W.K. Hancock, *Smuts*, I, *The Sanguine Years, 1870-1919* (Cambridge University Press, Cambridge 1962), 137

That British government which authorized its troops to imprison the families of their enemy, slaughter their livestock, and burn their farms had no reason to fear that some outside state, rallying to the victims of these atrocities, might obliterate the British Isles in a devastating assault lasting a few hours, or a few minutes. Half a century later such indifference was no longer possible. As the invading Anglo-French army stormed ashore at Port Said on 6 November 1956, Marshal Bulganin threatened what he called, in a message to Sir Anthony Eden, 'other means, such as a rocket technique ... to crush the aggressors and to restore peace in the East.' Eden writes in his memoirs that his government considered the Soviet threat to be a bluff which 'need not be taken literally.'[5] His ambassador in Moscow, summoned to the Kremlin in the early morning to receive the disconcerting news, was disposed to treat it not so lightly. 'There was,' as the ambassador recalls he cabled at once to London,

an element of bullying bluff in it. But I was afraid that the Soviet Government were working themselves up into a very ugly mood ... I thought they might ... take some violent independent action against our forces in the Middle East by submarines or aircraft.[6]

Even if, as Sir Anthony Eden contends, the Soviet threat played no part in the British decision to cease their fire, it ought to have played a large part. It certainly played a large part in the calculations of President Kennedy and his advisers at the time of the Cuban missile crisis six years later. 'We have won a considerable victory,' Dean Rusk remarked to his deputy on 23 October 1962. 'You and I are still alive.'[7]

The second fact of modern international life accounting for the impotence of force and the weakness of great powers is the nature of the only kind of war great powers are free to fight. This is not big war, thermonuclear war. It is little war, guerrilla war. And for Great Powers no experience is more frustrating.

It frustrates not least because the targets are so few, and so fleeting. The American strategy of bombing communication routes in North Vietnam would have worked fine had the Ho Chi Minh trail resembled the Pennsylvania Turnpike, the North Vietnamese railway system the New York Central system. But any resemblance is coincidental. The trail is patched, the line repaired, and the lorries and the boxcars, the bicycles and the runners, flow on. In guerrilla warfare supplies can be diverted but rarely destroyed.

5   *Full Circle* (Cassell, London 1960), 555
6   Sir William Hayter, *The Kremlin and the Embassy* (Hodder and Stoughton, London 1966), 146-7
7   Quoted in Elie Abel, *The Missile Crisis* (Bantam Books, New York & Toronto 1966), 110

It frustrates, too, because the enemy knows more about what's going on. After all, it's his country. He may be a stranger from the North. But his home's a few hundred kilometres distant, at most, he's fought in the delta for years, and he speaks the local dialect - if not perfectly, at any rate better than the young American shipped out three weeks ago from Pasadena, whom he is just about to kill. There's always an intelligence gap in these conflicts between great powers and their guerrilla opponents, in which the great power is invariably disadvantaged. So it was in the Boer War. So it was in the Irish War. So it is in the Vietnam War.

The third fact from which derives the impotence of force is the heightened constraint of opinion. The constraint of opinion's nothing new. What little news trickled back from South Africa outraged British Liberals sixty years ago: had they been fully aware of the extent of atrocity it might not have been permitted. Lloyd George and Churchill were surely spared humiliation by the Irish delegation's yielding, in 1921, to their threat of 'immediate and terrible war' if it did not meet their terms: the British public would not have stood for such a war, and their threat was but a bluff.

What is new is modern journalism, and its ability to place the news and images of war before an audience of unprecedented size with unprecedented speed, unprecedented accuracy, unprecedented vividness. Communications theorists may be left to debate among themselves which of these qualities is the most decisive. The most dramatic, without question, is television. With its ability to portray as it happens the helicopter-gunships firing on the villages below, the napalm searing the jungle, the Marine's cigarette-lighter held as an incendiary to the thatch, television quite properly receives the lion's share of praise - or blame - for the publicity in which the Vietnam War is being fought. But the role of the newspaper, though less dramatic, has been no less telling. With such inquiring reporters as Harrison Salisbury of *The New York Times* at large, governments can less easily than hitherto protect themselves by lying. If truth is the first casualty of warfare, untruth is a principal weapon of warfare. It is a weapon no longer to be used with impunity. Great powers are being compelled to divest themselves of it by great newspapers.

Even among the most liberally-minded of administrations there will be found hard-nosed men prepared to defy the opinion of all those publics save that which needs to be placated so that they may remain in office. There is on record the proceedings of a meeting of advisers of the Kennedy administration, convened to decide whether or not to recommend the resumption of testing nuclear weapons in the atmosphere. When someone opposed it, on the ground that it would not find favour with world opinion, John J. McCloy, then special disarmament adviser to the President, exploded in anger. '"World opinion? I don't believe in world opinion. The only thing that matters is power. What we have to do now is to show that we are a powerful nation and not spend our time trailing after the phantom of world opinion."[8] That view did not prevail. Nor did it prevail a year later, when many of the same advisers urged upon the President the wisdom of an immediate air strike against the Cuban missile sites. Kennedy would not have it. Surprise attack was not part of the American tradition. It was ruled out, he said, by 'a decent regard for humanity.'

There is such a thing as world opinion, and great powers are increasingly reluctant to defy it. Especially reluctant is the greatest of all great powers. The United States needs no outsider to remind it to pay a decent respect to the opinions of mankind. Its Declaration tells it to. Its conscience tells it to. Its people tell it to. It is a nobler country for that. It is a weaker country for that.

[January 1967]

8 Quoted in Arthur M. Schlesinger, *A Thousand Days: John F. Kennedy in the White House* (Houghton Mifflin, Boston 1965), 481-2

7

Weakness and power

The waning capacity of force to attain the goals of foreign policy provides the foreign ministers of great powers with some excuse for failure. An American foreign minister, or a Russian, may well point to that paradox of power by which force has been rendered impotent to exonerate his far from adequate performance. But it does not excuse the profession at large. The obverse of the impotence of force, which I have discussed, is the potency of weakness, which I now discuss.

The paradox of power operates to the advantage of small states, as it does to the disadvantage of the great. Great powers may aptly be compared to the albatross in a poem by Baudelaire. The albatross is the most majestic of the birds. Well may it take a certain consolatory pride in its magnificent dimensions. The spread of its immense wings inspires awe and wonder. But its wings are too heavy for it to take to the air. It is immobilized by its own weight. And so it squats, sullen and disconsolate, less awesome than absurd, as all around it the smaller birds – puffins and gulls, cormorants and terns – wheel and dip with abandon, snatching food within its range, sometimes from its beak. The paradox of power has made small states into great states, middle powers into great powers. Their foreign ministers are less justified than ever in seeking consolation in fatalism and invoking determinism in their defence.

When, at the dawn of the modern states system, Machiavelli presented Lorenzo the Magnificent with his classic exposition of the scope for free will afforded by foreign policy to those sufficiently wise and daring to take his advice, there was no such thing as great powers and small powers. Lorenzo's universe was confined conveniently to the Italian peninsula, in which five evenly matched units of power – his own Florence, Naples, Rome, Milan, and Venice – vied for an ascendancy as fleeting and unstable as the pattern formed by a kaleidoscope. What went on in other places was of no account to them. The realms of north-west Europe, shrouded in fog and mist, went their own way, forming, as we should now say, a regional sub-system within the states system. The Americas, as yet undiscovered, played no part at all in the calculations of statecraft. With the great civilizations of the Euphrates and further out in Asia, some tentative contact was being made; but it was contact for trade, not for diplomacy. Not until Perry's black ships dropped anchor in Tokyo Bay, three centuries later, would the lands of the far east enter the modern states system. Their entry, so long delayed, proved disruptive: we are still experiencing the shock.

One cannot speak of small states without great powers to compare them to; and the great power is a late arrival upon the international scene. It is not a new species of polity, but a permutation of the small state, several of which, more or less digested, go to make it up. By the end of the nineteenth century, the great powers of Europe had all been formed, with the Italian principalities among the last to disappear.

The small states, before the First World War, consisted of those regions or enclaves, in and about the European system, which for one reason or another had not been absorbed within the sovereignty of a great power. Their relations with the great powers may be simply described. It was a relationship of vassalage. Their independence of action depended upon the wishes of the great powers – not so much of any one of them as of all of them together. For this was the era of the Concert of Europe, when the great powers managed the states system collectively, so as to make sure that their individual peace and prosperity would not be rudely disturbed by unruly deeds in tiny countries. A small state, in such conditions, could hardly be a trouble-maker. Even its internal affairs were scrutinized by the Concert lest some instability in their capitals – a popular uprising, a dynastic dispute – threaten the stability of the system. The small state existed on sufferance only.

But then so did the Concert. It was only so long as the great powers repressed the desire to strike out individually on their own for whatever spoils their power might bring them that small powers could be kept in line. When the great powers fell out among themselves, the small powers could try to play them off against each other, perhaps to their advantage. By the end of the nineteenth century, the great powers were falling out among themselves. The Concert of Europe gave way to the rivalries of Europe, in which the small powers became embroiled. Their influence, in such an environment, was great. Their influence was the kind of influence a blackmailer acquires over a wealthy victim – potent while it lasts, but likely to be of short duration and to end abruptly in a manner unpleasant for them both. Their power, in such an environment, was also great. But their power was the kind of power wielded by a pyromaniac in a fireworks factory – the power to blow everybody up, including himself. It was a small state, Serbia, which has the distinction of having been the efficient cause of the bloodbath in which the old Europe drowned itself, drenching the rest of the world.

By the time the peacemakers had finished their work, the small state had come into its own as never before. What on the map of nineteenth-century Europe had been exceptional and aberrational became on the map of interregnum Europe – Europe between its wars – typical and commonplace. Out of the empires of the defeated powers, the new small states were carved. No master chef could have so surely aroused the appetite of his ravening customers with morsels more tasty or more tempting. Neither too small to be thought worthless nor too large to be thought indigestible, Czechoslovakia and Poland lay defenceless on their platters, until they were devoured. Their power consisted in what appeal their plight could make to the conscience of the community. But, like the screams of the political prisoner dragged away to beating and to torture, their cries came too late to save themselves, too late – almost – to save the community which they had sought to arouse.

I have spoken before of the lessons of history. Here was a lesson the peacemakers after the Second World War were determined to learn, and to apply. They sought security by reviving the concert system of the earlier nineteenth century. The four great powers – the 'four horsemen,' as Roosevelt called the governments of Britain and France, the Soviet Union and America – built the United Nations upon the cornerstone of great power hegemony. They, and they alone, should have responsibility for the safety of the society of nations. They, and they alone, should collectively determine when that safety was imperilled. They, and they alone, should decide if, when, and how that safety might be restored. They created a Security Council for the purpose, and assigned themselves commanding and unassailable positions upon it. They would protect small powers from aggression; the price for their protection was that small powers, like small children, should be seen but not heard.

For some small powers this price seemed much too high. And there were by this time – the year is 1945 – plenty of small powers willing and able to raise a ruckus. At San Francisco, where the Big Four offered the draft United Nations charter to its prospective membership on a largely take-it-or-leave-it basis, a few statesmen from the smaller states were almost inclined to leave it. The great powers, declaimed the delegate of Mexico in some disgust, wanted 'a world order in which the mice could be stamped out but in which the lions would not be restrained'; the Australians and New Zealanders were even more outspokenly indignant. But indignation is a notoriously poor basis for negotiation. Against the united front of the great powers it was to no avail. Occasionally a statesman of the great powers might consent to meet the small powers' protest by more or less reasoned argument – as when the United States' representative, Senator Tom Connally, pointed an accusing finger at a protesting New Zealander and demanded to know 'where you, Mr Berendson, would ... be today if the United States had to ask the United Nations for permission to defend your country even before the South Pacific had run red with American blood?' There was no good answer to this rhetorical question. There was no good answer, either, to Connally's still more flamboyant intervention. 'You may go home from San Francisco,' he told the delegations of the small powers, 'and report that you have defeated the veto. But you can also say, "We tore up the Charter." At that point,' the senator records with pride, 'I sweepingly ripped the Charter draft in my hands to shreds and flung the scraps upon the table.'[1] With them were flung as well the hopes of the small powers for an international organization in which they would control their destiny. Their indignation changed mostly to despondency, the delegates returned to their capitals to secure ratification of a charter not of their making and not to their liking.

God moves in a mysterious way. The United Nations, so far from proving a restriction upon the freedom of small states, has turned out to be the principal asset in their quest for power and influence.

Had the great powers continued their concert of convenience into the postwar era, one would not be speaking now of the potency of weakness. One would be speaking, if at all, about the potency of strength. But the Concert fell apart, if indeed it had ever really existed. Instead of great power unity, there was great power disagreement. The states system quickly fractionated into its two opposing camps. Small powers again became pawns of Great Powers, as in the late nineteenth century, but this time with a difference. What had already, by 1947 or 1948, acquired familiarity as the Cold War was no mere dispute over trade and commerce, territory and spoils. It was a war over principles, over the content of truth, an ideological war. When wars are fought for ideas, the fighters don't change sides. So it proved in the Cold War. Neither the allies of the Soviet Union – the Americans called them 'satellites' – nor the allies of the United States – the Russians called them 'imperialist stooges' – enjoyed even that limited room for manoeuvre that comes from selling one-

1 *My Name is Tom Connally* (Crowell, New York 1954), 265

self to the highest bidder: when the Americans offered aid to eastern Europe, Stalin put his foot down. The small power, whether Soviet satellite or imperialist stooge, had still to come into its own.

It came into its own during the later 1950s, taking advantage of the mutual paralysis of the great powers following their acquisition of thermonuclear weapons and long-range missiles, taking advantage, too, of the mellowing of Soviet policies following the death of Stalin. But what was most important was the tremendous swelling of their ranks, as the former colonies of the imperial powers – mainly of Britain and France – broke away from the metropolitan country like floes sloughing off from some great Greenland icefield and floating out into the open sea. Some of these new states were not much bigger than the ice floes, and almost as barren of resources. In an earlier era – after the First World War, for example – most of them would have been held to be unfit for independence and would have been made wards of great powers under the mandate system created by the League of Nations in order to dispose, in the words of its Covenant, of 'those colonies and territories ... inhabited by peoples not yet able to stand by themselves under the strenuous conditions of the modern world.' Conditions have become if anything more strenuous since then: but weakness was no longer allowed to serve as a pretext for delaying independence to any people who wished it. A General Assembly resolution, passed on 14 December 1960, made that official. Henceforward there could be no such thing as an unviable political community, for viability was held to consist in having the existing members of the states system prepared to treat new applicants for membership as if they were viable. This they have been only too ready to do, with the consequence that when the General Assembly met for its regular twenty-first session, it had more than twice as many member states as were assembled for its first session twenty years before. Among the first items of business was the election of the 121st member of the United Nations. The 121st member is Barbados. It has an area of 166 square miles and a population of 250,000.

If the presence of such tiny states within the states system is not altogether grotesque, it is their membership of the United Nations that saves them from ridicule. For it is the United Nations – once reviled by the small powers as robbing them of even that slight degree of independence of mind and spirit to which they felt themselves entitled – that has enabled the small powers to come into their own. More exactly, it is the General Assembly – that General Assembly which, in spite of, indeed, in defiance of, the Charter came in time to be entrusted with the work of security restoration and of peace supervision which the Security Council, because of the rivalry of its permanent members, had proved unable to perform. In the General Assembly, all states – large or small, strong or feeble, with 200 million people or 200 thousand people – become, in one aspect of their being, identical. They each have one vote. In the Assembly, the mighty are put down from their seats, and those of low degree exalted. Little wonder that nearly all new nations make membership of the United Nations the first and most important task of foreign policy. Of fifty or sixty new nations attaining independence in the last ten years, only one – Western Samoa – has declined, on grounds of economy, to accept a membership that would have been hers for the asking.

'The humblest nation of all the world, when clad in the armor of a righteous cause, is stronger than all the hosts of error.' With this recklessly extravagant quotation President Kennedy complimented the Irish nation, when he spoke to its parliament in Dublin on 28 June 1963. The Irish parliamentarians, well accustomed to blarney, may not have treated this proposition too seriously, and well they might not. Righteous causes have no more afforded protection to humble nations than did the ointment with which primitive tribes in Africa smeared themselves in the belief that it would repel the bullets of the white invaders. If the desire to live quietly at peace with one's own and with one's neighbours may be accepted as a righteous cause, the history of our times is a history of the frustration of that desire by ruthless and unprincipled bully states. In the long run, perhaps, they do not prevail. But in the long run, alas, their victims do not survive to enjoy the victories of righteousness.

To many of the small new nations of the modern world, such gloomy reflections seem wholly out of place. They have preferred to believe, as an article of faith, that power does flow from the righteousness of their cause, and that it flows with sufficient strength and force to enable them to prevail against more conventionally armoured rivals. The righteous cause in which they placed their trust was the cause of what they describe variously as positive neutralism, or positive non-alignment. Their emphasis is always on the positive, to contrast their position from the old-fashioned neutrality of the states of pre-war Europe. Certainly the fate of the little neutral states over-run by the Wehrmacht in April 1940 inspires no faith in the power of righteousness. Even those neutrals which escaped that fate – Sweden and Switzerland – endured severe restrictions upon their autonomy in order to survive. One authority describes them as 'rather like small sailboats, which used the more powerful elements to drive them obliquely along their course, tacking when necessary and constantly trimming their sails to gain the greatest advantage from the wind but never pressing too close to it nor venturing into the open sea.' This is not at all how the navigators of positive neutralism were prone to describe their feats of navigation. Recall Kwame Nkrumah: 'We face the hazards of the

high seas alone ... I proudly stand on the bridge of that lone vessel as she confidently sets sail ... and scan the horizon. There is so much more beyond.' What
gave them the confidence to embark was their belief that they were setting out
upon a civilizing mission. Seeing themselves in this role, they strongly objected
to the notion, sometimes put abroad by their critics, that they were in any
sense uncommitted or uncaring. 'We are committed up to the hilt,' the prime
minister of Ceylon told the General Assembly. 'We are committed to preserve
decency in dealings between nations.' And the prime minister of Tanganyika:
'We do care, passionately, about the development of justice, of well-being, and
of peace, throughout the world.'

It was one thing to espouse such righteous causes, another to try to corner
the market. All too often the positive neutralists implied, if they did not say
outright, that they and they alone were fit custodians of international morality. That new nations, just because they were new, that small states, just because they were small, that black peoples, just because they were black, were
somehow nobler, fairer, better, than the rest.

These are separate contentions, requiring separate examination. The argument from colour – black superiority – is a racist argument, no less potent for
that, perhaps more potent for that, but hardly requiring reasoned refutation.
Colour confers neither superior wisdom nor superior morality. There is something to be said for the argument from newness. To be a new nation is to have
had little time in which to engage in the iniquities of modern statecraft. But
history soon takes care of that. Finally, the argument from smallness. 'We
small nations,' remarked the prime minister of Trinidad not long ago, 'have
only our principles.' That may be so, but it does not make them principled.
There is no evidence that small states are more virtuous than great powers.
They may lack the instruments for doing wrong on the grand scale, so that
the great crimes of our century – aggression and genocide – lie beyond their
reach. But there's no virtue in necessity. Nor are small states necessarily virtuous. Their agents are among the most spectacular violators of the Geneva Conventions: North Vietnam condoning, without visible remorse, the decapitation
of civilians, Egypt engaging in poison gas warfare. This is not to say small states
are any more delinquent than the great powers. It's just that they're not no-
ticeably better behaved. Not enough, at any rate, to brag about it.

If President Kennedy was being more rhetorical than analytical in telling his
Irish audience that their small country, like small countries everywhere, derived power from righteousness, he was correct in telling them that it might
derive power from ideas. 'We need men who can dream of things that never
were,' he said, 'and ask why not.' And he went on to suggest that 'it matters

not how small a nation is that seeks world peace and freedom.' Its contribution may be great, however small its size. Force is the monopoly of the great
powers, for all the good it does them. But great powers enjoy no monopoly
over ideas. The foreign minister of a small state may not be able to summon
a gunboat in aid of his diplomacy, to carry a big stick let alone to brandish it.
But he can carry a brief-case well enough, and stock it with proposals.

Even more than great powers, small states may exploit this source of
power. Great powers, just because they have more than their fair share of the
wealth of this world, are not inclined to innovation except to protect and add
to what is already theirs. They are fearful of change, which for them is for the
worse. Opportunities for progress are best ignored, temptations to try new
ways are best resisted. The known present, unsatisfactory as it may be, seems
preferable to a future filled with uncertainty. They are solaced by the status
quo.

For small states it is all very different, or ought to be. They have no vested
interest save in changing the system that treats them so shabbily. Change for
them is for the better. Opportunities for progress are to be seized, temptations
to try new ways to be yielded to. An uncertain future, uncertain as it may be,
seems preferable to the present so unsatisfactory for them. They are solaced
by the prospect of change.

Having little to lose, and much to gain, the small states of the states system
are the natural innovators within the states system. The smaller the state, the
more acceptable its innovation, for its suggestions more than those of greater
powers are likely to be disinterested and directed towards the general welfare.
This point was made by Pope Paul VI when he addressed the General Assembly
of the United Nations in his capacity as temporal leader of Vatican City, the
tiniest state of all. 'We have nothing to ask for,' he told his fellow delegates.
'We have at most a desire to express and a permission to request: namely, that
of serving you in so far as lies within Our competence, with disinterest, humi-
lity and love. That,' added the pontiff, with exquisite irony, 'is so simple that
it may seem insignificant to this Assembly, which is accustomed to dealing
with most important and most difficult matters.' No message could have been
more significant - except perhaps that which Paul proceeded to place before
its members. 'If you wish to be brothers,' he told them, 'lay down your weapons.'[2]

Left to their own devices, great powers will never accept this advice. A
great power never goes into a disarmament conference intending to lay down
its weapons. It goes there intending to increase its armed force vis-à-vis that of

2   *The New York Times*, 5 Oct. 1965

its rivals. The gap between their preaching and their practice, between their declared purpose and their real purpose, has grown so wide and persisted for so long that today their governments sometimes don't even bother to conceal their cynicism and their insincerity. 'It's gotten to the point,' Dean Rusk has conceded,

where, in our conversations, we've been able to refer to the arguments by the numbers. He would make an argument – the [Soviet] Ambassador or Foreign Minister – and I can say: "Well, you know our position on that. This is Argument Number Five. Shall I repeat it, or shall we save time and go on?" And they'll smile and say: "Well, we'll perhaps go on to some other subject."[3]

It lies within the power of small states to prevent great powers going on to some other subject. They can compel them to stick with the subject at hand, whatever it may be – the spread of nuclear weapons, the testing of nuclear weapons, the demilitarization of outer space. They can compel them to negotiate seriously, rather than by rote and ritual. If serious negotiation on Plan A produces no agreement, they can compel them to consider Plans B and C. The methods by which the small powers may hope to coerce the great consist in their persistence and determination, their fertility of device and idea, and their readiness to invoke the sanction of public opinion. The motive for the small powers wanting to compel the great is the motive of self-interest, than which none is more effective. So long as the great powers remain deadlocked on disarmament, the interests of small powers are bound to suffer. Stalemate may suit the strong but it is intolerable for the weak. It perpetuates their misery, it intensifies their danger. 'Those terrible weapons that modern science has given you,' Pope Paul reminded their custodians, 'long before they produce victims and ruins, cause bad dreams, foster bad feelings, create nightmares, distrust and sombre resolves; they demand enormous expenditures; they obstruct projects of solidarity and useful work; they falsify the very psychology of peoples.'[4]

The responsibility borne by small states for the peace and prosperity of the states system, so far from being small, is really very great. There is much for them to do, much which only they can do. And it is not unrealistic to expect them to be equal to the challenge. They have not done too badly in the recent past, for it is out of the briefcases of the foreign ministers of smaller powers that many of its significant initiatives originate. It was Lester Pearson

3 Quoted in *Our Generation Against Nuclear War*, II, no 3, 40. Rusk made these remarks in a CBS interview in Jan. 1963.
4 *The New York Times*, 5 Oct. 1965

of Canada who contrived the United Nations Emergency Force; Adam Rapacki of Poland who developed the idea of disengagement in central Europe; Frank Aitken of Ireland who first proposed a non-proliferation treaty; Östen Undén of Sweden who first suggested the formation of a non-nuclear club; Per Haekkerup of Denmark who first exposed, like the child in the fable of his countryman, the nudity of NATO doctrine.

All this being so, the foreign ministers of smaller countries have little to excuse them when they tell us, as they often do, that their hands are tied by Fate, that nothing can be done. Either they deceive themselves, or they deceive us, or they disclose by their admission that they do not understand what makes the modern world go round. For any or all of these reasons their usefulness to us is at an end. They should make way, or be made to make way, for those who are ready, at long last, to allow Will to take charge.

[January 1967]

8

Stupidity and power

Suppose, for a change, we judge statesmen not for effort but for result. (We all know Dean Rusk put in a sixteen-hour day, no one accuses Andrei Gromyko of slacking.) Statesmen of the super-powers, if they don't deserve an 'F' for failure, can't be rated higher than a dismal 'D.' They've fouled their environment. They've squandered patrimonies which, prudently invested, could have made the lives of their nations, and of their neighbours, decent, prosperous, and secure.

Much is written lately of the excruciating aspects of power – its agony, its arrogance, its impotence. A chapter should be saved for the stupidity of power. It is hard to tell which front has been allowed to sag more – the foreign or domestic. It is hard to tell which super-power has messed things up more – the Russian or American. The failure of super-power statesmanship is not the whole story of world politics in the sixties, but it may serve to sum it up in half-a-dozen words.

What follows are comments on American folly. That is because Americans obligingly put their folly on the record, allowing us to account for it as well as make an inventory of it. The Russians are more secretive. But while they may conceal their motives they cannot conceal their record. It is no less messy than their rival's. Khrushchev's infantile attack upon the United Nations in 1960. The reckless gamble that he could put missiles into Cuba and get away with it. His breach with his Communist Chinese ally. The elementary blunders in farm and factory management. The brutal silencing of artists and intellectuals. These add up to a policy as erratic and destructive of Russian power and prestige as might be wished by the most bitter anti-Soviet emigré. And Khrushchev's successors haven't done much better. Is 'F' for failure too harsh a grade for leadership which first arms the Arab states, lets them off their leash, stands by mute and inglorious while the Israeli air force shoots up billions of roubles' worth of sophisticated Soviet weapons, then re-arms the Arabs for another round? Or for a leadership which, unable to tell liberal communism from social fascism, sends the Red Army into Czechoslovakia, tipping the scales of power the other way and forfeiting respect throughout the world? Khrushchev at least had *chutzpah* going for him; the most that may be said of the vapid stewardship of Brezhnev and Kosygin is that it has survived.

Nor does stressing super-power stupidity imply small-power sapience. On the contrary. Small-power statecraft of the sixties is marked by rancour and short-sightedness. Tiny federations fail, sandcastle sovereignties clutter up the system. Delegations from micro-states harangue the United Nations with maxi-speeches, sending it to sleep. From one of the tiniest states comes one of the sorriest policies: Vatican City is keen on arms control, not so keen on birth control. 'The Church is consistent with herself when she considers recourse to the infecund periods to be licit, while at the same time condemning, as being always illicit, the use of means directly contrary to fecundation, even if such use is inspired by reasons which may appear honest and serious.' These words are the operative part of Paul's encyclical *Humanae Vitae,* which might more aptly be called *Humanae Mori*; for, unless rescinded, unless ignored, it will lead millions to untimely death.

Historians deal harshly with the Eisenhower presidency. But Ike didn't leave America in such bad shape. The United States in 1960 was at peace with her enemies and in reasonable harmony with her friends. Neither his predecessor nor the three presidents which followed could claim as much.

In 1960, new weapons systems – the underground Minuteman missiles, the undersea Polaris submarines – were coming into service, placing American security on a firmer foundation of assured destruction capability. De Gaulle, restive in NATO, had yet to rend its fabric. Cuba could still be lived with. The Soviets were truculent, but that was nothing new. China was inscrutable, but the familiar mushroom cloud was still to climb above her deserts.

As the world outside seemed tranquil, so the land within seemed calm. Students sallied forth on raids, but of women's dormitories, not deans' offices. The man from Dow was welcome on the campus. Down south, the Negro plodded patiently towards his rights. A desegregated Woolworth lunch-counter seemed a major blow for freedom. To be poor was an un-American activity. Poverty happened in other countries, frankly known as 'backward.' The air was fresh, the rivers ran pure.

Borne by a strong current in favourable weather, the prudent oarsman rests on his oars, conserving strength for treacherous waters ahead. That was not how, in 1960, John Kennedy could hope to wrest the presidency from its heir-apparent, Richard Nixon. Instead he had to talk up a storm, and he did.

When the presidency became his, he did not let the storm of talk subside. 'Let the word go forth from this time and place, to friend and foe alike, that the torch has been passed to a new generation of Americans – born in this century, tempered by war, disciplined by a hard and bitter peace, proud of our ancient heritage.' 'Let every nation know, whether it wishes us well or ill, that we shall pay any price, bear any burden, meet any hardship, support any friend, oppose any foe, to assure the survival and the success of liberty.' A bluster inaugural from the pulpit. But it wasn't bluff – unfortunately.

From that pulpit, like Teddy Roosevelt before him, JFK preached 'not the doctrine of ignoble ease, but the doctrine of the strenuous life.' The strenuous life was more cheaply led in Roosevelt's time. Kennedy's cost billions of dollars and millions of limbs. Who would now say it was worth them?

The Kennedy style of *Sturm und Drang* was not dictated by expediency alone. It came naturally to one who, as an undergraduate, precociously excoriated appeasement, lambasted England as a nation of sleep-walkers, seized on Churchill as his hero. But where in the early sixties was the scope for the Dunkirk spirit? Where was the Luftwaffe, where was Goering? There was no Goering, there was only Gagarin.

The Kennedy quality of grace under pressure required pressure for the grace to show. The president raised the pressure in the White House basement, as retired teachers raise mushrooms or baby alligators in theirs. His hero called the Second World War 'the unnecessary war.' Kennedy's thousand days were crammed with unnecessary crises.

Within a hundred days came the first, and least necessary of all. Those who were there have since told of how Kennedy listened, with mounting scepticism and foreboding, to his advisers as they assured him that the Cuban masses, groaning under oppression, would rise against Castro when the tiny band of exiles waded ashore at the Bay of Pigs. After the fiasco, filled with remorse, Kennedy was aghast at his own credulity. 'All my life,' he told himself bitterly, 'I've known better than to trust the experts.' But before his thousand days were out he trusted them again. It was on their assurance of the need, and their estimate of success, that he sent Americans to fight on far more swampy soil.

The scene of his searing humiliation was also the venue of his famous victory. The Cuban missile crisis, like that of the Bay of Pigs, was a crisis by his choice and of his making. It takes two to tangle. Had Kennedy followed the advice of his Secretary of Defense, he would have accepted the move as a fait

accompli: 'A missile is a missile,' McNamara argued, 'it makes no great difference whether you are killed by a missile fired from the Soviet Union or from
Cuba.'[1] Had Kennedy followed the advice of his ambassador to the UN, he
would have bargained his way out: Adlai Stevenson suggested withdrawing
American missiles from Turkey and Italy in exchange for a Soviet withdrawal
from Cuba, throwing Guantanamo into the deal if necessary. Instead he chose
to compel the Russians to withdraw through fear of all-out thermonuclear war.

Kennedy's statecraft in those fateful fourteen days – the meticulous attention to detail, the careful selection (once the general strategy had been determined) of the least provocative move and counter-move, the studious avoidance
of the temptation to corner his opponent and to crow once he backed down,
above all the vaunted grace under pressure – is greatly admired by every student of crisis management. He rates, in their estimation, an 'A' or 'A plus.' In
crisis management nothing succeeds like success. Yet a child in the kindergarten of strategic studies might devise without difficulty a score of scenarios
wherein the Cuban missile crisis could easily have culminated not in a dazzling
success for Kennedy's statecraft but in disasters ranging from a brief but bloody
bout of city-swapping (Pittsburgh for Omsk for Chicago – US backs down; Pittsburgh for Omsk for Chicago for Leningrad – USSR backs down) to an apocalyp-
tic frenzy of destruction after which no students of crisis management would
be alive to grade the final competition in risk-taking.

'If the Soviets control space they can control earth, as in past centuries
the nation that controlled the seas dominated the continents.'[2] This mindless
maxim, reminiscent of the ravings of some demented geopolitician, was John
Kennedy's campaign pitch for the aerospace vote. It led as well to his decision
to race the Russians to the moon. Statecraft in the sixties knows no more disastrous error. The Russians could – and did – declare 'no contest' when they
wanted to drop out, leaving the United States (as Eisenhower's Commission
on National Goals had explicitly warned it would be) 'driven by nationalist
competition into extravagant programs which would divert funds and talents
from programs of equal importance.'

Worst of all, in the long run, was the mandate given by the space programme to technetronic expertise. It encouraged confidence in the capacity
of an élite of 'organization-oriented, application-minded intellectuals' (as one
of their number[3] admiringly described it) to guide America's foreign and

1 Quoted in Elie Abel, *The Missile Crisis* (Bantam Books, New York & Toronto 1966), 31
2 Quoted in Erlend A. Kennan and Edmund H. Harvey, Jr, *Mission to the Moon: A Critical Examination of NASA and the Space Program* (William Morrow, New York 1969), 74
3 Zbigniew Brzezinski

domestic policies with the same cool assurance of success shown from count-down to splash-down by the wizards of Mission Control. Just as the United States might surpass Russia's achievements in space by spending more money and applying more science, so it might counter insurgency abroad by spending more money and applying more social science.

But Saigon was not Houston. Anyone not bemused by technetronic tricks knows that. Applied social science counselled denying shelter to the Vietcong. GI's, obeying orders, touched their Zippos to the thatch. Watching yet another Vietnam village burn on television – the vignette typifies our times – Arthur Miller suddenly saw the light. 'How is it,' he asked himself,

that we never see Vietnamese peasants burning down their own houses? This is not as ridiculous as it sounds when we recall the Yugoslavs, the Russians, and, if a dim memory is not mistaken, the Americans during the Revolution who destroyed buildings to deny them to the enemy. Frankly, I am amazed that our Psywar people haven't thought of this. Here we are, pumping blood and money into a fight to help these people retain their freedom, and we can't even find a native pyromaniac, let alone a patriot, to fire his own roof. Since it is we and not the Vietnamese who are burning down their own houses, it can mean only that they don't share our urgency and would much rather live where they have always lived and work the land they have always worked, Vietcong or no Vietcong.[4]

A simple perception, blindingly true. But such perceptions lie beyond the ken of technetronic expertise.

Lyndon Johnson was not, any more than John Kennedy, what you could call the gullible type. He brought to the presidency his Texan's scowling distrust of the 'overbred smart alecks who live in Georgetown and think in Harvard.' But once he picked his man he stuck with him, for the reason the Lone Ranger stuck with Tonto – the scout's ability to heed the warning signals in the pitch of a coyote's howl, the footprints near a dry creek.

W.W. Rostow had more than the Indian's sensitive ear or eagle eye at work for him. At his disposal lay all the paraphernalia of technetronic social science – content analysis, factor analysis, operations research, war gaming, computer simulation – with which its practitioners imagine themselves able to confound the cunning of history, to frustrate the knavish tricks played on statesmen by events. In spite of them all, really because of them all, he paid no heed to the warning signals from Vietnam. They filled the sky like thunderheads and lightning, but Rostow, poring over his charts of pacified areas, his tables of

4 'The Age of Abdication,' *The New York Times,* 23 Dec. 1967

the latest body-counts, was impervious to the gathering storm. With the same airy assurance with which he had earlier told the statesmen of the western world that 'the tricks of growth are not all that difficult; they only seem so, at moments of frustration and confusion,'[5] he devised those sequences of search-and-destroy, those patterns of targetting, which he pledged to his president would win the war in nothing flat. The tricks of victory in Vietnam were not all that difficult; they only seemed so, at moments of frustration and confusion. So the bombs began to fall. Three years later, with an expeditionary force of half a million men mired in the mud and the home front seething, a frustrated and confused Lyndon Johnson was driven from the presidency, his Great Society a shambles.

Richard Nixon has history on his side, for it has become the lot of Republican presidents to end the wars of their Democratic predecessors. On his side as well is an adviser more promising than LBJ's. Well aware of the hubris to which technetronic experts so readily succumb, Henry Kissinger knows the limits of gimmickry in foreign policy. In an essay written while still a Harvard don, long before becoming Nixon's Number 1, Kissinger warned the intellectual presuming to advise the policy-maker against turning into 'a promoter of technique.' So far from that, the intellectual's mission in Washington 'is to demonstrate the overwhelming importance of purpose over technique.'[6]

On Vietnam, Kissinger had written little, but a few words can speak volumes. In guerrilla warfare, he noted, 'the guerrilla wins if he does not lose; the conventional army loses if it does not win.'[7] That made star-crossed from the start the Kennedy commitment to counter-insurgency, for in such operations the conventionally armed United States had stacked against it all the odds. The Marines might storm the beaches but they would find no enemy there, only (as one eye-witness reports) 'a dozen giggling Vietnamese schoolgirls who sought out the Leathernecks with garlands of yellow dahlias and red gladioli.' The enemy lay inland, deep in the elephant grass where he had prepared, with exquisite care, his pits and traps and ambush.

An odd couple. The Harvard scholar, nuclear metaphysician, a Hamlet among the strategists, rendering in convoluted prose and Dr Strangelove accent his abstruse speculation about the ways of states. The California politician pouring in his elocutionist voice a bland and oily rhetoric upon America's sea of trouble. Yet in their conception of leadership the odd couple thought as one. They believed in a presidency of prophylaxis, in the politics of prevention.

5 *The Stages of Economic Growth: A Non-Communist Manifesto* (Cambridge University Press, Cambridge & New York 1960), 166-7
6 *The Necessity for Choice* (Harper & Brothers, New York 1960), 352-3
7 'The Viet Nam Negotiations,' *Foreign Affairs,* XLVIII, no 2, Jan. 1969, 214

'The question before America is whether it can muster the dedication and creativity *before* the worst has happened.' 'One of the criteria by which I will measure success will be the extent to which problems can be solved before they reach crisis proportions.'[8]

Yet close to the worst, if not the worst, had already happened. By the end of 1969, their slate, so far from being clean, was smeared by slime and blood. And now so are their hands. Early in 1969 Kissinger met at the White House with a delegation of college students. He pleaded for their patience while he worked to end the war. 'Come back here in a year. If nothing has happened, then I can't argue for patience.' His year is up. His game is up.

[December 1969]

8 'Preface,' *Six Crises* (Doubleday, New York 1969), x

Part III **RIGHT AND WRONG IN FOREIGN POLICY**

1

The ways of statecraft

It is more than four hundred years since Machiavelli advised his Prince in what ways he should keep faith, and in what ways not. During this time, the scope for wrong-doing in foreign policy has greatly expanded; and of its expansion governments have not been reluctant to take advantage. In their dealings with other governments, and with other peoples, their behaviour is characteristically bad. It is deceitful. It is treacherous. It is cruel.

Deception is central to most of the techniques of statecraft. Consider negotiation. I am not concerned with the white lie, the half-truth, the repression of what one really thinks. Without such mild deceptions, there could be no diplomacy at all. No, I am thinking of the *grand guignol* of negotiations. Of Japanese ministers smiling and bowing at their American colleagues even as the Imperial Fleet steamed towards Pearl Harbor. Of the British refusal to disclose to their closest ally their plans for the imminent invasion of Egypt. Of Andrei Gromyko's assurance to the president of the United States that no strategic missiles had been sent to Cuba, while locked in a safe ten feet from where they talked was indisputable evidence that Gromyko was lying. Of the first minister of Kenya promising the British that once independent, Kenya would work for federation in east Africa – a promise, Jomo Kenyatta later gleefully told his countrymen, he had never intended to keep. The examples fill a book. No one government, no type of government, has a corner on the market. Great powers do it. Small powers do it. Even middle powers do it.

Consider propaganda. Not all propaganda is deceptious – though much of it is. But all propaganda is tendentious. Governments do not wish to tell the world of their shortcomings. In deciding what to tell the world – the truth as one sees it, part of that truth, what is known to be untrue – expedience prevails over ethics. What matters is not the truth of the message but the credibility of the message. And the estimate of the credibility of the message is determined by the estimate of the gullibility of the masses.

At one extreme is the assessment of fascism. The masses are craven and gullible. They lack the independence of mind and spirit to denounce as false anything bearing the hallmark of authority. The greater the falsehood, the more readily acceptable as fact, once stamped with the imprimatur of state. Propaganda to be credible should be a compound of monstrous untruths. And Hitler and Goebbels made it so.

At the other extreme is the assessment of liberal democracy. It thinks not of masses but of the man in the street - Bagehot's bald-headed gentleman at the back of the bus. Of his intellectual discrimination it takes a lofty view. It believes he can distinguish not merely between truth and falsehood, but among shadings across the spectrum of veracity. Propaganda to be credible should be scrupulously fair and rigorously unbiased.

Some governments today cling to the technique of the Big Lie, practising without remorse a sort of psychic genocide. A few - a very few - try to be fair. Most fall in between. Their apparatus for persuasion, usually called ministries of information, might better be called ministries of mendacity. They accept with zeal the job of putting out versions of events they know to be untrue. Never before have so many statesmen with so little scruple been engaged in the deception of so many people.

Deceit is commonplace in foreign policy. Betrayal no less so.

Treachery, in private ethics, is a grave offence. You do not flatter a man by calling him Judas. Jean Genet, casting perversely about for ways of soiling the moral precepts of a society from which he is so spectacularly alienated, settles unerringly upon betrayal which forms, with thievery and homosexuality, his satanic trinity of categorical imperatives.

Treachery, in foreign policy, is not such a grave offence. Consider three cases, in an ascending order of moral difficulty.

The betrayal of Abyssinia, in 1935, was easily done. A remote country. A people alleged to be of inferior race. Benighted creatures, they were thought to be scarcely capable of knowing whether they were betrayed or not. 'No interest in Ethiopia, of any nature whatever, is worth the life of a single Canadian citizen.' So said Ernest Lapointe in Quebec City, with Mackenzie King nodding approval at his side. That was one judgment, and it happened to prevail. But it was not the only judgment. The next day, from the rostrum of the Palais des Nations at Geneva, the delegate of Haiti uttered another: 'Great or small, strong or weak, near or far, white or colored, let us never forget that one day we may be somebody's Ethiopia.' But on this occasion, as on many others, it was not easy to apply to foreign policy even so diluted a version of the Golden Rule.[1]

The betrayal of Czechoslovakia, in 1938, was less easily done. The operation was delicate and tricky. It involved the dismemberment of a state at once an ally and a friend. Here was a civilized country in the heart of Europe, free, white and – dating its independence to the Peace Treaties – almost twenty-one. Canada considered it remote: Lapointe cabled frantically from Geneva to insist that 'immediate cause of war namely minority problems in Eastern Europe not of a nature to enthuse our people.' Britain and France found it too close for comfort. Gratefully their governments fell upon the doctrine of national self-determination: wasn't Sudetenland full of Germans? But that was dangerous doctrine: wasn't Scotland full of Scotsmen, Algeria of Algerians? No, the justification for the betrayal of Czechoslovakia had to be found elsewhere.

We all know about Munich, so we all know what it was. The sacrifice of Czechoslovakia was said to be a small price for peace. (That it had bought not peace but time to prepare for war is an argument contrived after the event.) There was no more ecstatic endorsation of the deal than the Canadian. 'On the very brink of chaos,' Mackenzie King cabled to Chamberlain, 'with passions flaming and armies marching, the voice of Reason has found a way.' Again this judgment prevailed, though not for very long. But it was not the only judgment. Out in Winnipeg, one of the greatest of Dafoe's editorials asked rhetorically 'What's the Cheering For?' A free people had been handed over to a tyrant: that, said Dafoe, 'is the situation; and those who think it is all right will cheer for it.' Almost everybody did.[2]

The betrayal of large numbers of Rumanians, Hungarians, and Bulgarians, in 1944-5, consigned against their will to the kind of people's democracy favoured by Stalin, was assented to by the United States and the United Kingdom governments as the price to be paid for appeasing the Soviet Union. What was done at Moscow and at Yalta differed in degree of wrong-doing from what was done at Munich: what was betrayed on this occasion was not so much a people already under the yoke of the Red Army as the ideals for which the war had ostensibly been fought. The Atlantic Charter makes painful reading when set beside transcripts of allied negotiations four years later. Of what then went on Winston Churchill has left a dramatic account:

1 See my *In Defence of Canada,* II, *Appeasement and Rearmament* (University of Toronto Press, Toronto 1965), ch. 1, 'War in Africa'
2 See ibid., ch. 3, 'Appeasement,' 61 ff.

The moment was apt for business, so I said [to Stalin] : "Let us settle about our affairs in the Balkans. Your armies are in Rumania and Bulgaria. We have interests, missions, and agents there. Don't let us get at cross purposes in small ways. So far as Britain and Russia are concerned, how would it do for you to have ninety per cent predominance in Rumania, for us to have ninety per cent of the say in Greece, and go fifty-fifty about Yugoslavia?"

During the translation, Churchill wrote out the percentages on a piece of paper. His account continues:

I pushed this across to Stalin, who had by then heard the translation. There was a slight pause. Then he took his blue pencil and made a large tick upon it, and passed it back to us. It was all settled in no more time than it takes to set it down ...

After this there was a long silence. The pencilled paper lay in the centre of the table. At length I said: "Might it not be thought rather cynical if it seemed we had disposed of those issues, so fateful to millions of people, in such an off-hand manner? Let us burn the paper." "No. You keep it," said Stalin.[3]

The people of small states, with a faith more touching than reasoned, believe such inequities to be the failing of great powers only. That is not always true. A former American minister to Canada has recorded his shock on learning how cheaply the Department of External Affairs appeared to value the liberty of the Baltic countries in 1942. He was told by the permanent head of that department that 'nobody [in London or Ottawa] worried about Finland, and that Estonia, Latvia, and Lithuania was a small price to pay to convince Russia of Britain's trust and earnestness ...' He remarked that 'what the British Government was suggesting and what [the Canadian government] was endorsing could certainly not be reconciled with the Atlantic Charter.'[4] But the Canadian government, or at any rate the Canadian prime minister, did not hold the Atlantic Charter in such high regard. 'To me,' wrote Mackenzie King in his diary, 'it is the apotheosis of the craze for publicity and show.'[5]

I have written of deceit, and of treachery; I shall write now of cruelty in foreign policy.

Cruelty is not confined to the maiming and killing of innocent people – though we know only too well how often governments practise this kind of

3 *The Second World War*, VI, *Triumph and Tragedy* (Houghton Mifflin, Boston 1953), 227-8
4 Nancy Harvison Hooker, ed., *The Moffat Papers: Selections from the Diplomatic Journals of Jay Pierrepont Moffat* (Harvard University Press, Cambridge 1956), 381
5 J.W. Pickersgill, ed., *The Mackenzie King Record*, I, *1939-1944* (University of Toronto Press, Toronto 1960), 233

cruelty. Those who passed indifferently by that certain traveller between Jerusalem and Jericho were cruel in their behaviour – this is the point of the parable – even though they were not guilty of his wounds.

The ethic that it is wrong to be cruel is more widely accepted today than ever before. Few of the world's religions, few of its ideologies, remain unaffected by it. The injunction to love one's neighbour has been sent bounding across the world's communications systems. Only about half its inhabitants have never heard of Jesus; and of them maybe half have heard of Gandhi. All the same, the scale and scope of cruelty in statecraft are greater today than ever before. Why is this so?

Twentieth-century war is increasingly an instrument of doctrinal conviction. Doctrinal war, more than war fought for gain, or to pre-empt attack, is likely to be total war and brutal war. Crusades are notorious for their cruelty. 'I implore you,' Martin Luther wrote to a friend, 'if you rightly understand the Gospel, do not imagine that its cause can be furthered without tumult, distress, and uproar.[6] Luther meant the gospel of the New Testament, but his words apply to other gospels and to other testaments, to Lenin's and Mao's, Wilson's and Johnson's – to all who wield great power linked to an idea. 'Bismarck fought "necessary" wars,' an historian[7] has noted, 'and killed thousands. The idealists of the twentieth-century fight "just" wars and kill millions.'

When wars are fought for ideals, everyone gets hurt. The distinction between soldier and civilian becomes obliterated. The battlefield is everywhere: in village huts, a market square, a smart restaurant, an embassy compound. Terrorism begets yet more savage terrorism; reprisal yet more insensate reprisal. We know this warfare well, from our newspapers better than from our history books. None know it better than Albert Camus knew it; he wrote in 1956 of the anguish of guerrilla war: 'Anguish as we face a future that closes up a little every day, as we face the threat of a degrading struggle, of an economic disequilibrium that may reach the point where no effort will be able to revive ...'[8] To revive what shattered country? Camus meant Algeria. But he could just as well have meant Ireland forty years earlier, Vietnam ten years later. Clemenceau once wrote of 'the grandeur and misery of war.' Guerrilla war is devoid of grandeur. There is only misery – and cruelty.

As Camus is the laureate of guerrilla warfare, so Auden is the laureate of the nuclear age, the age of anxiety. In 1947 he wrote of the barbarity which had already settled upon an atomically armed America, a barbarism unlike any the world had ever known:

6 Quoted in Robert Endicott Osgood, *Limited War: The Challenge to American Strategy* (University of Chicago Press, Chicago 1957), 67-8
7 A.J.P. Taylor
8 *Resistance, Rebellion, and Death* (Alfred A. Knopf, New York 1961), 133-4

> ... the new barbarian is no uncouth
> Desert-dweller; he does not emerge
> From fir forests: factories breed him;
> Corporate companies, college towns
> Mothered his mind, and many journals
> Backed his beliefs ...[9]

And, on the occasion of the twentieth anniversary of the ordeal of Hiroshima and Nagasaki: 'Our world will be a safer place and healthier place when we can admit that every time we make an atomic bomb we corrupt the morals of a host of innocent neutrons below the age of consent.'[10]

As to safety, Auden is no authority: strategists better than poets may determine whether we really would all be safer by unilaterally dismantling the apparatus of deterrence by which we believe ourselves preserved. But as to ethics, Auden is as good a guide as any strategist, possibly more reliable. Surely he is right to force our attention upon the plight of the innocent. Why do we punish a kidnapper more condignly than a robber, even sometimes a murderer? It is because we abhor, and properly abhor, the crime of holding innocent life as hostage. By what sort of reasoning, then, does our society not only condone but indulge in the holding as hostage the lives of millions of innocents?

The issue has been posed in this way: 'Nuclear-missile weapons hold out the prospect of conflict which may be neither subject to restraint nor meaningfully described as defensive. Can such a war be justified? Can there be a moral sanction for threatening to take a measure which, if circumstances ever required carrying it out, could find no justification?' On 22 October 1962, speaking on television with all the emphasis at his command, the president of the United States uttered the following words: 'It shall be the policy of this nation to regard any nuclear missile launched from Cuba against any nation in the Western Hemisphere as an attack by the Soviet Union on the United States, requiring a full retaliatory response upon the Soviet Union.' By what moral law, by what sacred text, by the precept or example of what saintly figure, in response to what promptings of his own conscience, could John Kennedy dare to serve a national interest by risking the mutilation of mankind?

If you put this question to a statesman, he will have an answer – of sorts. He will say that it is not a fair question.

If you put it to a strategist, he will lecture you on the distinction between 'action' policy and 'declaratory' policy. Action policy, he will tell you, is what

---

9　*The Age of Anxiety* (Random House, New York 1946), 19
10　'The Corruption of Innocent Neutrons,' *The New York Times Magazine,* 1 Aug. 1965

a government intends to do. Declaratory policy is what it says it intends to do, very likely without intending to do it. The President's statement, he will assure you, is declaratory policy, not action policy. This answer is hardly more satisfactory than the statesman's answer. It does not explain how the distinction between action policy and declaratory policy, which the enemy is not supposed to understand, will be readily apparent to those who are not the enemy. Nor does it answer the question of the ethical right of any statesman in any circumstances to indulge for whatever reason in such dire and dreadful threats, action or declaratory as the case may be.

So what happens if you put the question to a moralist? Up to now, the moralist has asked to be excused. He has no answer to the question. He has not even considered the question. 'I find myself profoundly in anguish,' an American scientist has lamented, 'over the fact that no ethical discourse of any weight or nobility has been addressed to the problem of nuclear weapons. What are we to think of such a civilization, which has not been able to talk about the prospect of killing almost everybody, except in prudential and game-theoretical terms?'[11]

Not without reason have moral philosophers and theologians shied away from questions of this kind. The predicaments thus posed are so macabre, so horrific, that to apply to them the traditional apparatus of ethical discussion results only in black humour and sick jokes. Our playwrights, frustrated because reality is so much more lurid than any plots they can devise, have created the theatre of the absurd. We are still waiting for our moral philosophers and theologians to create an ethics of the absurd.

The work may have already begun. At the meetings last year of the Ecumenical Council of the Roman Catholic Church, the committee charged with formulating positions for the Church in the modern world was faced with the task of contriving some ethical precepts for nuclear warfare. The committee could not reach agreement. One of the formulations causing its members to set the task to one side was the following:

Although, after all the aids for peaceful discussions have been exhausted, it may not be illicit, when one's rights have been unjustly hampered, to defend those rights against such unjust aggression by violence and force, nevertheless, the use of arms, especially nuclear weapons, whose effects are greater than can be imagined and therefore cannot reasonably be regulated by men, exceeds all just proportion and therefore must be judged before God and man as most wicked.

11 J. Robert Oppenheimer, quoted in Nuel Pharr Davis, *Lawrence and Oppenheimer* (Simon and Schuster, New York 1968), 329-30

This may not seem an extreme position for those who profess devotion to the gentle carpenter of Galilee. But it was too extreme for some of the more worldly Churchmen on the Council. 'It is important to make clear,' one of the dissenters argued, 'that there may well exist objects which, in a just war of defence, are legitimate targets for nuclear weapons, even of vast strength ... To attack a ballistic missile or a satellite missile in the outer atmosphere would be a legitimate act of defence, and with just proportion duly preserved might require the use of a weapon of vast power ... The Council should not condemn the possession and use of these weapons as essentially and necessarily evil.'[12]

At the deliberations of these divines, solemnly debating the morality of a nuclear anti-missile system, one does not know whether to laugh or weep. They recall recondite discussion within the thirteenth-century church. They recall as well Oppenheimer's image of morality as a flying trapeze,[13] and Kierkegaard's comparison of the man of faith to an acrobat. But funambulism is not enough. If we keep our balance, if we keep our faith, if indeed we keep our sanity throughout the ethical inanities of the atomic age, it is not by acrobatics but by an operation on the inner ear of conscience, rendering us impervious to height, and to the depths below.

Suppose we assume, with Niebuhr, that within the immoral society which is the states system there dwells a moral mankind. How should we react? Should we accept its inequities with resignation, or with indignation? Ought we to come to terms with it or ought we to declare war on it? Is it a condition to be borne or a situation to be changed?

The literature of political theory provides two traditions in which to find an answer. They are usually described as the realist tradition and the idealist tradition. I shall accept this terminology for convenience, but so as not to over-simplify I shall identify the principal strains which occur in each.

Plato's Thrasymachus, asked to define justice, replied that it conforms to the interests of the stronger. Here we have the first two strains of the realist tradition. I will call it brutal realism.

The brutal realist is a *realpolitiker* of an extreme kind. Ethics, he insists, have no place in politics. Might makes right. What is good for the state is good. Characteristically, the brutal realist takes pleasure in his brutal realism. He prides himself on his tough-mindedness. His nose is hard. He enjoys the company of hawks.

12 *The Times* (London), 11 Nov. 1964
13 *The Flying Trapeze: Three Crises for Physicists* (Oxford University Press, London, New York, & Toronto 1964)

The brutal realist is not so fashionable a figure as he used to be, perhaps fortunately; specimens are hard to find. But not that hard, for there is at least one old State Department hand, still an important figure in the Washington policy community, who waves his brutal realism about like a bull-fighter's cape. Some months ago, Mr Dean Acheson recalled with evident satisfaction how lightly moral considerations weighed with those, among whom he was one, who in 1949 took the decision to produce the hydrogen bomb:

A respected colleague advised me that it would be better that our whole na-tion and people should perish rather than be a party to a course so evil as pro-ducing that weapon. I told him that on the day of Judgment his view might be confirmed and that he was free to go forth and preach the necessity for salva-tion. It was not, however, a view which I could entertain as a public servant.[14]

Here is the authentic voice of the brutal realist: rasping in tone, sardonic in de-bate, crushing in rejoinder, sure that he is right.

To belong in the realist tradition one does not have to be a brutal realist. There is another strain, which we may call sceptical realism. The sceptical realist is no disciple of Thrasymachus, proclaiming the mighty to be right and throwing the weak to the wolves. Still less is he a disciple of Nietzsche, extolling an anti-ethic of force and violence. He is realistic not because he is sadistic, but because he is sceptical.

He is sceptical of the supposition that if his own government dealt impec-cably with others, those others would deal impeccably with it. A unilateral declaration of morality would cause the rest to take advantage of such a curi-osity as a government determined to make its foreign policy conform to what is right. Machiavelli, often thought to be a brutal realist, is for this reason a sceptical realist. He does advise his Prince 'not to keep faith when it would be against his interest': but this is counsel not of perfection but of necessity. 'If men were all good,' he immediately concedes, 'this precept would not be a good one; but as they are bad, and would not observe their faith with you, so you are not bound to keep faith with them.'[15]

He is sceptical, as well, of the supposition that moral judgments may be made with confidence in such a welter of confusion. The skein of history is so tangled, the motives of statesmen so mixed, the cause of events so obscure, that rarely is he sure of what is right and what is wrong. If a gifted historian[16] can trick out so obvious a villain as Hitler in such a way as to exonerate him

14   'Ethics in International Relations Today,' *The New York Times,* 10 Dec. 1964
15   *The Prince* (Mentor Books, New York 1952), 101-2
16   Again, A.J.P. Taylor

from responsibility for the Second World War, with how much less assurance does one approach the more morally ambiguous figures of our times. Lenin, for example. Or Neville Chamberlain.

Hard as it is to judge the statesman, it is harder still to judge his statecraft. 'There is no standard of right and wrong applicable to conflicts of political interests,' wrote the permanent head of the British Foreign Office in 1912. 'Was Alexander right or wrong in invading the Persian Empire and erecting on its ruins the foundations of a flourishing Greek civilization? Was William III right or wrong in putting an end to the reign of James II? Is Great Britain right or wrong in holding dominion over India?'[17] There is no shortage of similar examples in our own day. In the conflicts over Kashmir, over Berlin, over Rhodesia, over Vietnam, each disputant is convinced of the justice of its cause, and views the struggle as one between good and evil, right and wrong. The sceptical realist views the struggle as one between two conflicting conceptions of right.

It has been said that when John Kennedy was president, it was his habit to ask not whether a proposed course of action was good or bad, right or wrong; he asked instead: 'Can it work? Can it help? Can it pass?' Such are the concerns of the sceptical strain in the realist tradition.

I now turn to the idealist tradition, where again two strains are found. One is brightly hopeful, blithely optimistic. I will call it the strain of liberal idealism, for it carries within itself two of the tracers of liberal thought: belief in the sweet reasonableness of mankind, and belief in the certain improvement of mankind. Keynes has told of how he and his young friends at Cambridge at the turn of the century believed so passionately 'in a continuing moral progress, by virtue of which the human race already consists of reliable, decent people, influenced by truth and objective standards,'[18] and Stephen Spender relates in his autobiography how he was taught at school of the

terrible things which had happened in the past: tortures, Court of the Star Chamber, Morton's Fork, Henry VIII's wives, the Stamp Tax, the Boston Tea Party, slavery, the Industrial Revolution, the French Revolution, Bismarck, the Boer War. Weighing in the scale of human happiness against these were the Reform Act, Wilberforce, Mr Gladstone, Home Rule, Popular Education, the United States, Health Insurance, the League of Nations. If the history books were illustrated, they gave the impression that the world had been moving steadily forward in the past thousands of years, from the vague to the defined,

17   G.P. Gooch and Harold Temperly, eds., *British Documents on the Origins of the War, 1898-1914*, VIII, *Arbitration, Neutrality and Security* (HMSO, London 1932), 549
18   *Essays and Sketches in Biography* (Meridian Books, New York 1956), 253

the savage to the civilized, the crude to the scientific, the unfamiliar to the known. It was as though the nineteenth century had been a machine absorbing into itself at one end humanity dressed in fancy dress, unwashed, fierce and immoral, and emitting at the other modern men, in their hygienic houses, their zeal for reform, their air of having triumphed by mechanical, economic and scientific means over the passionate, superstitious, cruel, and poetic past.[19]

For the future of international politics such an outlook was heartening. Every day in every way international politics would get better and better. Its inequities stemmed from some mere malfunction of the system, not from some inherent defect or fatal flaw in human nature. In a speech to the Congress on the eve of war in 1917, President Wilson forecast what the future surely held in store: 'We are at the beginning of an age in which it will be insisted that the same standards of conduct and of responsibility for wrong shall be observed among nations and their governments that are observed among the individual citizens of civilized states.' Only a liberal idealist could risk so reckless a prediction. Two decades later, nations and their governments stood silently by while Italian airmen dropped mustard gas on Ethiopia, and Nazi troopers killed Jews on German streets. Much worse would follow.

The strain of liberal idealism accordingly has weakened in the west; but elsewhere flows more strongly than ever. Leaders of newly independent states in Asia and in Africa do not accept *realpolitik* as real. Its characteristic deceptions, betrayals, cruelties, they construe not at all as characteristic, but as a species of deformity. For the deformation of international society they blame the shackles of colonialism. When these are cut away the system will be transformed.

But what if the shackles are cut away and the system remains? If nations are freed but keep on fighting? There is still no need to despair. Colonialism has given way to neo-colonialism. Its shackles are less visible but no less deforming. And in time these, too, can be cut away. And then the day will dawn.

The second strain in the idealist tradition I will call pharisean idealism. (Luke's Pharisee, you will remember, 'prayed thus with himself: "O God, I give thee thanks that I am not as the rest of man, extortioners, unjust, adulterers ..."') Pharisean idealists, like liberal idealists, are optimistic. There are such things as right and wrong in foreign policy, for is not their foreign policy nearly always right?

Pharisean idealism in recent years has been practised most spectacularly by the United States government; and of all Americans, John Foster Dulles has

19   *World Within Worlds* (Hamish Hamilton, London 1951), 1

the most celebrated reputation for pharisean statement. But the pharisean idealism of which his speeches are so perfect an epitome by no means ceases with his death. One of President Johnson's addresses dealing with American policy in Vietnam provides an exquisite example:

For centuries nations have struggled among each other. But we dream of a world where disputes are settled by law and reason. And we will try to make it so.

For most of history men have hated and killed one another in battle. But we dream of an end to war. And we will try to make it so.

For all existence most men have lived in poverty ... But we dream of a world where all are fed and charged with hope. And we will help to make it so.[20]

And a month later, explaining why he found it necessary to send troops into Santo Domingo, the President declared: 'This is required of us by the values which bind us together,' and went on – or rather, his speech-writer went on – to quote the great Bolívar: '"The veil has been torn asunder, we have already seen the light, and it is not our desire to be thrust back in darkness."'[21]

The Pharisee of whom Luke tells us may have been a hypocrite, and pharisean idealism may be hypocritical. But it does not have to be, and in its American manifestations there is usually no hypocrisy at all. When Conor Cruise O'Brien writes that the face of Adlai Stevenson at the United Nations, 'with its shiftily earnest advocate's expression,' was 'the ingratiating moral mask which a toughly acquisitive society wears before the world it robs,'[22] he gets it all wrong. The pious utterances that I have quoted are not at all a façade behind which a cluster of cynical manipulators go about their dirty business. Dirty business it may be, but it is not thought to be so and it is characteristic of pharisean idealism that it is thought not to be so. What caused the look of pain that from time to time crossed the features of Adlai Stevenson when defending the United States at the United Nations was not his hatred of hypocrisy: it was his distaste for the insensitivity of his political masters, whose voice he had allowed himself to become. When McGeorge Bundy remarks that 'measured against the record of others ... the break-down in the relation between what we do and what we believe seems less severe in the United States than in any other major nation,'[23] there is no reason to think him insincere. He really believes it. That may be the problem.

20 *The New York Times,* 8 Apr. 1965
21 *The New York Times,* 4 May 1965
22 *Writers and Politics* (Pantheon Books, New York 1965), xiv
23 'The Battlefields of Power and the Searchlights of the Academy,' in E.A.J. Johnson, ed., *The Dimensions of Diplomacy* (Johns Hopkins Press, Baltimore 1964), 8

Between realism on the one hand – whether brutal or sceptical – and idealism on the other – whether liberal or pharisean – is no easy choice. We face not an embarrassment of riches but an option of difficulties. Still, I would not be the good Canadian I like to think I am if I did not try to open up a middle way. Let us call it practical idealism.

The practical idealist knows the ways of statecraft well. He knows their deceptions, their betrayals, their cruelties. He knows how pitiless are their laws. He cannot hope to do away with them. He cannot, accordingly, share the outlook of the liberal idealist. He cannot hope to be exempt from them. He cannot, accordingly, share the outlook of the pharisean idealist.

But the practical idealist knows just as well how much wrong-doing may be done by statesmen whose moral mandate is too permissive. He will on this account refuse to allow *raison d'état* to be their guide. They are not to be trusted with so dangerous a doctrine. It leads straight to massacre and genocide, to total war with terrible weapons.

And so the practical idealist, his idealism at once prompted and tempered by his realism, clings to a more stringent ethic in international life than may be warranted by the facts of international life. If international morality did not exist, he would find it necessary to invent it; for he knows that if international morality did not exist, people might not exist.

Practical idealism may be found in the thought of Ernst Troeltsch who, knowing how obvious are the philosophical difficulties of the concept of natural law, urged its acceptance in a last despairing effort to save Weimar democracy from fascism.[24] It may also be found in Freud, to whom ethical systems are shocktroops of the reinforcements called up by culture for battle against the aggressive instincts of mankind.

Imagine, then, a meeting of the cabinet. A crucial foreign policy decision is to be taken – whether or not to run the blockade of Berlin, send troops to Korea, send troops to Vietnam. Various divisions of labour take place. The Prime Minister worries about national unity. The Finance Minister is concerned at the cost. The Defence Minister is anxious about logistics. The Secretary of State for External Affairs frets about effects on friends and foes. But there is no Secretary of State for Conscience to speak up to ask two crucial questions: Is it good? Is it right?

Lacking a Secretary of State for Conscience in the organization of our government, we should, as practical idealists, insist that his function be performed by statesmen whose portfolios bear more prosaic titles. Otherwise we are in trouble.   [November 1965]

24 'The Ideas of Natural Law and Humanity,' in Otto Gierke, *Natural Law and the Theory of Society, 1500-1800* (Cambridge University Press, Cambridge 1950), 220-2

2

The ways of keeping faith

'In every system of morality, which I have hitherto met with, I have always remark'd, that the author proceeds for some time in the ordinary way of reasoning ... when of a sudden I am surpriz'd to find, that instead of the usual copulations of propositions, *is* and *is not,* I meet with no proposition that is not connected with an *ought,* or *ought not.* This change is imperceptible, but is, however, of the last importance.' So David Hume complained two centuries ago. It is a fair complaint, and I am anxious not to give you cause to reproach me with it. Let me therefore announce that I am changing gears. Before, they were (more or less) in neutral: now, they are engaged. They are shifting from the *is* and *is not* to the *ought* and *ought not.* Before, I attempted to describe the ways of statecraft. Now, I am concerned with the ways of keeping faith. What ought we to expect of moral man caught in the coils of the inequitous states system?

A critic of the policy of appeasement practised by the governments of the United Kingdom and the Dominions before the Second World War wrote of its practitioners: 'One could not blame them, one could not admire them, one could not admire anybody.'[1] Why not blame them? Is it just because they did their best? Are statesmen to be excused their follies if they act in good faith? Are we to judge them for effort in a world which usually judges for result? What is so special about statesmen that when their plans miscarry and their statecraft goes awry we are not to call them guilty men?

1 *The Mist Procession: The Autobiography of Lord Vansittart* (Hutchinson, London ·1958), 529

A theological answer holds that statesmen, being instruments of God, are beyond reproach by lesser mortals. Thus the Professor of Religion at Princeton University opens a discussion of the ethics of intervention – by which he means Suez, and the Bay of Pigs, and Santo Domingo, and Vietnam – by observing: 'Religious communities need to stand in awe before people nowadays called political "decision-makers," or rather before the majesty of top-most political agency. Political decision and action is an image of the majesty of God.'[2]

A secular version of this doctrine requires not so much deference to the makers of policy as compassion for them. It is not the divinity of their position but its poignancy which entreats our indulgence. Those who ask this of us are usually those set in authority over us: naturally so, for they stand to profit by our forbearance, just as they stand to lose by our condemnation. And so they say to us: 'Look – you do not know, you cannot know, how it is. You do not understand the agony of taking decisions in an imperfect world. If you knew, if you were one of us, you would not judge so harshly.' Or else they say: 'Unless you have been one of us, you have no right to judge so harshly.' They may even say: 'Unless you have been one of us, you have no right to judge at all.'

What are we to make of special pleading such as this? Is it simply self-pity? Is it, less simply, part of the defensive fortification by which statesmen seek to protect their niche in history? Or is it a genuine manifestation of the poignancy of power?

Much depends on circumstance, much depends on personality. Certainly in reading those portions of Mackenzie King's diary where he compares his lot as prime minister of Canada to Christ's agony in Gethsemane, one's inclination (if not too offended by the blasphemy) is to recall Harry Truman's advice: 'If you can't stand the heat, get the hell out of the kitchen.' But this is not really very helpful. Cooks are temperamental creatures; some of the best chefs give notice at the crucial stage of the preparation of a banquet. But a prime minister who quits in the middle of some grave international crisis just because he finds the awfulness of taking decisions too heavy to be borne doesn't deserve our gratitude, and doesn't get it either.

But perhaps the advice is harsh as well as unhelpful. Power *has* its poignant aspects. Those who dispose of it can never do the perfect thing with it. Always the policy-maker is robbing Peter to pay Paul, the poor to pay the veterans, the old to pay the young, the farm to pay the factory, the Maritimes to pay Ontario. (Or, of course, the other way around.) Nor, it is said, can he do the gen-

2   Paul Ramsey, 'The Ethics of Intervention,' *The Review of Politics,* XXVII, no 3, July 1965, 287

erous thing with it. Behaviour admired in individuals – kindliness, compassion, benevolence – is not permitted to statesmen. An individual who gives everything to the poor, who lives his life by the Sermon on the Mount, may be as admired as he is hard to find. But a statesman who guided his statecraft by the Sermon on the Mount would bankrupt his country within a week, invite aggression within a month, accomplish the destruction of his country within a year.

If the profession of statecraft is unlike other professions, should we then not judge the statesman by more lenient standards? A physician whose patient dies through malpractice or neglect faces an inquest or a suit for damages; an engineer whose bridge collapses through faulty mathematics or through too much sand and too little cement faces a royal commission or a penitentiary sentence. But the statesman whose policies bring ruin to a nation does not even ask forgiveness. There is, he says, nothing to forgive.

Why this should be is hard to understand. No doubt the purely political leader cannot perform the purely perfect act. But there are no purely political leaders, just as there are no purely perfect acts. These exist as constructs and abstractions only; they are not found in this world. For analytical purposes we may separate the public figure and the private man. But there is always a private man in every public figure; and often he bursts through to tell the public figure what to do. Not even the most dedicated, the most ruthless, the most public-centred, the power-hungriest of statesmen can always keep his emotions from intruding upon, and giving final form to, his statecraft. Nor is it desirable that he should.

In 1946, the British government entered into negotiations with New Zealand. It needed food badly, and had very little to pay for it. The minister involved has since recalled what happened:

I expected a bargaining session as difficult as any other. Instead, the leader of the New Zealand delegation opened the proceedings in words I shall never forget. "We have not come to ask you, 'What can you give?' We have come to ask, 'What do you need?' When you stood alone, you preserved our freedom for us. Now tell us what butter, what meat, what grains you need, and – whatever the sacrifice may be for the New Zealand people – we will supply it."[3]

And they did. Some years later, the New Zealanders were the beneficiaries of magnanimity in statecraft. In 1962 the delegates to the Common Market discussed the probable effects of British entry upon New Zealand's economy.

3 Rt. Hon. Hilary Marquand, quoted by Harold Wilson, United Kingdom, *House of Commons Debates,* DCXLV, col. 6155, 3 Aug. 1961

These were thought to be disastrous, but the foreign minister of France remained unmoved. 'What obligations,' asked M. Couve de Murville, 'have we towards New Zealanders?' The foreign minister of Belgium answered: 'The fact that twice in our lifetime their men have come over to be killed for freedom.' M. Couve de Murville was unimpressed. 'Why are we bound,' he persisted, 'to do anything for them?' 'Because,' M. Spaak replied, 'because we are sitting around this table organizing their ruin.'[4]

For no good reason, then, theological or secular, are statesmen exempt from judgment. But how are they to be judged? What is the criterion of guilt? Not, certainly, failure. The history of foreign policy is replete with failures, of which some are ignoble and others magnificent. Churchill's failure to prevent appeasement; Attlee's failure to prevent partition; Hammarskjold's failure to prevent war – these are magnificent failures. In each case the statesman concerned tried to do the right thing. He is not guilty just because he did not succeed.

Not the failure of his enterprise, but the pursuit of the wrong enterprise, ought to bring upon the statesman the wrath of others. And he pursues the wrong enterprise through asking the wrong questions. In the preceding section I wrote of the creed of the sceptical realist, of which I was critical; and of the creed of the practical idealist, of which I was not. The sceptical realist asks: 'Will it work? Will it pass? Will it help?' To the practical idealist, the last of these questions is of the first importance, and he asks it in an amended form. Not just: 'Will it help?' but: 'Will it help to relieve human suffering, here and now?'

The statesman who treats this question cynically, or to whom it seems irrelevant, or to whom it never occurs, has broken faith with the political community which is his trust. He does not deserve its admiration, and he should not escape its blame.

Political obligation is for Machiavelli a problem for people at the pinnacle of power: he is concerned with the way princes keep faith. But what of people lower down? What of those who serve the Prince and execute his commands? How may they keep faith?

'A diplomat is an honest man sent to lie abroad for his country.' This weary pun, now more than three hundred years old, may not flatter the profession, but it conveys well enough its occupational hazard. It is striking how few of its members protest against the sort of things it requires them to do. This is not at all because what they are required to do is always clean and

4   Quoted in Nora Beloff, *The General Says No* (Penguin Books, Harmondsworth 1963)

decent. Rather it is because the whole ethos of the profession is designed to quell the moral sensibilities of its members. It is as though foreign offices have built into their basements some sort of low temperature chamber where fledgling foreign service officers deposit their consciences on recruitment for redemption only on retirement. By then they are too deeply frozen to thaw out in time.

Satow's *Guide to Diplomatic Practice* tells how to write despatches and warns against accepting bribes (though not against accepting gifts). But it offers no hints to the junior diplomatist on how to go about expressing to his superiors his qualms about his country's policy. These are dangerous thoughts which the seasoned diplomatist will long since have learned to suppress. For, as Satow cautions, 'those in whose hands is placed the supreme direction of foreign relations are alone able to decide which should be the main object of state policy.'[5]

Diplomacy is not an art but a craft. Its practitioners, with loving attention to detail, take satisfaction not in creation but in workmanship. If the object of their labour turns out to be some hideous gargoyle, that is not their fault. They are executants of the designs of others. These may be squalid as well as grand.

The modern diplomatist is fortunate in having little time for brooding. If there were not so many cables to read and despatches to draft and parties through which to whirl, he might go quickly to pieces. Even so the strain is great. Occasionally it shows.

The local equivalent of Satow's *Guide* is Cadieux's *The Canadian Diplomat*. This contribution to the literature by the present Under Secretary of State for External Affairs alludes to 'a certain tenseness, an uneasiness, which can be occasionally glimpsed beneath the unruffled exterior of the diplomat, whose profession consists in a curious blending of freedom and of restraint, of the changing and of the stable, of splendour and of simplicity, of crests and hollows, of coming and going.'[6] M. Cadieux is himself too much a diplomat to explain just what he is getting at in this mysterious passage, but what he really means is this: the diplomatist is a tragic figure. An artist compelled to be an artisan, a painter forbidden to paint, a poet who must spend his most creative hours grinding out the gibberish of state.

Not for a moment is any foreign service officer on this account entitled to our sympathy. 'The tragedy of his position,' Louis Halle has written, 'is implicit

---

5 4th ed. (Oxford University Press, London 1957), 99-100
6 Marcel Cadieux, *The Canadian Diplomat: An Essay in Definition* (University of Toronto Press, Toronto 1963), 110

only. Since the measure of tragedy is always the quality of the victim, the implicit tragedy is realized only to the extent that the diplomat represents intellectual and moral distinction. Most career diplomats, like most of us others, have no aim except to get on with their careers.' But there are exceptions.

Consider Adlai Stevenson again. As a politician his career is among the select company of magnificent failures. As a diplomatist it was a tragedy. 'For six weeks I had to sit there in the United Nations,' Adlai Stevenson told a friend soon before his death, 'and defend the policy of my country in Santo Domingo although it was a massive blunder from beginning to end ... Those six weeks took several years off my life.'[7]

My other exception is a Canadian. In 1938 Loring Christie was the second ranking member of the Department of External Affairs. Like one or two others who have climbed to the top of that greasy pole, he was a man of profound and even passionate sensibility, which he went to great lengths to conceal. What happened at Munich was too much for him to bear in silence, and he poured out his feelings in a letter to a friend:

I have been reflecting on what I have to do to earn my keep. I am a member of one of these sovereign creatures – Canada. I am paid by the other members, the people of Canada, to help manage and express their creature in its relations with the others. The ultimate test on my desk is: "Will this 'save' the people of Canada? Will it advantage them?" The chain of responsibility allows no escape from this.

I am not at the moment recoiling from having to mess around in the filthy mug's game which is called "diplomacy" and "international relations." I am simply illustrating ... I have seen the inside of this creature; I have had to concoct and even mouth his gibberish; I *know* how lost these monsters are ... I do not yet know what the job of being one of their servants will eventually do to me ...[8]

Those who serve the state as warriors are largely spared these emotional stresses and strains. They are protected by their training and their ethic which, more than in any other profession, cultivate the ideal of unquestioning obedience to higher command. They are protected as well by the nature of their mission. The diplomatist may well experience malaise when required to execute policies which seem to him likely to result in war; for the onset of war is to him a signification of his failure. But to the military the onset of war

7   As quoted in the *Globe and Mail* (Toronto), 15 July 1965. Stevenson's remark, made in the presence of David Schoenbrun to Averell Harriman, evoked an official denial from the White House.
8   Christie Papers, Dept of External Affairs, Ottawa

signifies opportunity, not failure. It enables the military to serve the state in the traditional way. The motto of the Strategic Air Command notwithstanding, war is its profession.

Even so, the military servant of the state is not wholly free of ethical dilemmas. The most disciplined warrior may confront the issue of conscientious objection. It does not happen often. After all, the soldier is trained to kill. He is a professional at cruelty. He does not balk at bloodshed. To be sure there are exceptions. General de la Bollardière resigned his command in Algeria because, as he said, he was a paratrooper, not a Gestapo torturer. But such men are rare. The bombers of Hiroshima and Nagasaki (leaving aside the curious case of Major Eatherley) seem marvellously untroubled. The airmen who daily scourge the villages of Vietnam have ready replies to those who exhibit concern on their behalf: this, they say, is war, and war, they say, is hell. There is a story that at the time of Suez, when the Soviet Union threatened the United Kingdom with nuclear bombardment if the Egyptian operation was not abandoned, President Eisenhower called his Strategic Air Commander to order an attack alert. 'Very good, Sir,' came the instant reply. 'Which side?' General LeMay was a real professional.

The amateur warrior, unused to the cruelties of war, is less able to rise to such heights – or to sink to such depths. And since much military power is today provided by amateur warriors – civilian soldiers conscripted by the state – their situation is worth attention.

Civilized society makes provision for conscientious objection. That might be more strongly put. Civilized society demands conscientious objection. It holds that when a citizen finds he has to disobey the state in order to obey his conscience, he is the better citizen for obeying his conscience.

When conscientious objection becomes a virtue, so that the conscientious objector is in a sense the ideal citizen, it is because society holds as valid two basic assumptions. First, that the defection of a small number of conscientious objectors will not imperil the safety of the state. Second, that the society, being civilized, will not act in such a way as to provoke conscientious objection on a large scale.

Neither of these assumptions can today be held with much assurance. The behaviour of states in the modern states system, characterized by deceit, by treachery, by cruelty, is precisely of a kind to provoke large-scale protest among any morally sensitive citizenry. And small-scale defection may have the gravest consequences. When a nuclear physicist goes over to the enemy, taking his secrets with him, the entire balance of power may be changed. When a civilian soldier refuses to embark for a theatre of war because the war to him seems evil, his refusal may touch the national nerve, causing it to fail; or touch the national conscience, causing it to stir.

That publics more than statesmen are morally fastidious about foreign policy was the confident belief of those liberal idealists who survived the First World War. 'Throughout this instrument,' said Woodrow Wilson of the League of Nations, 'we are dependent primarily and chiefly upon one great force, and that is the moral force of the public opinion of the world – the cleansing and clarifying and compelling influences of publicity.' And Lord Robert Cecil: 'The great weapon we rely on is public opinion ... and if we are wrong about that, then the whole thing is wrong.'[9]

It turned out they were wrong about that. Public opinion between two world wars was not cleansing; it was not clarifying; and if it compelled at all, it compelled as often as not in the wrong direction. Expected to exert a constructive influence upon the conduct of foreign policy, public opinion proved instead to be fitful and gullible, fickle and craven. When the need was to rearm, the public clamoured for disarmament. When the need was for belligerence, the public was pacifist. When the need was for defying the dictators, the public was for appeasing dictators.

Has it done much better since? That, I suppose, is a matter of opinion; my own is that it has not done much better since. There is as much gullibility about as ever; and there is something else. We seem to have developed an addiction to violence, a morbid fascination with crisis. Albert Camus has noted the reaction of people during the Hungarian Revolution: they spared 'neither applause nor virtuous tears before returning to their slippers like football enthusiasts after a big game.'[10] The week must be crammed with catastrophe, so that at its close the hour may have seven days.

A new form of public protest has recently appeared among us. It operates in a twilight zone between violence and non-violence. Its techniques are varied, sometimes very daring. The protestants paddle tiny boats where great powers prove their nuclear prowess. They cling to the hulls of atomic submarines. They march on missile bases and lie on tracks in front of troop-trains. They withhold taxes. They burn draft cards. Norman Morrison has burned himself.

Of their effectiveness it may be too soon to speak. Their ranks, we know, are few. They consist of knaves, and fools, and heroes – in what proportion who can tell? They may give aid and comfort to the enemy. They may give the President sleepless nights. But will they change his mind?

Hey, Hey, LBJ!
How many kids did you kill today?

9 Quoted in Hans J. Morgenthau, *Politics Among Nations,* 3rd ed. (Alfred A. Knopf, New York 1960), 260
10 *Resistance, Rebellion, and Death* (Alfred A. Knopf, New York 1960), 157

If this cruel rhyme is representative of their attitude, one would think not. They may mortify; they will not convert.

Nor will they reach, save as irritating noises, the ears of the man in the street. He has neither taste nor temperament nor time for such shenanigans; he is preoccupied with second cars and second mortgages. He is likely to look upon the protestants for peace as shrill and sour and cranky, outside the mainstream of national life, offering nothing of relevance to the making up of his own mind.

Foreign policy, in societies like ours, is meant to be an expression of the contents of that mind - biased, addled, empty as it may variously be. Only when it is straightened out will foreign policy straighten out. But can we wait so long?

If, as I have argued, neither the public service nor the public at large is specially equipped, and therefore specially obligated, to confront statesmen with their wrong-doing, can no one do the job?

Someone can. The intellectual.

There may still be Canadians who smile or snigger at this suggestion. I suppose them to be in the same condition of arrested development as Canadians forty years ago who thought a professor was 'a man who plays the piano in a house of meretricious entertainment.' All of you will share my conviction that the intellectual is uniquely a custodian of the national conscience. All of you will be more interested in discussing the difficulties the intellectual faces in carrying out this assignment than in arguing over whether or not it is properly his to carry out.

There are as many ways of defining intellectuals as there are intellectuals to define themselves. I like the definition Camus once jotted down in his notebook: 'An intellectual is someone whose mind watches itself.'[11] An intellectual breaks faith when he allows his mind to give up the watch, to go off duty.

No kind of intellectual has more spectacularly broken faith than the scientific intellectual. The scientist has lugged Pandora's box into his laboratory and left the lid open for years on end. Only a fiend could knowingly do this: and it is fitting that the Arch-Fiend in Hochhuth's drama is not a Nazi politician, not a storm-trooper, not even Eichmann, but a doctor:

Brain tissue from a pair of Jewish twins,
two kids from Calais, preserved in formaldehyde.
Rather interesting comparative sections.

11 *Notebooks, 1935-1942* (Modern Library, New York 1965), 28

> I brought the specimen with me for a girl
> who's taking a first course in histology ... [12]

In the presence of such a monster we are in the presence not of sin, but of Absolute Evil. It knows no guilt. It knows no shame.

But there is another kind of scientist who knows both guilt and shame. Typically he invents and produces weapons of mass destruction. Typically he is a physicist, a nuclear physicist.

It is not his intention to do wrong and, at the beginning, he was not conscious of doing wrong. One is struck by the gusto, the enthusiasm, the almost school-boy exuberance of the scientists of the Manhattan Project, working to perfect a product to kill one hundred thousand people. Only the deed itself shocked them into recognition. Then guilt fell on them like radioactive rain. Many of those who had cheerfully worked on the atomic bomb shrank from work on the hydrogen bomb. A majority on a scientific committee advised the President not to make the hydrogen bomb: such restraint, they argued, might help to end the arms race. A minority flatly proclaimed that 'this weapon is an evil thing.... We think it is wrong on fundamental ethical grounds to initiate development of such a weapon.'[13] But their protest was ignored. The work went forward. Thermonuclear weapons were designed, built, tested, mass-produced.

It could not have been done without scientists to do it. Enough came forward, their moral burden lightened by a minute division of labour. 'Men work on gyromechanisms,' Ralph E. Lapp has written, 'on micro-miniaturized electronics, on plasma physics. It is easy to forget the monstrous machines of destruction to which their work is a contribution.'[14] Fragmentation is the mother of amnesia.

But in the subconscious guilt remains, never to be driven out. 'In some sort of crude sense which no vulgarity, no humour, no overstatement can quite extinguish,' one of their number has testified out of the depths of his torment, 'the physicists have known sin; and this is a knowledge which they cannot lose.'[15] No wonder the dramatists have had a field day with physicists: Brecht, and Durrenmatt, and now a play based on the transcript of the proceedings in the case of J. Robert Oppenheimer, than which no stage drama could be more bizarre, or poignant.

12 *The Deputy* (Grove Press, New York 1964), 70
13 Quoted in Robert Gilpin, *American Scientists and Nuclear Weapons Policy* (Princeton University Press, Princeton, NJ, 1962), 94
14 *Kill and Overkill: The Strategy of Annihilation* (Basic Books, New York 1962), 21
15 Quoted in Gilpin, *American Scientists and Nuclear Weapons Policy*, 25-6

First cousins to the scientific intellectuals, often coming from their ranks, are the defence intellectuals – that group of scholar-strategist-consultants (not necessarily in that order) who, it has been said, prowl the corridors of the Pentagon as Jesuits moved through the courts of Vienna and Madrid three centuries ago. Their profession is to think about the unthinkable – about the circumstances in which nuclear wars might be fought, about the consequences of nuclear wars being fought. It is not a pretty subject. But can one fairly be charged with lacking moral scruple just for thinking of such things? Herman Kahn's lectures on thermonuclear war were treated as Hitler's *Mein Kampf* ought to have been treated (but, alas, was not): an 'evil and tenebrous book,' someone called it; 'a tract on mass murder: how to plan it, how to commit it, how to get away with it, how to justify it.'[16] I add at once that no reading of the book undertaken with any intellectual discrimination could possibly sustain so perverse an interpretation of its thesis and its purpose.

All the same, preoccupation with the problems of nuclear war, while not itself morally reprehensible, tends to make those so preoccupied somewhat deficient in moral sensitivity. All too easily, all too frequently, they succumb to the sickness of brutal realism in its most sadistic and disagreeable form. Consider the sort of scenario on which the members of the Hudson Institute are wont to sharpen their wits:

The military balance of power has changed and US forces become so vulnerable that after a Soviet first strike at US forces the US no longer has a devastating second strike capability. At that point the Soviets warn that for every Soviet city we destroy, they will demolish five of its American counterparts. The ultimatum concludes: "You know better than we do what kind of country you want to have when the war is over. Pick whatever major cities you wish to be destroyed and we will destroy them."[17]

The exercise consists in figuring out what Washington does next. The game is called 'Urban Renewal.'

I recognize, of course, the need to allow to intellect the freest possible play and the widest possible latitude. But surely its prolonged attention to these sorts of problems is not very good for the human spirit. It may not be so very good for the human race either.

But what of the rank-and-file, run-of-the-mill, intelligentsia – those of us who work well within these outer limits of science and strategy? Our moral dilemmas are less spectacular. But they are no less troublesome.

16 James Newman, in *Scientific American,* CCIV, no 3, Mar. 1961, 197-8
17 Quoted by Frances Fitzgerald, 'Herman Kahn: Metaphors and Scenarios,' *New York Herald Tribune Magazine,* 4 July 1965, 41

One temptation is to enter the service of the state. It is a temptation to be resisted.

I do not intend to demean the public service in any way, or to diminish the importance of what it does. I am told that the life of the civil servant is deeply satisfying. Dean Acheson testifies that 'to everyone who has ever experienced it the return from public life to private life leaves one feeling flat and empty.' It may well be so. I take his word for it.

But the public service is no place for the intellectual. The intellectual cannot do it justice. The environment is alien. Particularly the environment in which foreign policy is made.

An intellectual, displaced from his proper preoccupation to advise governments on foreign policy, tends characteristically to under- or over-react. He under-reacts if, as is likely, he is unduly deferential in the presence of power. Arthur Schlesinger tells in his memoirs of the Kennedy presidency of his failure to protest against the Bay of Pigs operation despite a strong premonition of disaster:

One's impulse to blow the whistle on this nonsense was simply undone by the circumstances of the occasion. It is one thing, for a special assistant like myself, to talk frankly in private to a president; and another for a college professor, fresh to government, to interpose his unassisted judgment in open meeting against such august figures as the Secretaries of State and Defense and the Joint Chiefs of Staff.[18]

Or else, and just as likely, he is unduly scornful of events and circumstances, ignoring or belittling their capacity to frustrate his favourite project. 'As he could mould the printed word to suit his ideas,' Hans Morgenthau points out, 'so he now expects the real world to respond to his actions. Hence his confidence in himself, his pride, his optimism'[19] – his over-reaction. Hence also his almost invariable record of failure. The history of recent international relations is strewn with the litter of the schemes of intellectuals-turned-policy-makers, or of intellectuals-turned-policy advisors: schemes contrived in haste, put forward in conceit, and abandoned, as soon as may be decently possible, by the professionals in government who know from hard experience what policy-making is all about.

But the intellectual as policy-maker not only makes a mess of policy; he largely destroys himself as an intellectual. 'It is only knowledge freely acquired that is disinterested,' Walter Lippmann wisely remarked many years ago. 'When

18 *A Thousand Days: John F. Kennedy in the White House* (Houghton Mifflin, Boston 1965), 255
19 'The Sweet Smell of Success,' *The New York Review of Books*, 30 July 1964, 6

those whose profession it is to teach and to investigate become the makers of policy, become politicians and leaders of causes, they are committed. Nothing they say can be relied on as disinterested. Nothing they teach can be trusted as scientific.'[20] It is a harsh verdict, but fair.

So if the intellectual is to remain a useful critic of foreign policy, retaining his capacity for detached analysis and informed condemnation, he must stay out of government.

He must also stay out of the consulting business. A mind whose function it is to keep watch on itself cannot function properly when rented out to special pleaders. The practice is too common for comfort, too common for comment. A conspiracy of silence muffles the activities of what one authority has described as 'a new kind of *condottieri*, mercenaries of science and scholarship hooded with doctorates and ready for hire on studies to contract specification.'[21] The intellectual should keep his distance from those who want to buy his thoughts. Keeping his distance will help him keep his principles and, in keeping his principles, he keeps faith.

If the intellectual experiences the crudest kind of degradation when he delivers his mind to someone else's payroll, or to someone else's charge, he is exposed to degradation at its deadliest when he is self-employed. Then it is that he may allow his capacity for moral protest to serve himself more than the community.

An article lavish in its praise for the first of the American teach-ins describes its origins in 'an idea which permitted the concerned professional to envision himself as the conqueror, not of governments, but rather of his own sense of impotence.'[22] Motives are always mixed, and it is foolish to expect simon-purity. But when the motive of protest becomes primarily therapeutic it places in jeopardy that sense of moral discrimination which it is the first duty of the intellectual to develop. He develops instead a craving for protest. The time comes when any cause will do. Unscrupulous parties flourish the appropriate symbols and imagery before him, sure of his response. Moral protest becomes moral pot. The intellectual, hooked by the needs of his addiction, no longer is able, no longer cares, to distinguish right from wrong. Here is the ultimate in *trahison des clercs*.

Confronted in the preceding section with a dilemma of my own devising, I sought escape through the device, so typically Canadian, of the middle way. This time there is no such exit.

20 'The Deepest Issue of Our Time,' 15 June 1936, in Clinton Rossiter and James Lare, eds., *The Essential Lippmann* (Random House, New York 1963), 388
21 Gerard Piel, quoted in *The New York Review of Books*, 5 Aug. 1965, 11
22 Marc Pilsuk, 'The First Teach-In: An Insight into Professional Activism,' in *The Correspondent*, no 34, spring-summer 1965, 6

Before the intellectual are two life-styles, and two alone. One is the life-style of detachment. The other the life-style of commitment. One has to choose.

My late teacher, Harold Innis, knowing better than anyone else how heavily mined and menaced are the slopes of commitment leading away from the ivory tower, begged the intellectual to remain within its precincts.

I used to think this good advice. Now I think otherwise. It is the intellect of commitment which in spite of all my cautionary tales I must finally commend to you. Not just because it is in short supply – although in Canada, God knows, it *is* in short supply. But rather because it alone enables the intellectual to do his job. A detached mind may keep watch upon itself, but it watches over wasteland. Only a mind ethically anaesthetized, morally lobotomized, remains detached from what statesmen are doing to our world.

[November 1965]

3

The words of world politics

'He hath sounded forth the trumpet that shall never call ... readjustment.'
Such is the battle hymn of a republic whose campaigns in southeast Asia are
turning out so badly that none of its officials dare admit in public what is
going on. If truth is the first casualty in war, language is the second.

Our political discourse is currently infected by the same disease that felled
German after World War II when the language of Goethe and Rilke collapsed
beneath the burden of guilt the Third Reich passed on to its inheritors, who
only wanted to forget. For twelve years there had seeped into their vocabulary the pronouns of the holocaust. Jew, Pole, and Russian had become syn-
onymous with lice, roach, and vermin. Words had lost their way in a language
which, in George Steiner's phrase, had gotten the habits of hell into its syntax. It was moreover pulped by lies.

So far we've not been called upon to ratiocinate a genocide. Yet after a
quarter century of nuclear deterrence, after a decade of evil war on the peri-
phery, the language of our politics is sick, sick, sick. Its words are blunted at
their cutting edge, their power to discriminate diminished. What Steiner wrote
of German in 1959 we may write of English in 1971: 'It will no longer perform, quite as well as it used to, its two principal functions: the conveyance
of humane order which we call law, and the communication of the quick of
the human spirit, which we call grace.'[1]

The responsibility for the purity of language, wrote Thomas Mann when
the Nazis took away his honorary doctorate, 'does not have merely an esthetic

---

1 'The Hollow Miracle,' in *Language and Silence: Essays on Language, Literature and
the Inhuman* (Atheneum, New York 1970), 101

sense. The responsibility for language is, in essence, a human responsibility.'[2] Politicians as well as artists have a duty to discharge it.

Politicians discharge it best by combatting the evasions of bureaucracy. Where the bureaucrat says 'readjustment,' the politician should admit 'retreat.' Where the bureaucrat says 'protective reaction,' the politician should speak of 'bomb attack,' and specify the tonnage and the target. Where the bureaucrat says 'unemployment' - or even more evasively 'redundancy' - the politician should insist that men and women can't find jobs.

Do politicians discharge their duty to speak plainly of such matters? Consider how L.B. Pearson commemorates the Battle of Vimy Ridge. (No one who calls a selection of his speeches *Words and Occasions* properly objects to scrutiny of the words he chooses to mark occasions.) 'Only by collective action for collective defence with collective strength under collective control can there be maximum deterrence against aggression.'[3] What is being perpetrated here is totalitarian prose - Pentagon or Kremlin, it doesn't matter which - a prose, as Norman Mailer says of it, that 'does not define, does not deliver.'

The reluctance to define, the hesitation to deliver, are readily explained. Pearson's clutch of 'collectives' conceal a reality too unpleasant to be shown without wraps - except by risking public indignation. 'Collective action through a strong and cohesive coalition for policy and defence' is a euphemism for the strategy which threatens millions of innocents with slaughter so savage, so gross, that its survivors would envy the dead - a perfect example of Orwellian Newspeak, which 'differed from most all other languages in that its vocabulary grew smaller instead of larger every year.'[4]

The failure of our political discourse to define and to deliver is reflected in the prevailing low estate of rhetoric. Rhetoric has come to mean bad rhetoric. Thus, an historian writes that the oratory of Huey Long was 'eloquent but shameless' - seemingly uncaring that it can't be both at once. 'The swelling anaphoras of a Southern Congressman,' observes John Illo (a student of rhetoric in its true sense), 'are not eloquent but ludicrous, raising irrepressible images of toads and swine ... But such is the tradition of vacant and meaningless political oratory in America, and such the profusion of the universally accepted and discredited rhetoric of advertising, that the public nods and acquiesces.'[5]

2 *An Exchange of Letters* (Alfred A. Knopf, New York 1937)
3 (University of Toronto Press, Toronto 1970), 265
4 George Orwell, *Nineteen Eighty-Four* (Penguin Books, Harmondsworth 1954), 249
5 'The Rhetoric of Malcolm X,' in Peter Spackman and Lee Ambrose, eds.,
   The Columbia University Forum Anthology (Atheneum, New York 1968), 260

Is this the tradition of political oratory in Canada? I've referred to the rhetoric of L.B. Pearson and (by implication only) to the rhetoric of J.G. Diefenbaker. What of the rhetoric of Pierre Trudeau? Has he done anything 'to purify the dialect of the tribe?'

One of many sycophants praises his speeches as 'models of steely lucidity.' That evaluation seems extravagant. (I refer to speeches made in English; I can't judge those he makes in French.) Trudeau does not indulge in totalitarian prose – though utterances like 'If we accept parliamentary democracy as a political system we must also accept the basic rules which govern this system' have been compared by Robert Fulford with the quotations of Chairman Mao for their 'sheer mind-numbing obviousness.'[6] Trudeau indulges in 'lady prose.'

Just as Pentagon prose is spoken far beyond the Pentagon, so lady prose is spoken by gentlemen as well as ladies. 'Lady prose,' a critic writes of it, 'can be so arch it would curdle a shark's blood. Lady prose is icky prose. Lady prose is genteel. Lady prose is next to impossible to read.' And next to impossible to listen to, even if Liberals pay $50 for the privilege. Here is their reward: 'It has long been the habit of the Chamber of Commerce to publish its views on what policies the government should adopt. "Adopt" is probably the right word, as the paternity of government policies is often difficult to identify.' The rhetoric of Pierre Trudeau is remarkable only for its ability to move so rapidly between the soporific and the scatological.

Along with all these trials and tribulations, the language of politics has lately to endure what Illo calls the verbal sniffling and stumbling of the New Left. That may be an improvement on the ranting of the Old Left, but not a marked improvement. The New Left's lexicon of 'freak' and 'rip-off,' 'like' and 'dig,' is limited, its unwitting anacolutha of 'uh' and 'you know' are a feeble fertilizer for the greening of America. 'A childlike, breathless sense of wonder,' writes Charles A. Reich, childlike and breathless, 'this is the quality that Consciousness III supremely treasures, to which it gives its ultimate sign of reverence, vulnerability, and innocence, "Oh wow."'[7] Oh wow.

'Languages have great reserves of life,' George Steiner assures us. 'They can absorb masses of hysteria, illiteracy and cheapness. But there comes a breaking point.'[8] It may be closer than we think. We are at the bedside of a language not far away from death. Unless we insist on higher standards of political discourse, probe the pollution of its vocabulary, we will be more than bedside witnesses; we shall have hastened its demise.

[March 1971]

6 'On Trudeau's Speeches,' *Saturday Night,* Aug. 1969, 17
7 *The Greening of America* (Random House, New York 1970), 263
8 'The Hollow Miracle,' 101

Browsing through some of those massive tomes recording for posterity the speeches of the chief executives of the United States, I'm struck by how shallow so many of their orations appear on second sight. Why does the prosing of the presidents, in our time especially, leave so much to be desired? Why has no president since FDR been able to use words to rise to an occasion, much less soar above it?

Harry Truman gave 'em hell while whistle-stopping, peppered his talk with pungent homilies ('the buck stops here'), but his state papers yield few remarks worth keeping for more than their historic interest. Eisenhower was a captive of his teleprompter, intoning flat and fatuous phrases about 'peace with justice,' 'a just and lasting peace'; cut adrift from speech-writers his syntax lurched and wobbled like Ulysses Grant's when in his cups.

Ike's rhetoric is platitude tempered by incoherence, LBJ's a relentless barrage of banality. 'Here in this slim volume,' Norman Mailer comments of a collection of Johnson's speeches, is a 'cove of presidential prose whose waters are so brackish that a spoonful is enough to sicken the mind for hours,' 'a prose which stirs half-heard cries of the death by suffocation of Western civilization.'[9]

The speeches of President Kennedy are vastly over-rated. Does it contain anything, a critic asks acutely of what is generally acclaimed as the noblest utterance of them all, 'that a commencement address does not? Indeed, the inaugural displayed the meaningless chiasmus, the fatuous or sentimental metaphor, the callow hyperbaton, of a valedictory.'[10]

On the speeches of President Nixon, finally, there is no need to dwell: an oily blend of sentiment and cant, slicking America's sea of trouble. Even the speaker, like Willie Loman on the skids, knows he hasn't got it any more.

Do not suppose that this steady decline in the standards of political declamation - I've traced it at the White House but they've gone downhill in Downing Street as well as Sussex Drive - reflects only a lessening calibre of leadership. Alfred Kazin observes that 'now, when power seems more centralized than ever but when American presidents are less imposing than ever, Texas-California commoners betraying all their hesitation and salesmen's ambition, Roosevelt seems more personable because he was the last gentleman in the White House.'[11] That's not just snobbish, it's way wide of the mark.

Roosevelt talked good like a president should because there were some things he didn't have to talk about. Two things in particular - global develop-

9 *Cannibals and Christians* (Dial Press, New York 1966), 49
10 John Illo, 'The Rhetoric of Malcolm X,' 261
11 'The Confidence of FDR,' *The New York Review of Books,* 20 May 1971, 3

ment, nuclear deterrence. Both have been high on the agenda of his successors.
Both have helped debase their words – and deeds.

People used to be rich or poor, regions were once prosperous or depressed,
nations advanced or backward. Then the development intellectuals took over.
Poor people emerged as under-privileged, depressed regions as development
areas, backward nations became under-developed countries, then – 'under-
developed' being thought too blunt – less-developed countries. 'And so we
find in the literature,' writes the Swedish economist Gunnar Myrdal, 'a flori-
legium of euphemisms,' 'the use of increasingly evasive terms.'[12]

Why? To hide increasingly unpleasant facts. 'The tricks of growth are not
all that difficult,' W.W. Rostow, doyen of the development intellectuals, used
to assure the statesmen of the western world, 'they only seem so, at moments
of frustration and confusion.'[13] If it were only true. The trouble, as we've
learned since then, is that frustration and confusion must be measured not in
moments but in decades.

Two decades of 'development' go by. The rich get richer and the poor get
children. The vocabulary of global growth is deployed so as to obscure these
stark statistics. What are the developing countries in the parlance of development? Brazil, Tanzania, Burma, Pakistan. But they are not developing, they
are sliding towards ruin. What are the developing countries in the real world?
The United States, the Soviet Union, West Germany, Japan.

Terms such as 'newly developing countries,' 'emergent countries,' 'newly
emerging countries,' 'lesser developed countries,' Myrdal has pointed out, 'are
used in connection with a tendency to de-emphasize the actual differences between the rich and the poor countries. And they thus become misleading. All
these terms express an escapist attitude.'[14]

Is any as escapist as the term devised for President Nixon's latest message
to the Congress on foreign aid? There the wretched of the earth are concealed
as 'the lower income countries,' and here is what the president says about their
future: 'Today the lower income countries are increasingly able to shoulder
the major responsibility for their own security and development.'[15] That will
be news in Dacca.

Strategic discourse is likewise disfigured by euphemism and evasion. 'The
language in which the strategy of deterrence is being discussed,' Fred Charles
Iklé, an American scholar, has written recently, 'tends to obscure the fact that
this strategy is based on a scheme of totally unprecedented cruelty. Various

12 *Asian Drama,* III (Pantheon, New York 1968), 1841
13 *The Stages of Economic Growth* (Cambridge University Press, Cambridge & New
    York 1960), 166
14 *Asian Drama,* III, 1842
15 United States Information Bulletin, 21 Apr. 1971

abstractions and metaphors help to insulate the design against the innocents who are its target. Owing to these metaphors, a scheme that would have been rejected as abhorrent in the Dark Ages by kings and the common people alike appears to reflect the humane ideas of modern civilization.'[16]

Here we are, cogs in the most frightful apparatus of destruction, where every citizen of every city in two continents – if he understands what the human condition has become – lives in fear of being reduced to fly-ash or a pulp of rotting sores. And we block out the horror by a gabble of 'ilities' – capability, survivability, penetrability, credibility, viability, destructability. 'The "ility" suffix,' Russell Baker observes of it, 'seems peculiar to those who deal with death on the grand scale. It may be that "ility" helps lighten the sombre cast of their thought, for "ility" has a light, gay, skipping sound.'[17]

Herman Kahn, doyen of the defence intellectuals, helps lighten the sombre cast of his thought by what he is pleased to call thermonuclear humour. 'Thermonuclear war is not a joke,' Capability Kahn explains humorlessly, 'but professional or serious discussions of thermonuclear war can include humor, at least in Europe or the United States. For various reasons,' Kahn concedes, '"thermonuclear humor" might be inappropriate or in bad taste in a talk by an American in Asia ...'[18] So audiences in Tokyo or Nagasaki are spared the scatological reference to city-swapping as 'a tit-for-tit' exchange. For such exquisite sensibility, O Lord make us truly thankful.

Joking about the apocalypse, Kahn claims, induces the right attitude of mind: 'People in a state of horror are not good analysts.' One might ponder that proposition profitably for hours. Perhaps if more people had been in a state of horror we would not now be quivering at the starting tape of yet another lap of the most dangerous arms race of them all.

'The language of a community has reached a perilous state when a study of radioactive fall-out can be entitled "Operation Sunshine."' To this remark the British critic D.J. Enright takes strong exception. Noting that in ancient China the drowning of unwanted babies was called 'bathing the infants,' the branding of criminals 'affixing the golden seals,' Enright sees euphemism as essential to existence. 'I am not yet so lost in lexicography,' he quotes from Dr Johnson, 'as to forget that words are the daughters of earth, and the things are the sons of heaven.' The daughters of earth are tough, says Enright, 'they can take care of themselves.'[19]

16 *Every War Must End* (Columbia University Press, New York & London 1971), 129-30
17 'Behind the Mask of the Ility Boys,' *The New York Times,* 21 Sept. 1967
18 *Thinking About the Unthinkable* (Avon Books, New York 1962), 282-3
19 'Speak Up!', *The New York Review of Books,* 12 Oct. 1967. (The remark about 'Operation Sunshine' is George Steiner's, whose *Language and Politics* Enright was reviewing.)

No. They cannot take care of themselves. They need nurture and respect. Instead they are degraded and debauched. God did not command his flock: 'Thou shalt not destroy, thou shalt not waste.' Christ did not single out for his especial grace and favour little dinks and slopes and gooks. 'Thou shalt not kill.' 'Suffer little children to come unto me.'

Escapist words are more than symptomatic of a sick society, they make its sickness worse. These nouns too nonchalant by half, these verbs overly evasive, conceal reality from those responsible for it. They who use a vocabulary of escape will with more impunity resort to evil for, as Emerson understood, 'words and deeds are quite indifferent modes of the divine energy. Words are also actions, and actions are a kind of words.'

[May 1971]

Acknowledgments

I am grateful to the Canadian Broadcasting Corporation for permission to reprint the first seven sections of Part II first published by CBC Publications in 1967 as *Fate and Will in Foreign Policy*. The first two sections of Part III were first published by the University of Toronto Press in 1966 as *Right and Wrong in Foreign Policy*.

'The Deliquescence of Diplomacy' (section 10, Part I) and 'Stupidity and Power' (section 8, Part II) first appeared in *Saturday Night*, while 'The Correspondent and the Diplomat' (section 3, Part I) first appeared in the *Canadian Forum*. With the exception of 'Principles for Receivership,' which is based on a lecture delivered at the University of Western Ontario, the remaining sections first appeared as columns in the *Montreal Star* and/or the *Toronto Star*. I am grateful to the editors of these various publications for permission to include them in this book.

JE